POEMS 1968–2004

Carol Rumens was born in Forest Hill, south-east London, in December 1944. She won a scholarship to grammar school (Coloma Convent) and her first poems and music reviews were published in the *Croydon Advertiser* when she was 16. She studied piano and cello, intending to become a musician, but gave up this ill-founded ambition and went to university to read Philosophy instead, a step she soon regretted. She left at the age of 20, after marrying David Rumens, with whom she has two daughters. They were divorced in 1984.

Carol Rumens has published eleven volumes of poetry, a novel, *Plato Park*, and assorted short stories and literary journalism. Several of her plays have been produced, and she has also worked as an occasional translator of Russian poetry with her current partner Yuri Drobyshev. She has edited two anthologies, *Making for the Open: The Chatto Book of Post-Feminist Poetry* (1985) and *New Women Poets* (Bloodaxe Books, 1990), as well as Elizabeth Bartlett's *Two Women Dancing: New and Selected Poems* (Bloodaxe Books, 1995).

In 1981 her collection *Unplayed Music* was joint winner of the Alice Hunt Bartlett Award. Carol Rumens has also received the Cholmondeley Award and the Prudence Farmer Prize. *Star Whisper* was a Poetry Book Society Choice in 1983 and *Holding Pattern* was shortlisted for a Belfast City Arts Award in 1999. 'Baby, Baby, Baby' won first prize in the Peterloo Poetry Competition in 2003.

A former poetry editor at *Quarto* and *The Literary Review*, Carol Rumens has held writing residencies at the University of Kent at Canterbury, University College, Cork, Queen's University, Belfast, and the University of Stockholm. She was Northern Arts Literary Fellow in 1988-90, worked as a Teaching Assistant from 1995 to 2003, and is now a Lecturer in Creative Writing at the University of Wales, Bangor. She is a Member of the Welsh Academi and a Fellow of the Royal Society of Literature.

Poems 1968-2004 (Bloodaxe Books, 2004) draws comprehensively on Carol Rumens' previous collections. It includes a short opening selection of previously uncollected poems, as well as material from an unpublished sequence set in Mexico City, *Aztec Sacrifices*, written in 1974-76. There is a final section of new poems. The volume excludes separately printed translations and the light-verse collection, written in collaboration with illustrator Viv Quillin, *The Miracle Diet*.

CAROL RUMENS

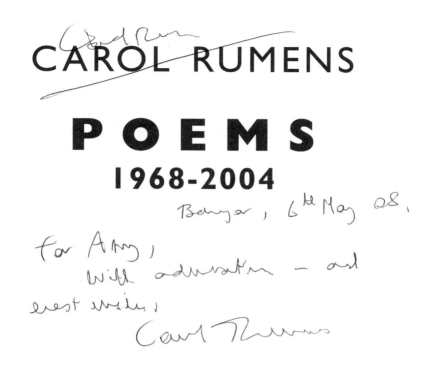

P O E M S
1968-2004

Bangor, 6th May 08.

For Amy,
With admiration — and
best wishes,
Carol Rumens

BLOODAXE BOOKS

ISBN: 1 85224 680 4

First published 2004 by
Bloodaxe Books Ltd,
Highgreen,
Tarset,
Northumberland NE48 1RP.

www.bloodaxebooks.com
For further information about Bloodaxe titles
please visit our website or write to
the above address for a catalogue.

Bloodaxe Books Ltd acknowledges
the financial assistance of
Arts Council England, North East.

Cover printing by J. Thomson Colour Printers Ltd, Glasgow.

Printed in Great Britain by
Bell & Bain Limited, Glasgow, Scotland

for Kelsey and Rebecca

ACKNOWLEDGEMENTS

This book includes all the poems which Carol Rumens wishes to reprint from her previous books and pamphlets: *A Strange Girl in Bright Colours* (Quartet Books, 1973), *A Necklace of Mirrors* (Ulsterman Publications, 1978), *Unplayed Music* (Secker & Warburg, 1981), *Scenes from the Gingerbread House* (Bloodaxe Books, 1982), *Star Whisper* (Secker & Warburg, 1983), *Direct Dialling* (Chatto & Windus, 1985), *Icons, Waves* (Starwheel Press, 1986), *Selected Poems* (Chatto & Windus, 1987), *The Greening of the Snow Beach* (Bloodaxe Books, 1988), *From Berlin to Heaven* (Chatto & Windus, 1989), *Thinking of Skins: New & Selected Poems* (Bloodaxe Books, 1993), *Best China Sky* (Bloodaxe Books, 1995), *Holding Pattern* (Blackstaff Press, 1998) and *Hex* (Bloodaxe Books, 2002).

UNCOLLECTED POEMS 1968-81: a selection of relatively early work draws on poems not included in *A Strange Girl in Bright Colours* (1973) and poems written over an eight-year gap before the publication of *Unplayed Music* (1981). Acknowledgements are due to the editors of the following publications in which some of those poems first appeared: *Ambit, Encounter, Outposts, The Times Literary Supplement* and *Vogue.*

POEMS 1974-86 FROM *SELECTED POEMS*: previously uncollected poems included in *Selected Poems* (1987) written after the publication of *A Strange Girl in Bright Colours* (1973).

OTHER UNCOLLECTED POEMS: four poems contemporary with two published collections are grouped with them. 'Greetings from Düsseldorf' and 'Digging' (from *The Poetry Book Society Anthology 1986-87*, ed. Jonathan Barker), after the poems from *Direct Dialling* (1985), and 'A Dialogue of Perestroishiks' (from *The Poetry Book Society Anthology 2*, ed. Anne Stevenson [Hutchinson, 1991]), and 'Rides' (from *Give Me Shelter*, ed. Michael Rosen [Bodley Head Children's Books, 1991]), after the poems of *From Berlin to Heaven* (1989).

NEW POEMS (2004): Acknowledgements are due to the editors of the following publications in which some of the new poems first appeared: *Agenda, Electric Acorn, Metre, New Welsh Review, Peterloo Poetry Competition 2003: Prizewinners' Booklet, PN Review, Poetry London, Poetry Review, Poetry Scotland, Skald, The Times Literary Supplement* and *Van Gogh's Ear*. 'The Weather of Scarves' is published in *Out of Fashion*, ed. Carol Ann Duffy (Faber, 2004).

CONTENTS

FROM **SCENES FROM THE GINGERBREAD HOUSE** (1982)

FROM **STAR WHISPER** (1983)

ICONS, WAVES (1986)

POEMS 1974-86 FROM SELECTED POEMS (1987)

UNCOLLECTED POEMS
(1968-1981)

Just Eve

Money can buy me love, it's true and terrible.
There's a swirl of colour in the air, spotlights
shaping my desire on every clothes-rail.
The DJ whispers loudly, like a wicked
uncle, gifts and bargains, into every
delicate ear, but any minute now
the songs will start again, and it'll be
real pain stabbing through the fan-whirl:
Stay with me, baby, please, stay with me, baby.
Pink and grey, a dress like petals fondles
my hand and slips. The price-tag
nestles inside me like a chip of glass:
I'm poorer than the pavement. Only money
would make me gleam until he couldn't doubt it,
and I not doubt myself, bringing him
slow flowers across the office, pink and grey.

Sibelius/Conception

Night-blue of spring in the small window-square:
we lie without touching
under the ocean, the huge, cold, northern allegro
plunging and rolling from the disc you've spun
to soothe us after love. We listen, we watch
the curtain of green icebergs slowly parting.
Sun strikes the water, brass instruments soar.
Your blue eyes are still strange to me.
Are they land, are they sea, how far, how near?
And the music cannot look forward, the music turns
as always and mists with grief for the old order.
Vengeance. A harsh jostle of new rhythms
worries it, grasps it and roisters off like a dog.
My blood will jump, in spite of me,
to obey the calving cell, the busy skeining
of mirrors I can find no face for.
Sibelius combs back the bergs again
on a parting of blue water, a smell of land.
This time, he says, go forward, take it.
Soon this small bedroom will not hold all our future.

Letter to a Two-Year-Old

Eldest child, blond and heavy,
coiled in your uterus of sleep,
already your mouth moulds a scowl,
already you're once bitten.
When I brought home the baby
you tottered round me dumbly
in your panda playsuit. How big
you'd grown! Face like a sunflower,
you stared at me without smiling.
Two days had passed and we,
forced to forget each other,
now stiffened to remember.
I laughed, and lifted you high,
but my milk, my anxiety, my pride
were for someone else. A death
formed and stuck in your knowledge.
This later love, these caresses
of words and remorse can't touch it:
your self springs from that stone.

A Marriage: Poems in Six Snapshots

1

We would make marriage human, standing proud
in jeans and flowers, taking it on ourselves
to melt the ruled certificate with tears
and furnish draughty rooms with long, slow kisses.

2

Where does money come from? A battered tin,
Solid with black, sour-smelling coins!
Your childhood sails away in ha'penny ships.
We eat the florins first, like dainty silver biscuits.

3

In the sixties, marriage was "out", love was in.
We clinched our compromise, and shook hands
with those mean-eyed relations, Pinch and Punch.
'Love is all you need,' sang the stylus, blindly grooving.

4

We have tasted the world with our feet and hands.
Others went by in cars. We walked
all the way to the flowers. Sometimes, you plunged through brambles.
I followed, bare-legged. You held the map.

5

I queue at the call-box. Someone inside
keeps adding pence. The blizzard softly whitens
my coat-sleeves, children blaze like clumsy robins.
A warmed hand-set. Your smooth pick-up gesture.

6

Have the sixties gone to Heaven, or are they in Limbo
like a love-child stillborn in a doorway?
Though old, we are unripe, have scaled too quickly
our learning decade, toppling now behind us.

View of Senility

A stare on a sinewed neck, a circuit broken,
the old mouth gapes its emptiness. O what
if I should come to this and not have spoken?

Heir to the treasured key that failed to open
his parents' book, the child forgets the plot.
A stare on a sinewed neck, a circuit broken

enskull the fossil of what might have woken
once, in one mind. There'll be no photostat
if I should come to this and not have spoken.

So soon each sense, each making sense, is taken;
the most permissive surgeon can't abort
a stare on a sinewed neck, a circuit broken.

I need no grave-feast, silks for when I waken.
Dust for all time my hope, my heart, my throat
if I should come to this and not have spoken.

To stamp the running sands with some hard token
is to survive, and youth was nothing but
a stare on a sinewed neck, a circuit broken,
if I should come to this, and not have spoken.

Seascape with Woman

Always the body of the land
savaged by the many-mouthed sea, extremities stripped
to heavy bones that jab skywards,
iron-red torso carved to a fall of meat
crumbling into the bay's sunlit dish
where childish fingers sift pre-history's mountains...

A soft thing, over-ripe, inadequate
for the lewd bikini, I tread
the grainy corpse in its pox of limpets, tensing
to a landscape of dark-jacketed men
with fishing-lines and imitative sons;
they shout through the wind at an angry, graceless woman.

I catch their sly contempts
and loud ambitions, a haul of slippery bait,
and turn in panic to the rock's stiff sinew
which claims the power to wreck, draws token blood,
yet in its vast disinterest cannot break
the concaves of my footsure innocence.

At last, where the water finally twists
out of the land's dead grip, I throw my body
to the blue muscled gullet; cold eyes
follow me, then waver. In a flash
the woman is nothing, her caverns
lost in deepening green, her cliffs foam-broken.

I give up my years like lies, the waves
lifting them to a vaster timescale.
I am a gull or driftwood, of no consequence
my smiles and measurements to the preoccupied anglers.
They look elsewhere; they have cast off their desires
to the slow infinite drag of money or meat.

Later perhaps they will notice and dislike
a strange transfiguration of the rock
where a woman in love with sea and seasons, asking
no oils or surgery, no promises, no mirrors,
but the rough glittering of the wounds she carries
from the past, accepts herself and is ready for ageing.

Advice Before the Act

The cat's
a real live raver of a
crazy hot-hipped all-girl go-girl   wow
she's fizz-fizz-fizzing over   hey you
nu-type super doll with the EYES ARE
IN look   hit the charts WHAM make it
front-page and punchline flash-snapped over
Soho swinging those sheerest-joy legs
sky high   honey you've switched on heaven
for that aston-martin-ad-boy showing you
his plastic fantastic split-level swing-pad   you're
so wantable   and today there's no
bad odour no mess no strings and all
but all the go-wild-go-to-bed-
in-nothing honeys do it   only don't
slip up will you   always take
that twenty-one day precaution   there's a pill
to medicare your passion   if you
    conceive you know
    you die?

Soho Square, April

An animal wakes expansively as love,
and thinks of a grass island in the hot city
where the play of voices would be a soft excitable
ostinato to the traffic's discords
like a thicket of birds stirring at first light,
or water twisting its future
down the shoulder of a hill.
The sky touches the animal through a small window
and already its heart has sidled
into the kingdom of light, already it hears
the soft husks dropping from the plane trees
like tiny peeled fur coats.
Now the building is honeycombed with abandoned lairs,
each with its empty machine mirroring
the futile journey of fluorescence.

24

The animal lies down awkwardly in its new element
of damp and wallflowers, an extraordinary glamour
where the green-plumaged pigeons are always nodding
at fear and escaping upwards.
It bares its delicate skin to search for splinters
of time, finds nothing that the sun won't cure.

Birth

I held you tight in me
like a solid gold Easter egg,
like a melon of cream-pale marble
while you kicked against

the bloody entanglements, the web
of capillaries and the rock-hard
cord I held you with,
determined not to let you go

an hour too early.
But when you forced the issue,
suddenly I changed my mind.
I hated you inside me.

I fought, convulsions of me
conspired with you
to be free of my body.
I still fight today

and scream for you to be born.
I've a lifetime of tugging at
freedom through the chinks of your daughterhood
and teething on the uncuttable cord.

For the Pioneers: Poems from a Kitchen

This room's my home, scoured bare of history;
its glaring panes of chrome and PVC
carry my only family portraits, blurred
faces that might be mine, askew, absurd.
The shelves sprout plates instead of books. The bread,
broken, will be made flesh, but raise no dead.
Where is the cup encrusted by the thumb-
prints of hands, chained centuries back to one
that tooled the first flint, scrawled the first crude line
and, as I deeply drank, would link with mine?
Should I drill tunnels, hack the floor's cement
for charrings from cold fires, excrement?
I sweated at the stove while lyres were played
but heard my heart's drum throb. My body swayed
as old modes were perfected by old men,
and new, wild-bowed by boys of seventeen:
I frowned, and served. And still I recognise
the remnants of those pentatonic cries
filtered into the living-rooms of tired
women through the latest amplifiers.
But let a Doric note be struck. Let love
give way to anger. Summon from the stove
the servant blending gravies for fierce greeds;
though the pot's chilly and the meat still bleeds,
let the men clench their hunger, cool their throats:
the aproned woman plucks a shower of notes.
They dance like phoenix feathers, and her feast
is music, words, machines, hypotheses.
I stoke the furnace where the naked dark
of time will buckle, and receive her mark.

Scars

Better to be defaced than deceased.
My vaccination scars resist the sun's
brushwork like drops of wax, sealed proof
that I was a "welfare" child, planned, vitamin-reared,
armed at thirteen against the ancient killers.
Health must be holier than skin, experience
equally so. The hieroglyphics scrawling
white across my belly surely preach
that to live and to bear life are the true vocations:
and yet I dream, a sun-baked objet d'art,
camera-tamed, fit for a million eyes,
scarcely human, wholly beautiful
and resigned to sterility or the crippling virus.

Destinations

I hear the strident children of midsummer
crying their hurts along the dusty crescent:
echoes of small-town crises, squabbling marriages,
put-upon mothers, border-guarding neighbours
rise baby-fleshed from the Triang-cluttered verge,
then pedal away towards their inheritance
of fences and the letter of the bye-law,
intimacy laced with loathing. Overhead,
the roses put on airs, bleed and despair
in torrents of petals. Only thorns survive
all seasons. For a time, the children dare
high walls, forbidden zones of love, footsure
between barbs, but soon feel the world turn chill
like a neighbour's eye, and go quickly home.

Addington Village Road

Horses' heads,
turned ash-blond in the wind,
and hills of roof-piled tarmac
gnawing the sky...

up there, they say,
live witches who beat their children
and eat fish-fingers. Do they
mean me? Perhaps.
I have forgotten
so much, frames of reference
misted over while I
was tugging the window blind
on one more morning,
one more one more one more.

Repetitiveness
is a dull husband.
He pours from the sun's
rush-hour and thumps
across my soaped tiles
fresh white footprints
of futility.

And here they are again,
his bawdy mates,
spruce-jowelled spring days,
one behind the other,
swinging like shaving mirrors.
If they'd brought me
instead of winks, a glass
with a clear long view,
that might have been crueller,
flashing, flashing
through a back-shed gap
the vicious distance,
the lost possibility,
but these cold eyes
that dissolve into
scuff-marks, that state
flatly there is nothing
for me but lying down
to a hank of dust
in the common grave –

they stop the heart
with their terrible cry:
no falling green,
no horses
only the worry of wind
with back legs tied
terrace to terrace to terrace,
constantly moving.

Lines of washing
whiten all day.
Their nylon lights,
black roofs, blank sky
oscillate
the guilt-hinged slits
of thin rooms
where I dilute
the pale blood of my
great-grandchildren
with tears and hang
the dead-eyed pans
one by one,
startling as the heads
of cancerous polyps
or too-small money.

Down there, down there
where the hill has not begun,
myth-creatures writhe
their necks at the sky
and toddlers, bare-fingered
push bundles of
disappearing grass
through brown lips, long teeth.

November Portrait

This morning the city has drowned in mist,
thick, plush, elderberry mist that might have poured
from a ghostly reunion of troop-trains.
Poppy-sellers splash the station forecourt.

A woman crossing the glistening street
between buses is mist-coloured too
with her long damp hair and inky denims.
On the train between home and work she read Chekhov,

or gazed out at the adolescent day
in its pinkish drowse, dreaming of many disguises.
Now she vies with the impatient traffic,
her mind a rainstorm of words.

How easy, she thinks, for poems to be born in gutters.
She'd like to be the eternal student,
her life always in flux, a stream of questions
to which there are countless answers.

Instead, she's supposed to be on time,
earn money, explain things
and be useful, as the years
etch fragments of dark into her senses.

But still she thinks how age might set her free,
cutting the strings her children strain at, how
she'll fly as well. Already, in her city,
there's the stirring of wet, iridescent wings.

One day, she'll travel like the mist,
or lean on steps, idle as a wreath of poppies.
One day, the heavy magnets of her love
will be tiny, piercing, star-like memories

and immortality will claim her
if she can only keep the sharp cold throbbing
in her bones, the blue November clouds
rushing beneath her feet.

November

The wind is sudden.
Leaves pass like millennia
rusting the hill.
One by one, the trees
will open to let in light,
each twig a small seed-fern,
a fossil of the air.

Funfair on Mount Tibidabo

What armies of magical children,
helmets clamped above starry eyes,
excavated this glittering Meccano
out of the mountain's skull?

What passionate strategist
sent the red cable-cars
skimming the precipice into the sheer smoke-blue
of a Barcelona morning

then swept them back to the crag,
quivering with daring,
or launched the Skymobile, great moon-shiny toy
for a restless age, pausing now on its flight-path

to buy up the infant jet-set?
This is the heaven dreamed by
hand-cranked and rusting horses
shambling away in some Latin American corner,

running-boards free to the swift
and shoeless slum-child.
Of a swastika tyranny,
the slick machine at the heart of the innocence,

the crowd says nothing, and we, like a judgement suspended,
float down the unhurried cables
into cloudy pine-tops, bound, so the signposts say,
once more for the Enchanted Castle.

Folk Song

Left school a no one
With nothing to keep me
From now to the tomb −

A no-life for no one
And my grey mother moaning
There's work to do at home.

The wheel wasn't turning,
The lift-shaft was empty.
Dad walked in front of me.
He was going home.

I stood on the platform,
The trains ran round me.
Two eyes found me
And took me home.

I dyed my hair.
I opened my window.
A smile stood beside me:
You're wasted at home.

If the grey days moan
There's lights in the Palais
So stuff your untogether
Old dole and doom.

I'll marry in leather
When I'm thirty-three
And nearly in the tomb.

My face will save me,
My savings befriend me.
My life will spend me
And chuck me in a home.

Circles

In the playground they'd started on the game of belonging.
Their hands were made of china that would not break.
Their faces smiled into the empty centre.
Run home, baby, they sang, cry-baby, run home,
And the left-out child ran home to the grown-ups
Who said, Never mind, one day it'll be all right.
You'll find the grown-ups don't play silly games.
It's bed-time, now, have pleasant dreams! Goodnight!

All through childhood the dream was pleasant enough,
And the child grew up. When she got to the world,
She found they were playing at playing the game of belonging.
Their hands were joined, but she laughed and easily broke them.
She stood in the ring, she smiled into the centre.
The faces round her weren't smiling. Nobody stirred.
Dance, won't you dance, she asked them, won't you sing?
Not, they said, till the stranger has left the ring.

And then they all joined hands again behind her
And the game began. She looked back several times
And saw that the grown-ups had certainly been lying
Or perhaps the world had changed since they were there,
Because everybody played the game of belonging:
They belonged to the game, and nothing was all right.
She'd dreamed of living, now she dreamed of dying
For the dead would surely not play silly games.
She'd dance and the others would dance, not quite belonging
But stretching broken hands across the night.

Objects and Shadows

Before their time, the child-red apples crown,
Birthmarked with gold. We have no child like these
Under the sun. We visit empty-handed.
In dark leaf-nests the children swarm and fatten.

Hard-fleshed desires surround these celibate nights:
Nights of gold wine, red flowers and dishes, sweetened
Out of the limitless artistry of hunger,
Not to be tried: nights of the nerveless conscience;
Nights of well-chosen words passed without fumbling,

Electrifying the tiny wire between
Host and guest, mourner and ghost. We pause
For the last time at a first imperfect kiss.
To see, to touch, to hold, to possess:
The infinitives multiply on the merciless tree.
Foresight refused to alter this, could not
Turn back the diver from his pool of flame,
Nor warn the desperate climber to renounce
The glimpse of burning apples, far or falling,
Falling absurd, untasted into winter.

At the Pool

Planted in winter at an uneasy hour
When the stars of wishful lives were changing courses,
My single fruit swells to the knife of summer.
It asks to be named, to be named beyond all caution;
Dazed with the endless human repetition
That ploughs the water's solid blue or docks
On banks of light to burn towards perfection,
Desire keeps finding monuments to itself
And whittles from all shapes the one chosen.

This is the stepping-out from half a year's
Snug deceptions. This is wind-warned skin,
The rush into total knowledge, iced and pure
And unbreathable. The water is sky that burns
Down to the starless limits of its silence.

Stormed by an unplanned birth, I run beneath
The forge of the sun working its flame-white circle.
The shorn green bank, bare paving, glittering pool
Frame the dark plunge and path of my distraction.

Autumn '77

'One summer must serve
for a decade,' we sigh,
grey islanders, keeping our nerve
under the craggy sky.

The season is finishing,
a colder begins,
though it feels no different. The sting
is harboured in every wind

that plucks at our stalled machine.
Today we queue for bread.
Fear shrivels us mean,
vulturish. So much is dead –

wharves where the tide creaks,
a crane glowing rust,
the obsolescent Works,
livings rammed into dust.

Leaves falling make more noise
than the unemployed;
their lobby went by without trace,
their banner, a blown cloud.

A harsher silence
folds on the lately closed
factory where, at a fence
of fresh barbs, the last

picket shifts cold feet,
and the old, clear image of right
fades with the outside-broadcast
vans into the night.

Which ever way you turn
the dials of politics,
principles blur and run.
in the end, to throw bricks

seems an act of desperate reason,
for how else define
the invisible moral lesion
between your stance and mine?

Words? But words are these
buttonless, stained and stale
"freedoms", "equalities" –
dregs of the jumble sale.

Blood and bread remain holy:
when the baker oils his trays
the queue's corporate belly
hymns private enterprise.

Along the High Street, still
June's washed-out flags are tethered,
stubborn as the people's will,
dancing blindly into weathers

propitious to nothing
but anger and doubt.
The gift, then, was to sing
at all, never mind what about,

and furl from rotted brick
colours that semaphore
not defence or attack
but knowing who you are,

or thinking you know. Somehow
we all belonged to one
Union then, but now
as the year turns, we're alone,

each tensed to the next privation,
squirreling what won't keep,
justifying the filched ration
with that tooth-mark, ownership.

Our dreams, great shapes of light
and complexity, run loose
like wind-snatched kites.
It's a relief to choose

the quick, brute, earthbound kill,
or, as justice flies away,
to say we were too frail
to fight on such a day.

Latest Model

I've been trying for years
to get him right. I scrapped
the old loud-mouthed straight-liner —
durable but inapt
for the subtleties of his mistress.
This one's much finer.
When I call him from paradise,
when I hide my presence in
his brow, his lovely eyes,
he appears to listen and look;
he answers pertinently.
He's also an excellent cook
and cares about his skin.
Where did I ruin him?
It's not that badge of assertive
appetite he wears
in the shadows of his thighs.
It's not that he satisfies it
too quickly or too coldly
(though sometimes he does).
It's not that he tends to vote
for the party with guns and money
(though he's fond of both).
I don't know what it is.
He's my best animal,
the bright crown of my skill:
I know him, and know nothing.
For hours I sit at his side,
invisibly praising him,
smoothing his discontents,
enumerating his talents,
stroking sleek his pride.
With all my creatorly will
I breathe and breathe on him,
yet something insensate, wood,
stays put, fails to get warm.
I think he's afraid
to imagine me beyond
some carved thing he has made.
I'd smash it if I dared:
but how can one artist harm
the work of another's hands?
I already feel how he'll grieve
when I die of his failure to live.

Bay Mirage

This swathe of light is not the open sea,
But the bare flank of the bay extending miles
Before it curves and hard-pressed blue becomes
Violet, a fantasist of depths
In shallows. We could be staring at the world,
But over there is always part of here:
The dream's parameters are all too fixed
In the skull's white bay. Still, I spend hours
Foot-slogging to outstrip those ranks and files,
The tongue-tied, sweating flower-beds, the sharp-edged
Promenades, the tide's polite adjournment,
And sail out into air. Your daily presence
Is like the sun's, unnatural, an invasion
That breeds glitter in water, fires the wingless
To dazed flight, lures skin-cells past their limits.

The Metaphysics of the Virgin of Torcello

The Ducal Kingdom has long since fallen to grass, to marshland
   But she isn't sad about that.
The tourists are slumped in the pews, flexing their toes in their sandals
And the only two innkeepers brood like Sicilian rivals
   But she isn't sad about that.

Her child has announced his right to die, and will die
   But she isn't sad about that.
And fury still burns in the human eye when it meets the eye of a stranger
Even if that eye should be threatless, blue – an infant's –
   But she isn't sad about that.

Nor is she sad because she is poor and homeless,
Nor because she is suffering from post-natal depression
Nor because she is only God's mother and never considered a person:
And though it is true that no man has ever made love to her
   She isn't sad about that.

Why she's sad is simply because the stone-setter gave her
Curveless lips and dropped a faint tear from her eyelid
So that all the worshippers, even the weddings and tourists
Are suffused with a gaunt, black limned, soft-golden, mosaic sadness
Mixed up by themselves and the artists. And she, wherever she is,
   May even be smiling at that.

Maureen's Magnificat

You were called Maureen, aged five
And chosen to play the Virgin
Because of your long red hair.
I thought it a little unfair –
You weren't even coached or tried –
But you looked so perfectly right
For the part, I had to forgive you.
All the house went hushed at the sight
Of the flamey stream that fell
Down the back of your sky-blue shift
As you knelt so still, so still
And the Angel mumbled: 'Fear not.'

Nothing else about you was rare,
You were squat, with a broad pink face
And pale eyes that seemed puzzled
By the rumour of your hair.
It was down to your waist by now.
You must have moaned when your mother's
Stiff, stout brush raked out
The sparkling knots, and on Friday
Nights, when she crowned you with foam
And it toppled down over your brows,
You must have shed scalding tears.
But at last she taught you to care.
You began to own your hair.

By the fifth form you'd grown tall.
You sat at the front of the class.
You were not very popular
Nor clever at anything much
Except having long red hair
Which you wore in a rope-thick plait, like a dare.

Nobody bothered to pull it.
Plaits, and you, were right out.
We had perms, we mocked you, no doubt.
Our laughter died that day you unravelled your hair.
Oh, you were more woman than any of us were.

You left school, your life
Knotted up in your red silk hair.
It must have been heavy at times.
You must have felt lonely and small,
High in your tower, locked,
And the boys all crying below,
'Maureen, Maureen, let down your hair!'
What a miracle when you did.
It rose like a twisty stair,
And the bravest one found you there,
Waiting with wide, troubled eyes
For his tender, evasive 'fear nots'.

A STRANGE GIRL IN
BRIGHT COLOURS

(1973)

Prologue

Quietly the sky measures
the lengthening days. Her blue

pallor is blotted with cloud messages –
the indecipherable

desires of chain-footed February.
Out of the garden's squalor

breathlessly climbing,
the trees enmesh themselves

in buds black as barbs.
The sky says nothing

about hope or rewards.
Newness is terrifying.

Now the birds resume
their tinselling cries

that dismiss starvation and snow.
There are eyes, flower-small,

opening in the hedges,
shedding a strange light.

Stones have been shifted.
A memory of love,

an impossibility,
pecks at barrenness.

O lonely month
with your hard frosts and soft tears,

you tap and won't be silenced.
You demand action –

a deed, a commitment,
a wound to be root-filled.

Like the shiver of catkins
I hang these words upon you.

Sonnet

I like the baby's song, raw and glad,
as we ride home in the bus, in the year's gut-end;
an ambulance shrieks, the sun is nobody's friend,
but the small voice sings and sings of love well-starred.

Though it cried, will cry again, and, some time, die,
it does not ask to be married or insured.
These rough-haired vowels my children also purred,
are whole and ample worlds. Too soon they'll try

the nervier pitch, the riddle of consonants
which now these grown-ups sift, or else have lost
in speechless doubt. Chainsmoking, moping past
waste-heaps of passion, dregs of indifference,

no lowly ancestor can sing them home.
They travel like poison to the child's sweet tongue.

Menopause

No pains, no midwife now;
this is the dud season
set between extremes,
when the travel agent prints

red skies, gold skins
on the flat eye of the future.
It shuts. A woman mounts
her ageing escalator,

treading the rutted years
for music, like a stylus.
She catches, catches.
Her body glides by

on a pitiless turntable.
The light drops from her hands
to another latitude where
thin girls laugh

in the fumey slipstream,
their lives blowing outward.
This way, please, this way.
Here is a wooden cold,

a night unfit for journeys,
a night for turning home.
It is the twelfth month.
No baby cries.

Christmas Greetings

Fog thickens on the rose-bush. The moon eyes
of slowed cars grope homewards.
                              Don't despair.
The old romanticisms sound real tonight –
a string quartet gesturing ultimatums –
on the other channel the blaze of war
is sterilised in twenty-inch black-and-white,
and if a censored scream escapes, turn off.
Through fragile walls my neighbour's child coughs
one cough for hours between the ads and silence.
Our local madwoman calls out for her husband;
her porch-light frying the grey air gold, she craves
homecomings, visitors, incessant chat
to radiate her mind's iced rooms.
                              Don't listen.
In stiff dark copses now the multi-mouthed
holly broadcasts weather hard as death.
Don't worry. All the tills are wide awake.
God smiles from these Caesar-headed metals.
Our country's peaceful, though it has its poor –
scar-faced behind grey windows. Don't touch them.
The electrified manger bleeps from its new wrapper.

Superstore

This is the factory that makes the master-race;
the place where the dead are sold, fully-processed,
and the starving swing on meat-hooks or drown in vats.

So, madam, take your choice
from these gutted scraps, these eyeless hunks
in their deep snow-shelvings,

this terrace of ripe-bellied jars,
this marble plateau stained
by fresh garbage of amputations,

beyond the citrus shores, the steep nut-beaches.
Dip your white fingers anywhere you please;
rub, thumb, select, discard

for your larder of gilded shrunken-heads.
This is the grist of despair
guaranteed, madam, to pack

a power-house of protein, contract
the first pulse of the master-heart,
and to gird an entire cell-structure –

bones like rocks, hair like branches,
eyes that see in the dark,
blood as dark as burning raisins.

How much, how much forgetfulness,
rich as pudding dough,
do you need to out-eat guilt?

We will sell you the lot, we have everything.
Our conveyor-strips ceaselessly slide.
This is the exit, here is the sky

carved from a nerveless blaze
where snow-crystals span their beaded
prayer-wheels over and over

the tunnel of the wind-iced street,
and the throats of the charity tins
cough on cold nickel, your hasty apologies.

Palaeolithic Incident

Wolves from the wolf-red cave,
and the sabre-toothed tiger
that prints the Mendip mud
with barbed soles, are moving.

The gorge drops her green
fogs like a witch-curse.
High on the falls of scree,
human feet

dart to where the trees thin
on distanceless rock –
ten anxious knuckles
that have lost their ape-grip, their

old steady rhythms
under the irretrievable
assurance of a tail.
Balked now by cold blades,

white quartz, black basalt,
the cave-man flattens.
His fingers scrape upward
for the scarred wet lips of owl holes

and momentary moss.
The first dews lightly touch
the leaves of the valley. He slips,
slips faster as rocks spin with elms,

pivots, and hangs magical
from a skein of dead tree.
Above him are grasslands, sky
and the small lamps of strawberries.

He will worship them with bites
whole off the stalk, will lie flat
and breathe levelly again.
One tug, and the plateau will be his.

He leaps from his dream, but the sky
plunges backwards, and he
knows that the tiger is standing
below, and he is falling.

Biafrans

She still has her woman's body;
she drags its empty skin
step by step from the well of cynicism.

Her youngest child at her hip
lurches with closed eyes,
his life between her toes like the dust of wheat.

She carries him all day
back through the starved field of child-birth,
back to the first hunger of her cervix.

She returns him to the shadows'
falling bayonets.
The night swells like oedema, like a womb,

and a man's curses smother her; she's
his lost mirage. Her mouth in his, he cries,
and the bones of her pelvis fill his belly like meat.

From a Diary

Dear one, the week
slowly steps towards you. I'm frightened.
Fine mornings turn to rain by noon. Spring comes.
My eyes cloud with superfluous scenery
where images of you hustle and fade.
I sit by the telephone. The room darkens
into a featureless grief, and it is night.

The liberation of dreams
brings you back; we close upon a breath.
Peace creeps into the space between two skins.
Waking, my hands shake even to unseal
the vacant envelope, the far-travelled lie.
Merely to catch your glance across drinks and smiles
and murmured riddles about the weather, could kill.

Time and its slow rhythms
somehow sustain me; the transparent days
that pass like dancers carry me towards perfection.
They cannot reveal that the dance has no denouement,
how soon and bitterly each scene must be stripped.
Spring shakes the throats of the flowers. Winter watches.
The next act is unimaginable.

Night Song

A day of footloose sweetness, disenchanted
already, it begins to travel on.
The free can't keep from their double-locked apartments.
The city's watch-dogs can't detain the sun.

Outlawed, I gather up the words we dropped,
strain faded smiles from bottles left half-drunk –
garbage of memories cleansed, assembled, loved,
to challenge this city's boredom, this room's dark.

Though time's barbed wall divides our continents,
wired to my desperate hunger, you return,
melting its shadows. Now the city lights
rise like the sun. Dream-trapped all night, we burn.

Distinctions

The green hill-spine bends
to the new development
where graduates raise tulips and two
denim'd kids apiece
in stucco semis; their
Condé Nast living-areas in glass cases swarm
along the poppy-field kept
by a rustic whim, begin
to claw that gravelly scoop
borrowed from the hill
and leased to artists all last summer. Strange
happenings of smoke-bombs, clowns,

masques and kinetic painting
brought down the TV cameras and the odd
police car, light buzzing, a throttle of rage
before the sightseers revved and tutted away
up the dirt road. I
walked it every night,
padding on secretive soles the miles between
July poetry readings in fierce sunlight
and the enclosed Blues of late September
under a skull of rain.
I came and listened, crouching, uneasy.
I didn't belong
to either sect whose sparse lords balefully glared
at each other across the sandy floor
as night fell. The poppies dripped away.
Taking their bits of poems in plastic bags
and flowered vans full of old mattresses,
pale girls and boys pitched camp.
The residents lowered their blinds,
smiled, and turned the switch marked apathy.
Again I climbed the hill
to where the old estate in scabby mounds
of rented concrete hangs;
it has no artistry, no wiles
but those of subsistence.
Its girls, with sober head-scarves and great prams,
shove for their lives.

The Inheritors

The street lights bronze the pale weatherboard
house-fronts. Beyond their heads, twelve bald
bulbs climb, one behind the other,
up Beech House, beechless as Buchenwald.

Plimsolls pound. A human shadow drops
and coils for cover behind the concrete stair.
The panda car is watching somewhere else.
The broken glass winks under the star.

Outside the fish-shop, knives are flashed.
Down in the play-park, five
girls curse and laugh and jounce the metal horse,
and wait all evening to be snatched alive.

These are the locks they'll wake behind, and these
hard sons the sort they'll struggle not to raise,
against the weatherboard and echoing stair,
down the cul-de-sacs as short as days.

A Future

The lights of the estate blink on at dusk –
little well-drilled municipals, one for each

porch. Through curtained panes, block after block,
the violet shadows flash

animus of some small-screen homicide.
Out in the real night, bottles are cracked

for real fights, real wounds. I can't escape;
nor can my children, making what the world

would call an ignominious beginning,
their landscape crowded, graceless and cut-price.

Fingers in mouths, they sleep beyond despair.
Toys colour at dawn. A new snow spills

its innocent stars over the pointed hoods
of anoraks shoving into the main street where

plate-glass defines the limits of free will.
Sweets for the unsweet. I take and share

the sugar gems, souring my children's teeth
in lieu of their inheritance. I weep.

Though no one's starving, and the poorest will
receive his little spring

by courtesy of the state and Montessori –
paints and clay, milk and imagination –

the landlord holds the clock's trump card. These hopes
he'll blot, despite all miracles but money,

and money he'll withhold against all odds.
The rooms are shrinking fast, the colours die.

With snow-clogged boots the bailiff wanders in,
talks to the baby, comments on the cold,

sneering, apologetic. It is fate.
The price-tagged dreams fall to the darkening street.

Survival

It is my second summer here. A flat dread
sits out each afternoon. I keep my head
trying to work off the dense, inflated, blue
nightmare of half-a-dozen paddling pools,
with my dust-brush and sink of dust-coloured clothes.
The garden's sand and stones where nothing grows
but a shaggy skull of grass; my neighbour's gnomes,
planed off by four low fences, mark the place
where civilisation clinches this disgrace.
Last summer, though, was worse. I slept
whenever the children slept, but couldn't get up,
and didn't comb my hair for a month.
Time swept that stranded death to colder nights;
I tied great Christmas stars around the light –
purple, green, blue, gold – and thought I'd learnt
how to survive.
                    Will this summer's dragging hurt
let me survive the lesson? I must hold
with all my muscles the summer's blue and gold.

Betrayal

The suburb climbs the hill. Like an eclipse,
its shadow falls across the broken wall
where the last garden dissipates her red metals
for spring's melting-down to the steam of tarmac.

The orchard trees shake and cower behind
their curtains of cold jewels. I am no sun.
My boots smash their aisles, one more town-planner
to snatch the green fruits and promise them pie-houses.

This death is precise. With one stroke it ignites
the rowan's thin fingers, the hawthorn and the rose
trapped in her arsenal of fertility.
Their fires spring in unison to the sky.

They should be left to question the heart, and die,
these doomed mothers cradling pods of blood.
Why do I need to gather their sorrows home
to be scoured and preserved for a winter of usefulness?

The spiders have hung out their murderous silver
warnings over the graves of old flower-beds
where the great golden-rain, the tiger, crouches.
He is gleaming but hopeless. He waits, but I am gone.

In my suburban kitchen I will shush
the awful riches, split the rose-branch stem,
and delve the peep-holes from the sides of the apples,
and shut their eyelessness with snows of sugar,

while the walls of the garden crumble to the screams
of witches with scarlet dresses and spider hair.
I was their friend once, but I betrayed them.
I have a full larder and two clean children; I am the hungry suburb.

Crossing the Border

The round-scalped Cheviots
retreat into North and South,
gathering sheep-whitened battlefields
to the blue clouds' rainy neutral.

How their lyrical distances
coarsen when you enter them!
To marry a landscape is hard,
its blemishes enormous

underfoot, as the quick ram
lurches to the summit.
The bloody claws of heather
chain each step to their Flodden.

We brood over lamb-skull, rabbit-pelt –
fresh relics that mark out
the strategy of the latest
territorial argument,

while the flash of an aircraft, trailing
through silence its long abuse,
recollects a cruder armoury
that poured from the hills, ablaze

with the gargantuan love of rivals.
On moss-soaked Humble-down
they resolved their differences.
Time and geography

have trodden the two nations
into one rough grave
here, where the gale skims
the border fence, and we celebrate

with biscuits and burn-water.
The small barbs have nothing to guard
but a dark sea of peat-rigs
where the fir-babies stiffen.

They promise devouring maturity –
a rank, black night of needles
that the spryest foot-soldier couldn't
unravel. But, in twenty years,

the forester's saw will have carved
an acre of ruin over the dirt-tracked hill,
its shape slowly returning,
and the small brown deer in exile.

Remembering Morning Prayers

Salve Regina; in honour of your feast
we'll etch our knees with wood-grain, red and white –
cricks in the back and indifference in the soul.
Will she, the pasteboard queen, attend our sighs,

as, blue on blue, the sulking armies drop
like thunder-claps, worn sandals tipped in pairs?
My eyes grip hard her mortal surfaces,
or close on venial thoughts. Her mysteries

lie somewhere else, the points of seven swords,
the angel's stance, the lightning, the dismay
glowing through dark like fierce high-altar jewels,
plucking the retina with fires of truth.

Alone, I saw her tears and felt the quake
of innocent blood out of the torn heart –
but here, even the martyrs yawn. Beneath
the shoals of virgin coughs I drift awake.

Poor, faceless mother, voice a patter of beads,
form lashed to rocks and walls, helplessly bent
to those who drown, these pious headaches slip
through history now. What blessings came, are spent.

At Puberty

After rain
a blue light settled over the convent arches;

the naked asphalt astonished itself with diamonds;
even the washed-out plaster virgin
in the Bernadette Grotto, and the mulberry tree
propped up and barren of silkworms,
stepped cleanly out of their decay.

From the back of the music lesson
a girl stared through a window
watching beam upon beam of realisation
incise the long mists of her childhood.

Her thirteenth spring
was born among the tattered pages
of the Older Children's Song Book.

Komme liebe Mai

sang the class, uneasily.
A new emotion,
innocent, classical,
yet making her shake and burn,
was softly unravelled
by the clear-eyed woman who sat

at the black Bosendorffer
with her coquettishness and her merciless
gentle arpeggios.

The elm leaves turned, silver-backed,
on a wind coarse as hunger,

and nuns in their distant sanctuary,
the dark-blue brides of Christ,
closed their ears to the sin, the soft
tired alto of girls at puberty;
heard still a child's soprano.

O impossible miracles, light
out of straggle-rowed chairs
and school-room floor-boards –

the girl, pale as clouds,
stares for a year, aching
at the vision which has no need
of the speechless peasant,

which will suddenly vanish, leaving
only the deep river between them –

the woman who needed nothing,
and the child who promised everything.

Heroes and Villains

The air-raid siren's wail, pitched on its edge
of hysteria, wavering up through tired
valves into the staring seventies, still
un-nerves my parents. It's an old flame
who drags them to their feet, panting a bit,
fills their glasses, remembers names,
while their cold-war sophisticate, their only
surviving child, sits yawning at the heat
of that red sky, fogged behind fumey glasses
where god's Churchillian-jowled above the spires,
where flying bombs silver into
mystic V's, and friends outlast thick fires.
Love fills their eyes. It was a holy war.

My parents, seven years wed
but festive still in silks and fresh khaki,
swarmed like liberators through S.E.,
laughing and ducking as the Blitz spat blood-
stars back at them, and missed.
All night while the incendiaries spawned,
they kept awake and close,
crashing each German skyline to a smoke-
filled void under the white planes of their thighs –
such heat, such vehemence – and still
Auschwitz an unnamed drumming in the belly;
Auschwitz a mumbled word for a private deed,
dumb and vague as the old error which stopped
the dark clock of my mother's monthly flood.

All that summer the Blenheim dragon pumped
the home-fires' heat to fever. I uncurled
my ear under the taut paunch where my mother
cast on new wool for her victory December
but no sound reached me. Five years on I probed
the tobacco tin my father 'd saved
for one bright button, Royal Artillery,
flame-winged, more bird than bomb, and felt my dreams
thunder with disappointment. Twenty more
years, and I see all life slump valueless;
my father, blond and young in pointed cap,
still holding that child, that flashing of white love,
fists up at the sun, and all the young, blond, fine-
boned patriots we had never understood
feeding to flames under the same black sun
a million more pale children, one by one.

The Making of the Dictator

The hungry pressmen can his mind;
headlines like jackpots spill its chat;

the words tickle the voter's dream;
the images nudge the consumer's fat.

The fists shake flame, the mascara winks;
the cameras plant their sparkling shocks,

and still the voter believes his ears
and the satisfied consumer jokes,

till censors switch the slogans off,
and aides flush out the image – there

the invisible shape forms on the daïs,
its shadow taller than the spare

young smiler in the armoured car
that drove across the living-room –

this sightless eye, mouthed howl, drab hand
in silence draft the laws of doom.

Poem for May Day, 1971

In Moscow, aerobats instead of tanks,
and flaming through Old Town a rampant east
wind. It strafes the bare playing-field
that once was green lake. Two willows still
search the old boundaries for lost glimmers
of themselves, the cinerama of water.
Dark over roofs, the last eye-witness of
still older, witch-ridden marshlands, the Parish Church
booms out tradition on its mechanised chime,
hustling for faith down Bishop-named terraces.
In Church Street traffic scrapes the courtyard where
god's rugged, four-square stance still flags us down,
bells bursting out over our heads
like almond flowers along grey streets; inside
among the drifting whispers no one prays.
Plaques are read, each altar-piece observed,
while the tableaux in each window still pretend
to filter mysticism from a common light.
The sightseers leave, shutting the west door
with care. Outside, unseen, the faithful keep
their wooden seats for fate or reformation –
one woman and a dirty child, conceived
each by years of hardship in Old Town,
and the village idiot's latest descendant
nodding his goat-face at an old hallucination.

Aesthetics

Caught off-guard by the impudent laser beam,
alienated by a delicate whim,
the new aesthetes excitedly prospect
with guidebook and credit-card the age of steam.

It is September. On warm holidays
when the West End flickers into humanity,
Pre-Raphaelite silks float sandalled feet,
and the subways speed enlightened coteries

seeking the dim hives of market stalls
where a Renaissance glory emanates
from the bland patina of Victorian industry –
daguerreotype, ivory, willow-pattern plate.

Meanwhile the 'Mystic Orient' sustains
Victorian travellers' tales. Its trinkets tipped
onto white cloth by a staring Tamil sell
competitively to the Sadhus of S.E.6.

And the great Hampstead violinist pays
his private guru, forgotten in Bombay.
Obsessed, they shape the lineaments of world peace
through many a 'finely-imagined phrase'.

Now Blackhill Enterprises close the last
festival marquee. The butterfly falls.
Though money sets ideals in perfect glaze
and transcribes the glamour of old movie stars

into a not-quite-accurate verbatim,
the microbe of death navigates deeper mud
than the epidermis. Science hangs her head
when the beautiful die; she can only donate a post mortem.

Me-Time

Been interviewing my latest grin all day,
but still smell daisy-fresh – a nice, tall boy

in a roll-neck shirt, John Stephen's aubergine,
who watches on the monitor again

that grin flashing through legends of trendiness.
Wheels spin, there's a girl in my Lotus, the smile speeds west,

swerves, brakes, and now it's on my face.
Somebody coughs. Relax. They love to hate.

All things bright and beautiful are fake
and that means me. Just hear those punch-lines make

the laughter-scene. Style mod, intentions trad –
that's what they dig. I pray. Calm down. A hand,

folks, cos I'm proud to have for our next guest
a movie-star who's quit the Wild West

for Vietnam. What's his name? O yes. Hi there,
James Henry. Tell us, what's it like, this war?

Uh huh. The hawks wear doves now? Want to win
only to pack up fighting and go home?

That's great news. Great. The loud-mouth's overrun.
No kid? That's great. Where did I put my pun?

Well thanks a lot for talking. That was great.
I'm sorry. Once again our time's run out.

I'm sweating. That's his best Vietnam thumbs-up.
'You're a pro,' he says. I am? 'I wish you luck.'

The Star Is Dead. Long Live the Superstar

The gods have bounced around the world,
jet-plane to Rolls and up again.

Now they've dropped at your feet, give them a big hand.
Who needs Jesus, who needs the King of the Ravers,

who needs Krishna, who needs Lucifer,
Dionysius, Moses, the Kamikaze?

These four make enough noise for the lot of them.
They are sprawling in the air,

nevertheless, pretending to be crucified,
the strobes pitching great shadows of stained glass

over the taut white faces.
Yes, this is the old religion, good as new,

and offering a million electronic miracles,
the snapped string a sacred sign,

the wild dances a raising of the lame.
The roadies may sweat, scurrying between wires

to soothe and adjust currents as high-strung
as their idols' souls, but the little girls

never get tired. They are burning
everlastingly. Their hair whirls like fan-wheels.

Meanwhile, the drummer is attacking himself,
attacking and attacking.

The battered molecules, trying frantically
to recover their shape, must see that he's obsessed,

his blood torrential, his stance impossible.
On the backs of cymbals, snares, octaplus tom-toms

be rides through the hammer and stirrup of his nightmare,
and is hurled among showers of disintegrating tin

into a dud trip called reality.
Death fixes him, white-eyed, from the bedside glass,

but the fiery acolytes keep dancing;
they shake the drops from their eyes and understand

that even before the first fat flame has licked
the box and its flower-load, a smiling resurrection

will be at the vacant drum-kit, announcing itself
The star is dead. Long live the superstar.

Local Boy Makes Good

Justin, Prince of Poplar,
the fantasist in the fruit-salad shirt,
a destiny on his mind,
and the Cotton Street washing-girl
he lived with a year
still in there watering
the floor he shouldn't have stepped on
with his dirty dreams
big as fruit machines,
and his disgust;
Justin of the docklands,
boarding a sun-bound bus,
taking off from Blackwater Basin, the cranes,
tenements and masts
reeling like Ferris wheels
as he sweats it out in the cockpit
of his jet-set acumen, schooled
never to look down
into the storms of laughter
and the white-faced wind:
Justin Adamant,
lifeman of one mind,
who laughed off every crisis,
having taught himself the simple sum
that in Cotton Street the rats
make love, but in Wassermann's
of W.1 there are
beautiful silk bedspreads, prices
slashed by more than half.

Ad

Depressed, dispirited,
tired of trying?
Or just plain lazy?
Don't despair!
Now you can make
your own amazing
Krazy Kathy;
all you need

is in this chic
zip-fastenered, jet-propelled,
super de luxe
persona-kit.
Look into it, there's
riches for you.
A genuine girl
from a peel-pack, she'll
rise and shine.
This soufflé-stick –
a quick lick –
will give you her face;
these luminous moons –
pots of paint –
will be eyes, this slick
instant atomiser,
hair, and her mouth –
you can make it
in the wink of a roll-top;
peach, plum or sun-streak –
your favourite tint
in a special-seal finish
to give kisses that shine
and words that spin.
The body is easy –
allure from a tube –
just pierce and squeeze,
and there you have it,
the curves of your choice
the tan and the little
sun-gilded hairs
all down the thigh.
Beautiful animal!
Catch your breath;
there is nothing more;
no Maidenform,
no little X-tra.
All you need now
is to dare
to speak to her.
The words, you'll find,
are everywhere.
Just read what you see,
and await your prize.
Radiant, smiling,
she will rise up,
reach out her arms

and clasp you tight,
radiant, smiling,
and you will freeze
as she starts to devour you
like perfect peas.

The Girl and the Thing God

Shining plate-glass crammed with clocks and faces staring at clocks,
Saturday being dedicated to the multi-media, many-faced, million-
armed Thing God

the girl passes gracefully the south-west window of W.H. Samuel,
seeking discovery of the self on this consumer sabbath in this mirror
of religious manifestations. Her reflection moves like the ghost of
an ad-girl struggling for form and substance in the brassy shrieking
forest of live time

its tall clocks fat clocks mod clocks trad clocks clocks with revolv-
ing golden testicles Disneyland clocks travelling clocks shocking pink
alarm clocks clocks with black faces stainless steel clocks digital clocks
spherical clocks sunflower clocks cuckoo clocks

all variously shelved and priced, all arms at various akimbo. A
chaos of times that does not, unhappily, equal timelessness, a terr-
ible multiplicity of inaudible, mixed-up crisscross times chewing
rapaciously at the girl's twenty-five pound, all-wool, boutique-styled,
sixty inches of paradise-green self-esteem. Her great mossy tree-
trunk of a coat flickers among burning questions

      – am I pretty
      lean enough
      and not too mass-produced looking
for the twenty-eighth day of november in the twenty-first decade
of the century of the many-armed, golden, atomic Thing God?

How his pendulums sway, how his fly-wheels sing. He is bright
bright brighter than girls' mere bodies, brighter than their mouths
nervously laughing, their voices lamenting, their minds dimly intuiting
the disastrousness of too little money or too much fat. He has ground
to the gold ashiness of a museum head-dress Helen, Simaetha, Garbo,
the Virgin Mother, Great Aunt Violet – their inimitable myths.
From now on all shall be beautiful, he decrees, for the price of
beautiful clothes and expensive cosmetics – sauna baths, kohl and
the labour of manicurists, nylon, sealskin and proteins in bottles.
But the palace of the Thing God is the shortness of time, his armies
are minutes and seconds who pour endlessly into the town on horses

black as funerals. And he has decreed that no person nor thing, however beautiful, shall remain so for longer than the distance between a scrawled short-hand burble of epithets and its eventual eighteen-point by-line on Vogue super-gloss

savagely scanned even by the girl who pushes home her pramful, and with worn heels shatters the puddles, and thinks seriously of suicide

on this star-studded, jostling, note-rustling Film Première of a Consumer Sabbath.

And, all over the town, infinitely glittering windows cloud with the curvings of breasts and thighs, the shadows of brown, grey, white and scarlet skirts and bodices, the wrinkled ankles of boots, the sharp eyes and pale, peaking lips questioning prayerfully the moon faces and numerously pointing hands of the great Thing God

– is this our moment, our orgasm, sainthood at last?

or even at the high noon of our festival spend-out are we still overtaken

worn-dated

by some star somewhere with limitless cash and limitless opportunity, who queens supernaturally on the crest of each new minute, the illimitably in, immortally beautiful high priestess of the church of Things Unlimited?

Even the Thing God pales. What a terrible baby to worship. Better to crawl home among the middle-aged failures, at one with every powdered-in wrinkle and slopping-over waist-line, chained by suspenders and sunken into fur-lined ankle-boots.

Dear God, mouthed the face in the window, let me hate you, let me detest all images, let me be imageless

let me be brave enough to let you devour the perfection of the identikit leaving only the sacred bloody-awfulness of the identity

eclipse yourselves, galaxies of shining faces whose lewd mouths open onto my twenty-five-pound sixty-inch paradise-green sell-out, mocking. Whose steely arms and glittering sun-heads enclose me with an image at every turn. Whatever I wear, however plain, square, subversive will cost too much and smother me in its masks.

Even blue jeans bear complex telegrams.
Even to wear no clothes is to take up a political stand.

The identity is the image, the image is the identity. The Thing God has eaten the girl long ago.

under the coat

there is nothing.

FROM
AZTEC SACRIFICES
(1974–76)

An English Wife in Mexico City

Three flights up, our pocket-embassy
is a room of shaded eyes, upholstered breath;
our seven-league plimsolls shuffle raggedly
to the conference of its stiff-backed dining chairs.
They'd like us beaten into shape. We know
we hurt the plastic orchids with our lack
of dollars, how unclean our white hands show
on hand-white sheets. It's the thin air, jet-lag.
Tomorrow we'll be saved, acclimatised,
a proper gleam in our pale Saxon eyes.

Already, you're at home enough to leave:
your briefcase bulges missions by the door,
and I've found the dim cleft beside the stove,
the lizard place, smelling of blood and fire,
you scarcely know is there. I'll hack a cave
in ice, pound chillis, scour with pumice-stone,
while you, the hungry pioneer, approve
my brilliant adaptation. Yes, I've known
this room, this land, since the pale soldiery
flashed rape. I too am conquered territory.

Exiles

Who lives in this city, this beached raft
of half-dried lake where the world's skin
splits when God frowns, and churches topple?
Far off, the grass is floating, flowery punts
moving funereal into river mist,
and here the city nomads shadow panes
lit with 'Tacos y Tortas', stripes of airlines.
Who looks for Anahuac? Who tries for a foothold?

...Your worklords, Lebanese millionaires, basking
in a sheen of glass and gold carpets,
their pleasure boat on the waters of Babylon;
the maids in the supermarket,
each with a small, white child in a wire trolley,
patiently clearing paths through a world of short weight;

we, deserting Gringos, circling each other
under the cypresses of the Noche Triste;
the orange-seller, crouched all day on his blanket;
street-corner cops, teeth glittering at bribes;
scorpions; the government in its white
armed mansion...But who will moor this city
in his own rootage? Whom does the city cradle?

A Song of Empires

To the bright ports of the East they came,
pirates and tyrants, a spreading stain
on the water they called the Spanish Main
      Soli Deo Gloria.

Their pox-pit mines were the land's disease;
they leached the lakes, silenced the trees,
but the slave-ships sped through the restless seas,
      Soli Deo Gloria.

From Quito and Cuzco they sucked the soul,
and the Inca king has gone blazing to hell;
beneath the white dome lies the begging-bowl
      Soli Deo Gloria.

Their Vera Cruz, a shining gun,
rose again and roared at the sun
until he cracked. The caked wheels spun
      Soli Deo Gloria.

What coins will be banked when the gold is gone,
when the might of the church is a hollow tomb,
who'll marry the dark and the light as one
      Soli Deo Gloria?

The dollar will rule when the viceroys sail,
and the Revolution lie stiff and pale
in the plate-glass kingdoms beyond the jail
      Soli Deo Gloria.

Tezcatlipoca and the Sorcerers

With our own eyes we saw him
as we worked our sorceries seawards –
drunk and lovely butterfly
of the high wooded pass,
small bones his muttering anklets,
the lank plumes swinging.
We tried to take his hands,
coaxed him for name and meaning,
but he raised a mirror-y shield.
His plugged lip struggled to fly
as he cried to us old errors
and a kingdom already dashed
by the wheels of the planets.
We watched as he leaped away,
leaving his voice ringing
like a lake-flung stone. No birdcall
pierced that vowel-embossed air.
We turned, and over the green
drowse of the valley rose
red smoke, a skirl of war cries
and the long keenings of capture.

On the high pass he left us,
trickster, *chapultepec*, smoky
moon-lord and truthful fool,
his basket heaped with green chilli.
Silent and ashamed,
we gathered our windy spell-scrolls.
All day, in a shroud of forest,
we dropped to the city, creeping
like fatted slaves to their slaughter.
Our war crimes, sanctified
no longer, packed black snow
into the pits of our hearts.
Lord, you have ruled unwisely.
Lord, you must give back the crown.
Sails, bright swords in the south;
north, a blown tress of flame.
With our own ears we heard it,
the cry of Tezcatlipoca:
'Those who are marching inland,
march with the heavens behind them.'

Las Brisas

A day after the first mosquito bites
our bodies flare with peso-sized stigmata.
They come between desire and us all night;
our book of dreams grows jumpy with errata.

Guilty, I try to recollect the crime,
and plunge again our river's coiled green flow,
parting the wavering maize and sky-washed palm,
the silk mud streaming from my swimming toe.

The game's to drift away from you, dissolve
in deeper, colder waters, then strike back
full of the thrill and fear I'll never have
earth's warmth again, your coat spread on the bank.

Thirsty towards dusk, we dropped some coins
at a shabby stall for gulps of melon ice.
And the mosquitoes' delicate, piercing rains
fouled our sweet red rivers of paradise.

Quetzalcoatl 1: The Muse

Across the million pleatings
of silver, he was my winged
stowaway, my dissolver
of miles both salt and stone.
Cloudy, he followed me,
and the sun dropped like a coin
to the Gulf. His face recurred,
mild as the dolphins of air
shouldering our undercarriage,
and when the black nightlands rose
in all their lights to meet me,
he was the basalt wind
scouring the breast of the runway.
He came, breathing white fire,
from the stalled machine of London,
ghost of my Noche Triste.
He was free will, the burning
outside the walls of marriage,
the poet, the opposer.

He was unavoidable
As self, the missing day
Found tamped like a jade sunrise
In the fine cracks and frayings
Of the official skyline.

Down the grey Autopista
where once the causeway cut,
double-lance-broad, through the salt lake,
he haunts like fugitives' gold,
sunk in black reeds, and tarred.
We sift Cholula's stones
for changeling evidence.
Even in his lifetime,
he was intangible;
even to those that loved him,
less than the ash that sang
as it hatched the red pot.
He is unforgettable,
runs like a seismic fault
unhinging seashell cities,
is inscrutable as volcanoes.
All that you failed to conquer
with wheels and slave labour –
your fear, your unfaithful wife,
the palms fisted in neon
arcades for a cent or a peso
lingers on his breath.
In the street of the Noche Triste
he will cling like a scorpion
to the heel of your survival.

Quetzalcoatl 2: Marriage

The stone eyes gazing meet the stone eyes gazing.
Quetzalcoatl, phoney, unabashed
municipal folk hero, basks his coils
in ornamental waters, not perhaps

entirely sham, not quite content to cast
his skin of symbols for the latest fashion.
We follow him along the broad lake-path
striped cool with palm, an effortless translation

of Europe into America. Sunday whites
flash at dark throats, the zoo birds flame, but you
lower your eyes. You're sick of cantaloupe
and orchid, the ripe hot-house of my hope,

and I'm unsure of victory when I gaze
at you emblazoned on the sun's fierce gaze,
the heroes' fountains hanging like white fires
above the wood, air sharp with battle cries.

You want your own Independenzia!
Will you kill for it, die for it? I know
the price of parks, this suffering white and green;
I see the tribesman fighting through a rain

of hurled pots to snatch the leaping spring,
and civilisation, like a tiny fish,
glinting in his blind pitcher. Would you fork
new flames across the mellowed paths of conquest?

Angry, you comb your fingers through the serpent's
granite quills. And if we faced each other
now, there'd be no truce, no tail-in-mouth.
The stone eyes gazing meet the stone eyes gazing.

Two Monologues for a Conquest

1 *At the Lerma Factory*

The top of the mountain is flat
as if the rocks had been ironed
one wash-day by a stupendous wad of metal
that left it yellow, gasping

but fit for use. The investors whistled in
then, their turbines hymning prosperity,
argued, calculated.
Next, the builders, the ants,

erected this second storey of seared flatness.
Now it owns you and us. We climb here mornings
up the piled snake-coils of the motorway
to watch you make money.

71

You have a desk, maize-coloured curtains, a bathroom,
pearly and green as onyx.
The children loll on the wall-to-wall. It's home
except when we visit the Plant's

cavernous zoo. Your machines,
rolling out paper miles or slicing them softly,
are brute logicians, scathing of mere hands.
A shuffle of workers tends them

warily. Their eyes
darken towards our trail of confetti colours –
pastel vignettes of wife-and-kiddies, scissored
straight from the pages of *Time* magazine.

We glide gratefully
into sunlit silence. But there's a cloud
blown in from the snow zone. Supplies
of an important chemical haven't arrived.

Elbowing swathes of light, come at last
into visible power, you must leave
on a mission too exacting
for workers or wives. Trapped in the picture window,

I stand and watch the gate open
to your steady, marching pace. The other watchers
cluster, patient as flotsam, along the railings.
We are the unemployed, whose eyes say nothing,

but follow the skim of your tyres over the scorch-marks.
I remember the red Paseo Tolucan,
A parched tongue quenched by a single thread of fountain.
My last lifeline, a blue carbon breath,

has expired in dust. I'm marooned,
a speechless, white, colonial puppet-face,
cringing like an apology behind
gold-toothed curtains. Here, for the first time,

the Plant becomes audible. It is nearer than hope.
It stands at the door and whispers, a guillotine
with voicey blades, drumming the sullen machine
of its hunger closer and closer.

2 *In the Jardin d'Espagne*

Two children swing through an ironware jungle
in the Jardin d'Espagne. You're so late
I'm almost out of breath. I try to stare through the trees
into the windowed heart of sub-Manhattan.

Which cube picks out in strip-lit migraine your
tequila-breathing deals and machinations,
or do you service the other wing of the city?
What klaxoning auto breaks your guilty run?

Can two children hold off my madness
with small, stained hands, or the worn toe of a shoe?
The orange slide swoops to white concrete.
Their colours wrestle in a clash of shadows.

Dusk, and the respectable families leave,
but the rusty-horsed roundabout keeps shambling
its sinews like a clock. The city brightens,
ringing our leafy island with pale fire.

Shall I set out towards one of the postcards,
lit with the names that mean money,
or try the high shrilling peaks of Mestizo Spanish,
my tongue already lost like a Nahua text

in the blaze of civilisation? How can I reach you
from a cancelled self? The date trees' shadows
claw the gravel. I am beyond one word.
Please, please, can you tell me –

How do you ask, how do you understand?
I pray to all the lost gods for a trochee singing
out of the dark, my name and my existence
on smiling lips: only the squeak and tick

of the roundabout, and scattered footsteps, answer.
Two children are making a game
of snipers and searchlights. Their bright eyes hold me.
I am in border country, wasteland of spies

and wetbacks, the running shadow, the aimed gun,
motionless, nameless. If I'm still alive
where is my voice, why do the words lie silent
under the scream? Why is the scream silent?

Wonder

When you watch the bird-limbed boy in a celluloid haze,
strung on the rack of his growing and his hunger,
dying an inch, a light-year, from your table,
remember your children. Wonder at their birth.

When the fatherly general with the strategic smile
despatches flame to some peaceful delta hamlet
and from every child the ground sucks a crimson shadow,
remember your children. Wonder at their birth.

When you count the dead in your heart's comparable desert,
when two stone figures meet without sight or touch
upon the last bright field where love was promised,
remember your children. Wonder at their birth.

And when you bleed in accordance with your season,
in time with the cold moon where men have stood,
congratulate those who escaped becoming human:
remember your children. Wonder at their birth.

Tricksters and Quetzals

Grasshopper Park: a lake about to burn
so everything must fly, or try to learn

quickly: trees, bearing their double cross
of leaded silver paint and Spanish moss,

tangerines in untopplable pyramids,
the cartoon carollings, *Feliz Navidads*

trickling down through pumice fog, hot beats
of light from streams of Detroit metal sheets,

fridges on wheels, with pinwheels for propellers,
and balloons in mass-revolt to launch their sellers.

When the side-saddle optimist on the Witch's Hat
(a child or the child's maid) squeals a scarlet

butterfly into the air,
it's a tiny heart set free, or the brilliant last idea

Moctezuma whispered to his sage:
design, he said, a hopping grasshopper-cage:

line it with Huitzilopochtli's golden shit
and lock the hopping Christians up in it.

Farewell

The giftshops beckon, siren-eyed through veils
of onyx beads. You long to buy up all
my heart's desires – rings, rivers, foreign lands.
We walk a vinyl desert, cowed and small.
The city carries on, not asking who
leaves or invades, take over or gives way.
Our futures vanish into air. We know
only that we will wake to different days,
and your America is solid, near,
and mine about to tilt and disappear.

I thread my finger through the Taxcan ring
of peacock eyes, round windows rainbow-stained
in a dark ritual of unmarrying
while clouds scatter like snowfall to the plain.
Now air grows tall between us, now the sea
interminably heaves its ruck of years,
but if our hopes crossed worlds to meet, still they'd
chafe with cross-purpose. It's no cause for tears:
the gift was real. I nurse the fierce green land
in circling shadows of my writing-hand.

FROM

A NECKLACE OF MIRRORS

(1978)

Portrait of the Poet as a Little Girl

When the old exchanged dark glances
and rumoured blacker wars,
the ears of the little pitcher
grew wide with metaphors.

Her cave was the door-lined box
of a basement flat, her sword
a finger tracing woodgrain,
herself, her minotaur.

She shone like an epithet
in a father's fantasy,
ribboned, soaped, uncurdled
by the world's sour simile.

Slowly, slowly the labyrinth
unfolded in her brain.
Its streets of narrative lured her;
she trod a winding town,

and banished her own shadow
with neon heroines,
pavement and playground bending
in her hands like plasticine.

But fiction belonged to children:
new times, new customs sought
a new, self-probing scalpel —
obsidian for the heart.

It gleamed in history's fist,
the patrilineal prize
which she, disarmed, betrayed,
must learn by craft to seize

Sappho

Alcaeus jewels her icon — 'violet-haired,
holy, sweetly-smiling' — a later hand
adds heterosexual tears like flecks of gilt

as Phaon blunders from her lyric flame.
One little push, and she's a woman again,
the dark hair swirling at Leucadia's foot!

Surely she ground her bread on sharper stone,
entering history beneath some stained
old flag of power, Amazonian spark
spurting under the boot of the patriarch?
She sizzles through the mesh sly Phaon trawls,
naming her lovers by an act of choice
as treacherous as talent: in its heat
are fused the stolen verbs – to love, to write.

Li Ju-Chen's Dream

> *A talented woman is not a virtuous woman.*
> CONFUCIUS

My thoughts were a thousand fireflies –
they spun towards the grass
and turned at its touch into women
tall as horses, red as brass.

They were wise, their wishes carried
the might of mandarins.
To the Palace of Curving Water
came husbands, lovers, sons.

They knelt before the women,
their ears were pierced with bone,
their feet so tightly bandaged
the silken rags seemed iron.

And they were pale as nightmares
when the lesson was complete.
The stars looked down in wonder
as the warriors left the gate,

hobbling and weeping homewards,
ears jewelled like wasp-hung pears,
while the laughter of their teachers
called through the dark like bells.

The Witch's Manuscript

*Any woman born with a great gift in the sixteenth century would
certainly have gone crazed, shot herself, or ended her days in some
lonely cottage outside the village, half-witch, half-wizard, feared and
mocked at. For it needs little in psychology to be sure that a highly-
gifted girl who had tried to use her gift for poetry would have been so
thwarted and hindered by other people, so tortured and pulled asunder
by her own contrary instincts, that she would have lost her health and
sanity to a certainty.*

VIRGINIA WOOLF
A Room of One's Own

How can I hold this tongue, this eels that skews
from heart to throat, rattles down the dales,
spreads frothing over cobbles, riots like ale
on market-days, spills barrels of green fruits,
swings like a barn-door till the stones fly in?
Lies pelt bare breasts of truth. Run, mother, run!

Hived in my hut, I gossip with the fire.
Wind calls through cracks, the raining's all of words.
'Hush,' I cry, 'Hush!' Rags of my cindery bed
nudge me with husbands. Yes, this flesh was byre
to many, but the wrung juice of my soul
sprang to the ceiling, left a dry corn-doll!

Wind has a song too, pipes a plainchant swell
from Abbey stone. There, wifeless men snare truth
with inks and snow-white vellum. No red mouth,
no herbs or snakeskins rhymed a stronger spell!
Words preen like bishops on a bench, strange flowers
softly entwine the capitals of power.

Cover me, seas of singing, stop my heart
and throat before another night's command.
In darkness every word's a furious brand
that lights an ankle-snapping fire. I mount
black clouds and ride upon a storm of cries,
hugging a stick as red claws reach my thighs.

Song for Puberty

Girl upon history's doorstep
dressed up in hand-me-downs,
are you a cleric, soldier,
troubadour, businessman?

La belle dame sans merci,
Beatrice and Lucy Gray
star in your cloudy sonnets
then laugh and run away!

Today it's easy as dreaming
to smash the safe of the past,
but the coins you clutch are worthless,
the sharp-eyed diamonds, paste.

Girl upon history's doorstep
take off your heavy clothes,
look at yourself in the mirror,
know what your body knows.

Somewhere, somewhere is waiting
the 'I', the active voice;
he'll build a house of words for you,
his rose, his swan, his muse.

He'll swear to you you're happy –
and how will you learn again
to wield your tongue's fierce silver
against your borrowed name?

The Cruel Mother

'There was a lady lived in York
all alone and alone-o
she fell in love with her father's clerk
down by the greenwood-side o.'

Baby in the long grass,
baby in my lap,
soft as April ferns, the hair
gathers on your scalp.

Frost salts the dandelion,
October fires the dew;
the reddest apple on the tree
is not as sound as you.

Lady with the penknife
outcast of the thorn,
has scattered bloody jewellery,
but her chains cannot be torn.

Baby like a spider
sucked up all the sky,
hair a darkening forest,
the moon in one blue eye.

Hide her in white blankets
quiet as a leaf.
The apple swells inside me,
the nib clicks from its sheath.

Eyes as bright as rosehips,
the ghost-child won't be laid,
but cries to break the chain of words,
and laughs to see the blood.

Sylvia Plath

Scatter my words to Atlantis
or the chill-lipped mills of the sea;
I am full as the Taxcan mountains
for the earth has married me.

Old patriarch dressed in marble,
I've hung your beard on a vine
and thrown your frown to the leopards of sun
that are leashed to my wrist, that are mine.

I've dropped a gleam of water
like a rock, and like a tree,
two heavy, bright-skinned children,
for the earth has opened me.

Blue-stockings with black notebooks
are howling jealousy,
the Sybil chokes on her cobwebs
for the earth has aproned me.

Old patriarch dressed in marble
why does your eye spark still
under the frown of the earth-haired man
who calls my tigers to heel?

His traps are as sweet as brambles
and old as the hills of the sea,
and the wound is deep and perfect
where the earth has married me.

Last Words of the Sybil at Cumae

I, who wanted never to cease flowering,
hate, hate, hate the flowers!
I hang like a tooth, old ache

in the mouth of time,
maddened by little fingers,
the pertinence of children

claiming to love ancient history
for the glimpse of a bloodied nerve.
Shall I tell them how this

priestess of millennia,
this poet of arrow-heads, bird omens,
microfilm, lipstick stains,

was visited by kings
and other heavy merchants:
how they rolled out their sorrows like silks:

how swiftly my secret eye
would gather the threads, improvise
a brilliant symmetry?

Or shall I describe the lovers,
creeping by night, their hearts
in their hands like starry torches?

They needled my thirst with sparks
and burnt me to ashes.
The children poke and taunt.

All the long spring day I've spat
like a broken automat,
the crooked coins, the answers

to questions that cannot be answered
now the flesh is nothing, nothing
but an even crueller question.

Go away little flowers, cold
little suns, don't distract me
from the winter I'm trying to die of.

The Housewife's Manuscript

I'm one of the favoured prisoners here, they say.
At eight o'clock when factory windows stream
brass, and the workers march to the machines,
I sit before the blank page of the day.
No orders come. The pen, that ancient fake,
watches me through my endless coffee break.

Can this be freedom, this pre-packaged bread
that can't be grasped or tasted? Coming home
each night, word-famished, numb as spoons, the men
jeer at my helplessness. An unmade bed
or half-filled page, they say, can't bend the mind:
how can the wheels of cobwebs drive and bind?

They'd build a masterpiece in half my space!
What would they build with? Light and shade, the stain
of blood or ink, a child's hunger-pains,
a fat womb or a shrivelled purse, perhaps?
Yet I can't wish their wages. Man and wife,
both have been stripped of tools, both jailed for life.

We move on wires. Our circuits, cruelly twined,
flash 'earn' and 'spend'. A pure sterility
x-rays our deepest yearnings. I can't say
why I must serve this power. I came here blind.
If now I see, I know the switch is set.
I picture freedom, and I cry – 'Not yet!'

FROM

UNPLAYED MUSIC

(1981)

Coming Home

The bar is full of English cigarette smoke
and English voices, getting louder —
a language lumpy as a ploughed field.
It's hard to believe our tongues have got it too.

People are growing drunk at the thought of home.
The sea patiently knits its wide grey sleeve.
No one else comes up to lean on the rail
where, damp and silent, we watch

the long white skirts of land drifting
sadly through mist, as if a young girl sat
by the shore still, waiting for a bluebird.
It's September, and already winter.

And now the toy-sized train
is creeping with its worn-out battery
and a cargo of sandwiches and arguments
over grey-green fields into grey-white suburbs.

We're playing a game with the streets —
spreading them out and tying them up again;
when they've caught us, we're home.
The lawn blows like a tiny English Channel.

We chug towards our own front door
anxiously, seeing as if for the first time
how tight the plot that locks us in,
how small our parts, how unchosen.

Almost in Walking Distance

Two centuries ago they would have taken
this same short cut through the farm,
the rough, scrubbed boys and girls to whom
cornfields were work-a-day. In tight best boots
for the Sabbath, laughing tumbled country vowels,
on mornings blue and full of bells as this one,
they would have skirted the plait-haired rows
all the way to the crumbly lanes of Chaldon
and the parish church, their star,
cradled in a cluster of bent yews.

What's altered in the scene
isn't just the split sack of pesticide, blowing
from a hedge, the tractor waiting on the hill,
or the bare sting of my legs against the stalks;
it is my aimless pleasure in the walk
and the edge of melancholy it lends the bells
calling me to a hope I cannot enter
across fields I know well, yet do not know.

Suburban

Smoke hour. Brown
death of the blue hydrangea.
Gardens of spilled rust.
So the season smudges over

the measured clarifies
of these hill-cut avenues.
Only the houses seem
still sure of who they are,

solid as bottles of milk.
No season alters them.
They exist, they are proof.
Their owners cherish them

and are in turn defined
by white stucco, black
stripes of thirties Tudor,
the cat, the snowy drapes...

or are they? Once
I'd have been sure, accusing.
Now I think of eyes
that wait, of quick hands moving

in windows not yet lit,
and words, less brave than money,
lying spilled and incomplete.
No hard-earned roof stands nearer

now, than the rims of stars
pulsing through time and dark.
The cycling schoolgirls laugh
past their parents' fences.

Love flickers to itself
like an unmatched television.
But the neighbours will say nothing.
The priest will bless it and bury it.

Pleasure Island, Marble Arch

Time and tarmac have ditched the last
Creaking ghost of Tyburn. A car-swathed island,
Wooded and sown with fine turf, is the navel
Of this oil-fed, pleasure-rich half mile,
Its jewel, a square grey lake, restless as silk
Under the wind. Dull, now, with November,
It wears the haunted, half-resentful look
Of an off-season resort, waiting for life
To be cheap and bright again, a gift of strangers.
Then the fountains will leap like marathon dancers
Pushing white-muscled shoulders and sparkling hair-do's
Hour after desperate hour into the blue,
And the grass lie kindled gold under the plashy
Coloratura of many languages.
Wilkommen, bienvenu, the faded placards
Shout to themselves in the subway corridors –
And a girl will move shyly in front of the fountains,
Smooth back her hair and smile into the future,
To be peeled from its eye, a tiny Hockney
Of blue light, spray and the delicate boldness
Of flesh in a mild climate.
Meanwhile, the grass dims, the stone faucets
Eat leaves. A gardener stoops to his heaped barrow.
The island is ours, though we possess it
Only at a distance, from office windows
Or the tops of circling buses. We approve
Its elegiac mood, its little image
Of transience. Whatever storms tug
Bigger seas to madness, we trust this water
To move within imaginable limits.
It is stamped on our days, part of the pattern,
An opaque poetry, revealing less
Our sense of failure than our certainty
Of what's provincial, gardened, small, enduring.

The Girl in the Cathedral

(for Andrew and Joanna)

Daring to watch over Martyrs and Archbishops
Stretched in their full-length slumbers, sharp-nosed Deans,
Princes and Knights still dressed for wars as dim
As bronze, slim feet at rest upon the flanks
Of long-unwhistled hounds; daring the chills
And dusts that cling to stiffly soaring branches,
This small eloquence is a stone so plain
It cannot go unread, a chiselled spray
Of drooping buds, a name, a date, an age.
Susannah Starr died at ten years old,
And no one knows why her timid presence
Should be commended here. While history filled
The log-books of these lives, she sat apart,
A well-bred child, perhaps, patient with tutors
And needlepoint, perhaps a foundling, saved
By some lean churchman, warming to his duty.
Quietly during 1804
The blind was drawn, the half-stitched sampler folded.
Whoever mourned her must have carried weight
And bought her this pale space to ease his grief
As if such sainted company could speed
Her journeying soul, or because he guessed
The power of one short name and 'ten years old'
To strip the clothes from all these emperors,
And rouse her simple ghost, our pointless tears.

A Poor Man

He never buys his wife chocolates
but brings her library books
chosen carefully, three-week gifts
she must learn not to love too much.
He mends his children's shoes
with small, awkward fingers,
using the toughened scraps
of unworn leather, prized
from outgrown heels and soles.
Such economies are in his blood,
though his wife frowns over them.

89

Their evenings are almost cosy.
A single red skein
of electric heat chafes
their knees as they sit,
he marking books, she darning
a small glove. The children watch
an old black-and-white TV set
where success flickers vaguely.
When he denies them things,
his voice is measured, bringing
the balm of moral right
to a pain he no longer shares.

His house is slowly falling
apart, while he looks on
with love and fear, as though
sole witness of something sacred.
For such dilapidation
holds memory fast: his sister
skipping her breath away
to die at six years old;
the small chipped kitchen, filled
with the patient, cough-like sobs
of his father's hammer, tapping
onto his worn school boots her unmarked soles.

Before These Wars

In the early days of marriage
my parents go swimming in an empty sea –
cold as an echo, but somehow *theirs*,
for all its restless size.

From the year 1980 I watch them
putting on the foaming lace.
The sun's gold oils slide from their young skin
and hair as they surface

to fling each other handfuls
of confetti – iced tinsel
and tissue, miniature horseshoes
of silver, white poppy petals.

I search their laughter in vain:
no baby twinkles there,

and Hitler has not yet marched on Poland
beyond the cornflower waves

this print shows pewter.
But that the possible happens
eventually, everyone knows...
and when they swim away

the unsettled water fills
with shuddery, dismantled weddings,
a cloud unfurled like an oak tree,
time twisting as it burns.

Over the Bridge

Cowboys, free-rangers of the late-night bus routes,
they're on the town again, sucked cigarettes
fizzing as they lean into the edges
of shrilling corners, talk in nudges
and taunts, three ten-year-olds, too tough
for girls, though girls they'll brag of, soon enough,
their long, pale hair brokenly raked
beyond the line of last year's makeshift
barbering, frayed shirtcuffs falling short
to flash expensive watches, newly bought.

The city's greased and rapid
machinery is their passion; they'll work it
to the last cog, discovering all the loopholes –
how to tilt the pin-tables
and not lose the game, when to slip
their pocketful and saunter from the shop.
School can't detain them; they've cut the nets
of that soft playground. The lesson drifts
above their empty desks like a will read
solemnly to the disinherited.

Westminster Bridge veers up. They clatter down,
jump for its back, are straggling shadows, blown
and tiny as they run to see themselves
V-signing back from windows of black waves.
Further and further now from from the controls,
they wander out of history, though its spires
rise in gold above them. The clock's proud face
makes no comment, shines on some other place.

Consumerlit

This bookshop is being dreamed by somebody
who sits behind a desk and smokes cigars.
It expands shinily over several rooms and levels –
as dreams will.

These are enchanted forests
where crisp new chart-toppers, pliant classics
recently televised, are waving and singing
thoughts that are everyone's, simple as dollars.

And it is simple
how the ideas fit their packages,
how the packages assemble the idea
exactly as we've learned to like them.

The Old Wolf is dining on a new author.
Literature is a colour-plate princess.
Lightly she slumbers, waiting for your kiss
in the shade of the *Silmarillion* calendar.

The Light of Reason

In the stone darkness flanked
by Queen Victoria and the War Memorial,
long panes of leaded gold
make a cloister of the Reference Library.

On endless walls they climb,
the creased, close-packed maroon and sepia spines,
out of the schoolmaster's reach,
beyond even the tip of his lifted cane.
The gaseous light
of turn-of-the-century classrooms
burns clear the small print
on dozed-over 'Births, Marriages, Deaths'.

Who will ever dust them down,
those dreams of scholarship, now?
The chairs creak
with rheumatic departures.

Tiny thysanura
are racing like grey stars
all over the unbroken midnight
of Prescott's *Inorganic Chemistry*.

Rules for Beginners

They said: 'Honour thy father and thy mother.
Don't spend every evening at the Disco.
Listen to your teachers, take an O level
or two. Of course, one day you'll have children.
We've tried our best to make everything nice.
Now it's up to you to be an adult!'

She went to all the 'X' films like an adult.
Sometimes she hung around the Mecca Disco.
Most of the boys she met were dead O level,
smoking and swearing, really great big children.
She had a lot of hassle with her mother;
it was always her clothes or her friends that weren't nice.

At school some of the teachers were quite nice,
but most of them thought they were minding children.
'Now Susan,' they would say, 'You're nearly adult –
behave like one!' The snobs taking O level
never had fun, never went to the Disco;
they did their homework during *Listen with Mother*.

She said: 'I'd hate to end up like my mother,
but there's this lovely bloke down at the Disco
who makes me feel a lot more like an adult.'
He murmured – 'When I look at you, it's nice
all over! Can't you cut that old O level
scene? Christ, I could give you twenty children!'

He had to marry her. There were three children –
all girls. Sometimes she took them to her mother
to get a break. She tried to keep them nice.
It was dull all day with kids, the only adult.
She wished they'd told you that, instead of O level.
Sometimes she dragged her husband to the Disco.

She got a part-time job at the Disco,
behind the bar; a neighbour had the children.
Now she knew all about being an adult
and honestly it wasn't very nice.
Her husband grumbled – 'Where's the dinner, mother?'
'I'm going down the night-school for an O level,

I am,' said mother. 'Have fun at the Disco,
kids! When you're an adult, life's all O level.
Stay clear of children, keep your figures nice!'

Days and Nights

It's a summer day very nearly like any other.
The pollen count rises in the afternoon.
An Arab child steals a lemon in Selfridges.
The discontent of the unions rumbles softly
like a pit disaster many miles away,
while, in a murmuring classroom,
a young teacher is telling her six-year-olds
about the Miracle of the Loaves and Fishes.
The first Royal Garden Party is held,
and afterwards the small hills of Green Park
stream dark suits, pastel hats, flowing skirts
and low, respectful conversation,
as if people were coming out of church.
Even the tired marquee-waitresses,
leaving by the Electrician's Gate
with sprays of yellow rosebuds, feel important.
Two nurses, one on nights,
one days, swop their only pair of shoes.
Along Park Lane there are lights and dinners,
young love and middle-aged lust.
It's a summer night very nearly like any other,
the traffic thinned, the stars keeping their distance,
the Chancellor not even dreaming about the bank rate.

Disco on the Dana Regina

The North Sea drags our keel from noon to noon,
And when she kicks, we, who have trawled the moon
And pinned those dead glass oceans to our maps,
Tumble below to flay with Scotch and Schnapps
The old god, Fear. An oil-rig, dressed to kill
In lights, our Messianic money-mill,
Stands starboard, crying: 'Blessed is the pound!'
And in the flickering Disco, to the sound-
Track from *Jaws*, elaborately we prey.
Our streamered hair glows pink, as surf makes way
For civilisation, with its fizzing measure
Of music, sex and hope, its will to pleasure
Edged like a stylus, bravely swinging north
Between the winter stars, the berg's white tooth.

Unplayed Music

We stand apart in the crowd that slaps its filled glasses
on the green piano, quivering her shut heart.
The tavern, hung with bottles, winks and sways
like a little ship, smuggling its soul through darkness.
There is an arm flung jokily round my shoulders,
and clouds of words and smoke thicken between us.
I watch you watching me. All else is blindness.

Outside the long street glimmers pearl.
Our revellers' heat steams into the cold
as fresh snow, crisping and slithering
underfoot, witches us back to childhood.
Oh night of ice and Schnapps, moonshine and stars,
how lightly two of us have fallen in step
behind the crowd! The shadowy white landscape
gathers our few words into its secret.

All night in the small grey room
I'm listening for you, for the new music
waiting only to be played; all night I hear nothing
but wind over the snow, my own heart beating.

The Strawberry Mark

(for Dave)

Every Sunday we'd set out at noon
and wear down the light to a dust of stars

before turning home. Our child went with us,
billowing the green sail of my smock.

Do you remember that farmer who disturbed us
on the shady edge of his corn? We ran like fire.

Monday would put us in our different places.
You worked. I queued, dragging the heavy basket.

The strawberries plumped as their price went down.
I ate them, craving you only.

Our walks got colder and shorter.
The house re-introduced us, two strangers.

Come November, I would find
the hem of the green smock suddenly drenched dark.

Alone, I walked and walked the edge of the world,
my breath the great wind there. You thought me lost.

Someone said: 'It's a girl!' You lifted the shawl
and saw the dappled scarlet on her thigh.

Twelve summers and many strawberries
later, the mark has gone,

the peculiar heat and fragrance of that summer
sealed, perhaps, in her smile. Or simply faded.

Late Gifts

They meet in the mornings over coffee,
their only bond work, and being married
to other people. They begin with jokes –
the chairman, the weather, the awful journey –
delicately pacing out their common ground.

Later, they expand into description.
Families, who might not recognise themselves,
are called up in brisk bulletins
edited for maximum entertainment.
(Gossip ignores their middle-aged laughter.)

She shows him a photo of her sons
tanned and smiling over fishing nets
one green June day, when her eye was steady.
He talks about his daughters, both away
at college. They admire everything.

Through the months more curious, more honest,
they cultivate small permissions, remember
each other in the fading summer evenings,
and suddenly get up from their lives
to hunt for a book or pick some fruit.

No quarrels cloud the gentle light between them.
They imagine how their adequate weekends
might shimmer with this other happiness,
and how, perhaps, they'd still end up with less
than haunts a gift of pears, a borrowed book.

A Latin Primer
(for Kelsey)

Today, a new slave,
you must fetch and carry, obeying
plump nouns, obstreperous verbs
whose endings vacillate
like the moods of tyrants.
Say nothing. Do as you're told.
Dominus servum regnat.

Tomorrow, a legionary,
they'll have you building roads.
Clause by clause you'll sweat
to span counties, withstand armies
Pack the stones tight and straight.
Don't stop to pick flowers.
Milites progressi urbum ceperunt.

One day, you may discover
that even Rome was young.
And this is literature –
to hear your own heart-beat echo
in the bright streets of grammar
where poets lark and sigh,
and girls, like you, are choosy –
Da mi basia mille, deinde centum,
dein mille altera, dein secunda centum...

The Skin Politic

Sails for the dark blue trade routes
Guns for the jungle
Mulberry trees for Brick Lane
White skins for England.

Smiles for a passport
Pavements for wet walking
Ramadan for emptiness
White skins for England.

Airmail for memories
Shudders for dark nights
Swastikas for bus shelters
White skins for England.

Long words for governments
Short words for street corners
Last rites for promises
White skins for England.

Floating Gardens

Dusk drifts down in speckles, a dull sootfall
sticking to each clean edge and blade.
Am I asleep awake? The marigolds
light sudden waxy lamps that flicker out
in moments, leaving me futureless,
and the mind's secrets open, clear as stars.

They show me another garden where the warm
breath of the dying grass you whirled like grain
and scattered, moving patient as the sun
along each brightening strip, scents the air
and makes your absence almost tangible.
Do flowers fear the dark,
and shiver for the hands that tended them,
busy now with dinners, conversation?
Rooms are real, glowing through their glass
where families root and bloom, solid as brickwork.
But the gardens are lost to this world.
They whisper. They know it is not easy
to be sure of what we are or whom we love.

Double Bed

She goes upstairs early,
lies wretched in the double bed,
letting its cool space ease her.
The curtains strain a thin daylight.
People move faintly beneath.

Tired out, she enters soon
those inner vastnesses
where wishes are almost naked,
pursuing new shapes
of desire, new solitudes.

She wakes fractiously
as the bed rearranges its sinews
for a heavier transport.
He brings her cold flesh
and delicate flattery:

and at length she plays her part,
breathless, half-drowning,
while he straddles her as if
he would life-save her.
He's not a brute;

she's not all innocence.
It's just that, by daylight,
they inhabit different angles,
no longer wave and smile
from each other's mirrors.

So, not unkindly,
he turns his back
(he can never sleep facing her)
and she will lie staring
at the dark for hours,

motionless, disarrayed
in the space he has left her.
It is too narrow to sleep in,
but impossible to leave,
she thinks, without robbing him.

A Marriage

Mondays, he trails burr–like fragments
of the weekend to London –
a bag of soft, yellow apples from his trees –
a sense of being loved and laundered.

He shows me a picture of marriage
as a small civilisation,
its parks, rosewood and broadloom;
its religion, the love of children

whose anger it survived
long ago, and who now return like lambs,
disarmed, adoring.
His wife sits by the window,

one hand planting tapestry daisies.
She smiles as he offers her the perfect apple.
On its polished, scented skin
falls a Renaissance gilding.

These two have kept their places,
trusting the old rules
of decorous counterpoint.
Now their lives are rich with echoes.

Tomorrow, she'll carry a boxful
of apples to school. Her six-year-olds
will weigh, then eat them, thrilling
to a flavour sharp as tears.

I listen while he tells me about her sewing,
as if I were the square of dull cloth
and his voice the leaping needle
chasing its tail in a dazzle of wonderment.

He places an apple in my hand;
then, for a moment, I must become his child.
To look at him as a woman
would turn me cold with shame.

In Pear Tree Road

Only plane trees stood
Now in Pear Tree Road.
My father mourned white orchards,
But I was glad,

Especially in autumn
When the wind laid tiles
Of their broad, delicate leaves
To colour the stone miles.

I kicked them high and wide;
Pleased with the patterns, took
A rustling quire of them
To page my heaviest book.

Many were merely brown,
Some still green as May.
The best had put on all
Their rich seasons to die,

Hanging tight until
That final crimsoning
When the small sun had pressed
A flame hand to each skin.

December Walk

(i.m. W.A. Lumley)

1

Late winter noon,
the sky blue-black as taxis,
the street below
brimmed with fluorescence.
Typewriters stutter madly
as if they kept trying
somehow to re-shape the words
for bread or anger.
My father stands
in the narrow doorway
where a dim room meets
a darker hall.
His bent hands dangle,
useless even to smoke
a farewell cigarette.
He has only the threadbare
decision he stands up in,
and when they come for him,
no straitjackets or calming
drugs will be required.
Easy as a child,
he'll tiptoe with the strangers
to their white car.
Fled into this city,
this cradling honeycomb
where all the girls shine
and shirt-cuffs are clean,
I know that I have simply
followed him here,
that this could have been his chair.
He stands at my side,
rubbing the cold from his hands,
amused by his child's
new game – the full in-tray,
the memos, the poems –
and saying with his smile:
no hurry, no hurry.
We all have to go home.

2

Pacing behind him,
I imagine how light he must be.
The bearers' tall, black shoulders
would never admit it.
They are braced for immensity.
The organ takes up the pretence,
and the chrysanthemums, quaking
their frilly gold baroque
through icy chapel air.
In plain pews built
too narrow for kneeling
we remove our gloves
and pray from small books.
He was somebody once,
but sickened, and lost
the weight of himself.
He forgot our names
and wandered for years,
words melting off his back
like snowflakes. Now
as the altar screen slides
tactfully across
to blot out doomed wood,
I recall only a mood,
a flickering of smiled
irony, betraying
that willingness, flat and English
as the whited winter sky,
to be always disappointed
He was an unbeliever
in everything he did,
yet would have had a hand
in this, perhaps, approving
our boredom, the sad weather
and what there is of ash.

Small Views

When a road ends in sky,
you know that the sea is breathing somewhere near;
that the land has admitted defeat,
signing its name regretfully, gracefully
in a scrawl of white hotels.

What happens now?
A string or two of lights, a timid pier,
damp huts to brew tea in;
a lack of view. Is this what matters most?
Is that why we're lured here?

We become child-minded
whenever we stare across water.
We cannot really believe
in a far coast rising to mirror ours.
So too we interpret the sky

whose clear gaze says we're its only world,
and if there are stars beyond the stars
they must be demons.
Down here on our tiny maps
we have heard no news of America;

no film-packed satellites
have retrieved the mist-wept fall of our horizon
How could we live without this prejudice?
How set sail without forgetting
that, sea by sea, we're merely travellers home?

The Great Silkie of Sule Skerrie

> *I am a man upon the land,*
> *I am a Silkie on the sea,*
> *And when I'm far, frae far from land,*
> *My home it is in Sule Skerrie.*
> ORKADIAN BALLAD

Who is he, come to startle reality,
awkward over rocks, climbing without caution
to the cliff-hung cottage where the empty days
bleach and flap, pegged tight against gales?

An unlucky woman, living alone
with her child, not especially gifted
for growth, despite her body's common usage,
her mind composed to a view of the sea's withdrawal,

she heard his knock and put away her broom,
and rinsed the dust from her hands before answering.
She was unnerved by the sight of him, appalled
when he stood close to her, salt-haired, warm-blooded,

104

no scar of deep-sea coldness in his gazing.
He played with the child a little, then left.
From her window she watched him, a long shadow
leaving the cliff-path, intent on its strange direction.

As he climbed to the sand, he felt his love
bled like a fish upon her human knife,
yet knew the dilemma would slowly resolve itself,
a small flame trodden into the floor of the wind.

He paused once, and imagined her face behind glass,
then turned towards Sule Skerrie, the last thread of light,
grieved but sure, already unattainable.
Among the dust of the house she stooped and cried.

Making a Sponge

Not one pinch of love, she thought, was needed
(whatever the ads said). To keep the rules
with a quick hand, and, sometimes, a patient one,
was sufficient to enchant the stolid ounces.
Machines would help (their anger wasn't real) –
a pair of bladed fists pounding the yolk
to a high, pale foaming. Odd, she thought
how the house had changed, as if she cooked that too,
its quiet flecked with the talk of steel and china,
the faint hiss of the sieve, the scratch and sigh
of buttered paper. Someone coming home
would taste the sweetening warmth in every room –
but it wasn't magic. She must keep the rules
still, clear a new space, and count in minutes.
Soon she'd crouch, a midwife, clothed hand
into the glowing dark. She'd lightly tap
the golden discs from their tins
and feel their moisture lift like dying souls
and float to the top of the kitchen. Only when
their fragile skins were cold beneath her palm
could she pile jam and cream, and flourish icing,
architect of a dazzling Winter Palace.
The mob would bring it down with peasant shouts
and swift knives, of course. And she'd play God,
not asking for a crumb of her creation.
She had acted without hope, simply kept

the rules, a quick hand, patience –
though years later a casual child might praise
the memory of that skill, and call it art.

The Freedom Won by War for Women

From hassock, cradle-side and streaming walls –
The fogs of faith and wash-day – thin lives beaten
Blank and hung to weep, the fair are gone.
Raw-fingered saints who've tipped their pedestals

And dried their hands at Father Empire's yell,
They chivvy cautious husbands, rebel sons
With bloodiest white. But they'll take the same poison,
Hands deft among his axle-trees and shells.

True warriors, they were furnace-forged when bombs
Jumped roof-high. From tongue to lung the taste
Of lead rolled death. Massed engines pumped their Somme.

It was a flowering and a laying waste –
Man's skills found shining at the heart of woman,
His vengeance, too, expediently unlaced.

Three Poets Play the Saké Cup Game

A print dating from the Edo period shows a group of Japanese poets
floating saké cups on a stream. One poet would launch the cup,
and another, standing at a certain distance downstream, try to compose
a haiku by the time the cup reached him. In the print, the resulting
poems are being hung to dry on the branches of a tree.

1

Tying his proud syllables
to a scented branch,
the poet hears laughter.
He turns and sees the cup
lodged winking in some reeds.
It will never pass him now.
As life begins, the poet muses,
so it stops, without warning.
Haiku is the game in the middle.
'Have I won?' he asks. 'Or lost?'

2

The orange saké cup
throbs on the bright stream
with petals, like a migraine.
It's only one word he wants,
one last, ripe cherry
brimming with the juice of his poem.
The cup weaves nearer. Demons
toss him a flashy adjective.
He sighs, and scribbles.
Sometimes he can't bear to be a poet.

3

The idea grows.
He must be careful, careful.
Never mind the jeering,
winter's a difficult season
and this could be its soul.
He mustn't let it slip by
as the saké cup slips by.
When he wakes from the poem,
it's dark, the cherry has dropped
many leaves, his friends have gone.

Death of Anna Pavlova

The swans are blue ice now. They remember nothing –
Katya, Marenka who snapped bread
out of my palm with spoon-cold beaks,
their eyes keen as copper. Another hand,
old and yellow-skinned, a tax collector's,
strains from the bank's shade. I swim closer.
It knocks, knocks at my chest. Only stage fright!
Naiads bring rouged cotton, little swans
fuss at my ankles. I shall run alight
in my own white pool towards the crowds,
and show all Russia the wingspan of my love.

Listen, the applause breaks like gunfire
as bruised roses spin through the smoky shine
to drop at my feet. Real birds die like this,
heavily, their broken wings ungathered.
Even the mooning swans, necks dipped to blue
mirrors, die like this. But I laboured

each night until I held another truth.
Shoulders, elbows melted into sighs,
my hands were little flames, their ripples perming
to pure air, my long feet curved
like the beaks of magic birds that never touched
land or lake. In dying there's no art.
When blood carved the snow in the palace courtyard,
I heard theatres weep. The old dance,
choreographed in bones, is disappearing
between these sheets. I rasp my last cries
to prove them right, young soldiers, real swans
whose wings flashed treachery, who fished in silence.

Akhmatova in Leningrad

Queuing at the gate of the Kresty,
The whole city hanging in ice
Like jet beads in a paper-weight,
The woman turned to me twice

As if to convince herself
It was mine, this wrecked white face,
Mine too, the song that had measured
Her hopes in warmer days.

The second time her voice
Was like the first seeping of spring
Wrung from the snow-blue lips
Of a mountainous sorrowing.

'Can you write about this?'
She opened her hand to the wall,
To the women, mute, as if
They queued for the price of a star.

She dropped her hand, she shrugged.
Locked out, I tried to guess
If I'd given her bread or a stone
In the burning clasp of my 'yes'.

SCENES FROM THE
GINGERBREAD HOUSE
(1982)

Secrets

Two families, under one roof.
Mine plotted privacies
while my grandparents, sharp-eared
in distant easy chairs,
logged our fate in a rent-book.

A grapevine straggled, fruitless,
outside, keeping light
from our tiny kitchen-diner.
On the wall, a sprout of bells
was dumb as fungus.

We were 'below stairs'
except for one shared bedroom –
cavernous linoleum grandeur!
I used to dream of escape
by jumping into the arms

of the pear tree that tipped our window.
The grown-ups had their secrets.
I had my rhymes and riddles,
my own room growing inside me.
That other child – God's gift

or Grandfather's punishment? –
came and mooned in our doorway.
I'd play with her and not ask
why her chest flopped, why
she didn't go to school.

She could juggle two tennis-balls,
yet queered her alphabet
in a babyish hand.
When she ripped my notebook of stories,
Mummy explained: 'She's not like other children.'

Mongol

An extra chromosome
has marked her out,
shaped every cell to strangeness.
She wears her foreign country
till we're almost used to it.

Her tiny feet
whisper in child's sandals
but she won't skip into my rope.
She wanders down the hallway,
squinting at an imaginary sun.

She's happiest when lost in music,
carries her radio
everywhere, a small red bag
with a switch-on heart-throb.
He sings to her. She sings back.

They call us 'the children'
but she has a past and I have none.
I wear her outgrown clothes –
expensive sun-dress, party bolero.
She's a tiny, portly woman,

the last Matrioshka doll
to be plucked from its fat, calm mother.
Grandfather savages himself
with guilt, makes jokes, loves nothing.
He wants my childhood in a box to give her.

Misjudgement

Bouncing a ball
in a garden not ours but 'theirs',
I 'mind' the cherry's white
bone china, the seedy ferns.
Grandfather watches.

In the big shed
he planked across the yard
to bite a square of darkness
out of the table-mat lawn,
he is at work, boot

rocking the Singer treadle.
He steers the rich maroon
of a high school coat-sleeve
beneath the ticking needle.
However soft I play,

his spectacles glint at me.
And now the ball, skewed
by a waiting stone, flips
off-side. My fingertips
smart from its escape.

It cracks into the fern-bed
and disappears. I plunge,
parting green waves, and freeze.
A spider gnarls at me,
her crystal all unravelled.

I sense a violation
worse even than smashed stalks.
Behind glass, the flicker
of rage goes out, the yell
hardly touches me.

Spoilings

I bore two vests in winter,
and encapsuled vitamins.
When my throat shut too soon,
the Haliborange pearl
melted into a fish.

My outings were chaperoned,
so I never learned to unravel
the roaring intersection
where cars grew teeth, flashed eyes.
I was kept from the library –

its million strange fingers
printing greased poverty
and the chapter of the streptococcus –
but still they nearly lost me,
at five, to a passing virus

that filled my lungs with stops
and hyphens. I recovered
in surfeits of self-importance.
It was a warm September
when I first breathed sun again.

I saw my X-ray plates
held high, the clean, twin shadows,
ribs fanning like the backbone
of a halibut from the shoals
that by now I must have swallowed.

It would have been much later
that I learned about the baby
whose death had left that silence
in the dark, polished hall, filled yearly
with the blaze of chrysanthemums.

First Loss

A six-months life —
how could it cast such years
of shadow? These were graves
no flowers or tears could seal.
They blamed the hospital.

The child was recovering
after minor surgery
in a ward with an opened window.
Grandfather stormed: 'The baby's in a draught!'
But Sister spoke crisply of 'fresh air'.

Next day, he found the cot moved.
The child lay burning
in woollen hat and mittens —
too late. The sharp autumn
had already sunk its knife.

How long and quiet the evenings
in the big front room
with its shut piano.
My mother twists her hair,
a six-year-old who's seen the grown-ups cry.

Sometimes, during the war,
Grandma would glimpse a young man in the garden,
wearing soldier's uniform.
When he came in, she knew,
he'd clasp her with hands of bone.

Sixth Sense

There's a pane of orange, frosted glass
in the door that opens
'Grandma's room'.
Forbidden to visit,
I loiter outside,

imagining the orange Christmas smell.
Perhaps there are jellies
glistening in waxed cases.
Perhaps the cat would furl
around my hand, and purr.

Goodnight God bless you pleasant dreams –
I chant from the stair.
My shadow devil-dances
to bed in front of me.
A faint 'goodnight' returns.

Why can't I be the child
of that golden room?
Why can't that room's own child
climb with me, mumbling, singing,
a funny sister-shadow? –

For in this darkness
I am turned on a pinpoint
of knowledge, I am pierced
with all the sharp keys
of locked hearts, embattled generations.

A Fairy Tale for Parents

This Hansel, this Gretel
had loved entrancingly, once,
a little before I was born.
They kept in fine tissue
an ashen tea-rose,

a miniature horseshoe,
to show me how they'd danced
towards fabulous dividends
of safety and sunlight and children.
They had one more step to go

when the great wolf, War,
leaped blackly upon their luck.
The sky fevered scarlet,
innocent corporations
crashed, good prospects lay

shambled among corpses.
This Hansel, this Gretel
wept for the lost path,
when 'Welcome home,' cried the Witch,
'Step inside,' cried the Wizard –

and there stood a little house,
dark, wolf-dark, but cosy.
Hansel and Gretel were tired.
They stepped inside, they tasted
again the moist gingerbread,

potent as childhood,
and the spell was heavy upon them.
They never understood
how daily, garment by garment,
it stripped them of choice, of love.

Denunciation

Maria Goretti was canonised
the year I started in Mother Columba's class.
The nun's eyes rolled saintwards
in her gnarled, white face,
as she pictured the knife, its blade

claw-curved in an ivory foot.
We tensed. A peasant girl
and a labourer merged on the fray of the cornfield.
The sky blazed in the moment of the scream,
and the girl broke like a poppy.

By pony and trap she travelled
to the city hospital.
Blood ate through all her bandages.
'Imagine the agony,'
whispered the gnarled, white face,

squeezing between our eyes.
How puzzling, how heroic
Maria Goretti's refusal!
She bled rivers for it,
died and was made golden.

We drew breath again
on the journey north, to Lourdes
and Bernadette, who coughed
as the little, unblessed stream
nipped icily over her sabots.

One day, through the playground fence,
I saw pale sky torn open
by a flame-haired Virgin. I sobbed,
but Mother Columba frowned like the Parish Priest,
and washed her hands of me.

The Second Vision

(i.m. W.A. Lumley)

This wasn't what my father wanted –
rented rooms, the mockery
of the suburb where he'd grown up;
the small city job, small politics
of the office and the in-laws.

His vision lacked assertion
and the final catalyst,
money. I remember his voice
for its wobbling Crosby croon –
another lost ambition.

On our walks together he noticed everything –
still the keen young clerk
scanning for the vanes of ships
from Dock House, Billeters Street,
charting dream oceans, distance.

Long-sighted, he'd always spy
some famous church or bridge
that was just grey mist to me –
but I did see France
as we stood on the pier at Folkestone.

A smear of cloud where water
fainted into blue air,
it united us at last
in the one keen focus, stirred
a seeing at the back of my eyes.

FROM
STAR WHISPER
(1983)

A Cold Dawn

This is the sky that drank its bitter greenness
from the waters of Gdansk Bay.

This is the sky of the world, its forehead smeared
by the faded sacrifices of industry

and breath. This is the sky
that always shines into my room and makes a picture

of the moment of childish tears after a parting.
The first machinery creaks awake outside

like ice at a thaw. Blind hammers
grow intent on their fathering.

Soon everyone's brain will be working,
shuttling the dark, slackened parts of an obsolete engine.

The Division of Reptiles slides
into the square, announcing its dialectic

to the shipbuilder, hurrying
with lowered eyes over the bridge.

He thinks to himself, 'Blood fades.
These stains were wept only by rivets.'

So the snowstorm of light goes on
filling up the day,

and all the small no's are said
and lost in the monstrous yes.

The Name of Names

Because we belonged to a place of crossed-out names
where letters posed with guns like border guards,
and even the trees, blasted and deadbeat,
quaked again at the thought of changing hands:
because the searchlights swung white corridors

down all points of the compass, and the wire
lay wreaths of twisted crosses on the snow –
and because the snow had lost all track of you –
I returned to the rubbled house that was our home.
Now I feel as if I'll never leave again.

I can't think of the past, the crossed-out names,
the burning stars stitched to the east of the heart,
without distrusting everything I am,
but you could trust words written by the hand
that stroked so lightly back the twins of hair
falling across your frown, their gentle aleph.
I can't think of the future's windswept map,
where trains invent enormous distances
past cities atom-fed, white-hot all night,
past forests black and dense as grammar-books,
without loathing the ruthlessness of time.
But if anonymously you should come back
one day, and learn how near the old place is –
no work-camps, yet, no dogs to leap and tear –
turn and approach softly whatever's there.
Look in the dark that might have been our home.
Among the words that fell from me like dreams
until a kind of liberation came,
you will find hidden, love, your name of names.

Geography Lesson

Here we have the sea of children; here
A tiny piece of Europe with dark hair.
She's crying. I am sitting next to her.

Thirty yellow suns blobbed on cheap paper,
Thirty skies blue as a Smith's Salt-wrapper
Are fading in the darkness of this weeper.

She's Czechoslovakia. And all the desks
Are shaking now. The classroom window cracks
And melts. I've caught her sobs like chicken-pox.

Czechoslovakia, though I've never seen
Your cities, I have somehow touched your skin.
You're all the hurt geography I own.

Heart Sufferer

He stands in his kingdom of cloth, the long rolls
heaped in a stifling rococo all around him,
and smiles at the visitors' compliments. His eyes
are calm, however. He is no emperor now,
merely a guide. Business is a small thing
compared to a Bach fugue or even a prelude,
though balancing by day his lost currencies.

He speaks his adopted tongue with a fluent crafting,
except for a few cut vowels. But the poets he quotes
are all Hungarian, all untranslated.
He is recomposing a suite of piano music
remembered across the noise of thirty years,
this businessman who makes out an order so briskly –
three metres of small-check gingham in muted green.

His customers tonight are an English couple.
The man beats him occasionally at chess.
The woman he doesn't know. The cloth is a gift.
She presses it to her face, smelling the sweetness
of an orange giving its gold to the treacherous north.
He waits upon her choice, feeling December
creep from the walls, whisper up through his soles.

Here are satiny linings, cerulean
glints from the rarest birds, the earliest summers.
Here are the stripes of crops, a snow of flowers;
and now the flattened cities, tanks, collapsed
angles of aircraft; table-cloths once dappled
by the Sabbath candles, ravelling up in flame;
small bodies sewn into the colourless dresses.

He turns off the lights (no one else is allowed to,
he explains shyly – it's an old superstition)
and thinks of his tall sons, how they will never
wake the switches of his dying kingdom.
He climbs the stairs slowly, examining
the coats of his two visitors – brash young cloth,
not lasting. His heart warns him, beat by beat.

With luck, he'll leave its music at the door
of his favourite cellar bar. A dish of prawns
is light, easily swallowed. He breaks the necks
deftly, sucks the juice from each stalked head,

and wonders at his sin, the sea-clean flavour.
At pavement-level, London chains its gods
in light; he worships none, but wins each day
by his own kind of fasting and atonement,
time become paper-thin as the map of prawn shells.

The Most Difficult Door

There is an ageing mirror by the stairs
And, next to that, the most difficult of doors.
This is where we live, the home's true heart.
Its furnishings, heaped for some moonlight flit,
Are combs and hats and scarves in slip-knots, all
Embodying the female principle.

I sometimes think they must have swum like clouds,
My daughters, through those sea-blue altitudes
Of birth, where I was nothing but the dark
Muscle of time. I bear the water-mark
As proof, but that my flesh could be so filled
And concentrated, heart to heart with child –

It mystifies me now. I want to draw
One back, and this time feel a proper awe
For the tiny floater, thumb-sucking on its rope,
Slumbering in the roar of the mother-ship,
Or let my palm ride switchback on the billows
Kicked in my skin by silvery, unborn heels.

Instead, through thinnest glass I watch them drift
At leisure down their self-sufficient street;
Their territory might be the whole of time
Like that of lovers in some midnight game,
This house their port where indolently they sight
Far out at sea the changing play of light.

Sea restlessness! It haunts the oldest vessel –
A shanty murmuring under a torn sail
That no harbour is safe, nor should be safe.
Only deep waters lend full weight to life.
The maths of stars is learned by navigation,
And the home's sweetness by the salty ocean.

This glass could cut a vista down the years,
Gathering suburban satins and veneers
To a sleepy London bedroom. Hair, long-greyed,
Glows animal again. They're half afraid
To see themselves, so shiny, crimped and pressed –
My grandparents, doll-perfect, wedding-dressed.

And now its stare borrows an older face –
My own. The moon inimitably displays
Her sun-love. Through these veils we snatch from death
Our dusty matter, light its eyes with myth.
Nature wants Children. Children sometimes want
The moon, the cup, the shield, the monument.

We've watched the comb reap sparks from our live hair;
Now for the putting-on of mock despair
As timeless as these little pouts and twists –
A rite we go through as the cold glass mists.
We know the brightness in each painted eye
Must often be the brightness of goodbye.

My floating daughters, as I leave I'll see
How you will one day look as you leave me,
How touch draws back, malingering, though the breeze
Of night is tugging gently at our sleeves.
Be wary, but don't fear the darkening street.
I give you this, my opened map of flight.

A Case of Deprivation

A shelf of books, a little meat –
How rich we felt, how deeply fed –
But these are not what children eat.

The registrar rose from his seat.
Confetti danced, and thus were wed
A shelf of books, a little meat.

We sang, for songs are cheap and sweet.
The state dropped by with crusts of bread
But these are not what children eat.

They came, demanding trick or treat.
We shut our eyes and served instead
A shelf of books, a little meat.

Then on our hearts the whole world beat,
And of our hopes the whole world said
But these are not what children eat.

Two shadows shiver on our street.
They have a roof, a fire, a bed,
A shelf of books, a little meat –
But these are not what children eat.

The Émigrée

There was once a country... I left it as a child
but my memory of it is sunlight-clear
for it seems I never saw it in that November
which, I am told, comes to the mildest city.
The worst news I receive of it cannot break
my original view, the bright, filled paperweight.
It may be at war, it may be sick with tyrants,
but I am branded by an impression of sunlight.

The white streets of that city, the graceful slopes,
glow even clearer as time rolls its tanks
and the frontiers rise between us, close like waves.
That child's vocabulary I carried here
like a hollow doll, opens and spills a grammar.
Soon I shall have every coloured molecule of it.
It may by now be a lie, banned by the state
but I can't get it off my tongue. It tastes of sunlight.

I have no passport, there's no way back at all
but my city comes to me in its own white plane.
It lies down in front of me, docile as paper;
I comb its hair and love its shining eyes.
My city takes me dancing through the city
of walls. They accuse me of absence, they circle me.
They accuse me of being dark in their free city.
My city hides behind me. They mutter death,
and my shadow falls as evidence of sunlight.

An Easter Garland

1

The flowers did not seem to unfurl from slow bulbs.
They were suddenly there,
shivering swimmers on the edge of a gala –
nude whites and yellows shocking the raw air.

They'd switched themselves on like streetlamps
waking at dawn, feeling wrong,
to blaze nervously all day at the chalky sky.
Are they masks, the frills on bruised babies?
I can't believe in them,
as I can't believe in the spruces and lawns and bricks
they publicise, the misted light of front lounges
twinned all the way down the road,
twinned like their occupants, little weather-house people
who hide inside and do not show their tears –
the moisture that drives one sadly to a doorway.

2

My father explained the workings of the weather-house
as if he seriously loved such things,
told me why Grandpa kept a blackening tress
of seaweed in the hall.
He was an expert on atmosphere,
having known a weight of dampness –
the fog in a sick brother's lungs
where he lost his childhood; later, the soft squalls
of marriage and the wordier silences.

In the atmosphere of the fire
that took him back to bone
and beyond bone, he smiled.
The cellophaned flowers outside
went a slower way, their sweat
dappling the linings of their glassy hoods.

3

My orphaned grass
is standing on tiptoe to look for you.
Your last gift to a work-shy daughter
was to play out and regather
the slow thread of your breath

behind the rattling blades,
crossing always to darker green,
till the lawn was a well-washed quilt
drying, the palest on the line,
and you rested over the handlebars
like a schoolboy, freewheeling
through your decades of green-scented, blue,
suburban English twilights.

4

In the lonely garden of the page,
something has happened to your silence.
The stone cloud has rolled off.
You make yourself known
as innocently abrupt
as the flared wings of the almond,
cherry, magnolia;
and I, though stupid with regret,
would not be far wrong
if I took you for the gardener.

Lines on the Shortest Day

(to Joseph Brodsky)

> *Since this / Both the year's and the day's deep midnight is.*
> JOHN DONNE
> 'A Nocturnal Upon St Lucy's Day, Being the Shortest Day'

It's the year's midnight (I won't count how many
Since your last candle shivered out); now only
        Dust has designs
On the lost She who aped attentiveness,
And clasped your hand, its clever helplessness,
        To Poetry's reins.

So you ride out love's sighs, and history's,
Across the pyromaniac centuries
        To these bright streets.
Hot-line and waveband mesh the stars above;
Down here, the snow grows sluttish at the shove
        Of booted feet.

As for the fact it's Christmas, there's no doubt
In London; neon and tinsel spell it out
              Wherever you're turning,
And though the sun was sepulchred all day
There's a warm flush in the four o'clock night-sky
              Of money burning.

Recruited to our throng, with a lean smile
You press your nose to these alchemical
              Gold-brimming panes,
And deftly lift from each department store
A pocketful of burnished metaphor
              For tawdry stones.

Dear ghost, dissolving inkwards, reinstate
The mourning tongue, the negatives we hate;
              Show hollow plenty
Your whiplash lines whose very commas bite
Until the tears that smart like crimson, light
              Our frozen city –

A grammar for all those who move less freely
Than snow before the wind, or darkness stealing
              Across the floor;
For hungry queues whose meat and bread are doubt,
Closing ranks as the angle from 'sold out'
              Grows more severe.

The law in armour stalks their public squares
And rust-thin words are hammered to new powers
              On anvils of dissent.
At home, and tight, we chant a milder verse
To 'Peace on earth' (from Harrods to St Paul's) –
              Fine sentiment –

Though not conceded by the governing will.
The West stages its cold-war vaudeville.
              And it's as though
We'd purposefully forgotten being schooled
That here our rulers rarely shoot the ruled
              For saying no.

Between our market-place of wind-up stars
And the gross state with its new breed of tsars
              What's there to choose
But this hair's breadth infinity where you speak
And utter your peculiar heart-break
              Part fact, part ruse?

Verse is the courtship dance that rarely fires
A Lucy dead in conscience or desires,
        Yet tyrants fear
That poets are the thin ice of their times,
Their stanzas, tiny casements where red crimes
        Brazenly peer.

Be patron, then, on an indifferent day,
Of every tongue's reluctance to betray
        Its love with silence.
Bless, if you've power, the art of negatives,
If not the zero temperature that gives
        Words iciness.

The Hebrew Class

Dark night of the year, the clinging ice
a blue pavement-Dresden,
smoking still, and in lands more deeply frozen,
the savage thaw of tanks:

but in the Hebrew class it is warm as childhood.
It is Cheder and Sunday School.
It is the golden honey of approval,
the slow, grainy tear saved for the bread

of a child newly broken
on the barbs of his Aleph-Bet,
to show him that knowledge is sweet –
and obedience, by the same token.

So we taste power and pleasing,
and the white wand of chalk lisps on the board,
milky as our first words.
We try to shine for our leader.

How almost perfectly human
this little circle of bright heads bowed before
the declaration of grammatical law.
Who could divide our nation

of study? Not even God.
We are blank pages hungry for the pen.
We are ploughed fields, soft and ripe for planting.
What music rises and falls as we softly read.

Oh smiling children, dangerously gifted ones,
take care that you learn to ask why,
for the room you are in is also history.
Consider your sweet compliance

in the light of that day when the book
is torn from your hand;
when, to answer correctly the teacher's command,
you must speak for this ice, this dark.

Star Whisper

(for Eugene Dubnov)

If you dare breathe out in Verkhoyansk
You'll get the sound of life turning to frost
As if it were an untuned radio,
        A storm of dust.

It's what the stars confess when all is silence –
Not to the telescopes, but to the snow.
It hangs upon the trees like silver berries –
        Iced human dew.

Imagine how the throat gets thick with it,
How many *versts* there are until the spring,
How close the blood is, just behind the lips
        And tongue, to freezing.

Here, you could breathe a hundred times a minute,
And from the temperate air still fail to draw
Conclusions about whether you're alive –
        If so, what for.

Museum

Pro bono publico,
bright wood, clear labels;
a tasteful history
of sand and fossils,

motto-bearing plates
and, along one wall,
like the Apocalypse,
'The Coal Coast' in oils.

Out on the concrete copy,
dogs are walked. The flat
water takes a slice
of sun from the smokeless sky.

The schools line up to go,
but the men in caps
linger shadowily
over toy-town mines, dolls' ships.

They get the place by heart
like the last day at the pit
or the drawer in the kitchen
where the strainer's kept.

March, Happy Valley

Days that are finely stretched and luminous
as the paper of a Chinese lantern, keep
the birds up late and whispering across
the valley, where a massive wind feigns sleep.
All down the heath-side, dangerously close
as heart-beats to a foot that wades deep grass,
hang violets in the strangeness of their blue.
Luggageless, perennially new,
with ancient heads that they can only bend,
they have arrived more quietly than the dew
to feel the perfect cold of where they stand.

The country has a used, dishonest face,
a look of sour back-streets where trade has died
though half the windows still pretend with lace.
Spring, the sweet spring, is a refugee child
grown old before his time, a hope displaced.

Regent's Park Crossings
(for W.H.)

> *It will quite eclipse Napoleon.*
> THE PRINCE REGENT,
> on seeing John Nash's plans for the Park

> *Love then and even later was the whole concern of everyone's life.*
> *That is always the fate of leisured societies.*
> *ATTR. TO* NAPOLEON BONAPARTE

1 *Grand Designs*

A perfumed handkerchief,
a bedspread of silk, a park.
His sun-sleeked horse carries him,

the seaside Prince,
away from affairs of state
at a glorious, graceful canter.

Taker of air and of slender
hands, he is the patron
of the three-hour lunch-hour.

In his memory, two glasses
kiss in a buried wine-bar.
He has left an art of dalliance,

its lovely formalities;
a path broad as four coaches,
a bank of encrimsoned silver,

drawn swords of fleur-de-lis,
ducks in fancy-dress,
footmen and maids abandoned in the grass.

2 *College Fauna*

The park is as broad as thought
but the little bridge over the lake

is only as long as my youth.
The students still take to the water;

their slow oars break the dreams of the punting classes,
tangling, braiding the silver hair of Isis.

I set out for Philosophy,
and left clutching Marriage.

How much safer it would have been
to have strolled these quiet paths,

like Socrates and Timaeus,
enquiring, luminous-voiced, into the Why.

Instead, we plunged for the groves
of Discovery of the How.

Yet the lesson continues still
as if it could never be learned –

that difficulty of virgins
with their own nakedness

when love strips '*cogito*',
from '*ergo sum*' and lays trembling

hands upon timeless fashions, veiled in sighs
and stutterings of leaves, and birds' scared cries.

3 *A Brooding of Mallards*

The females are crowding the bank
with moody silences,
heads tucked in, wings crossed.

I turn to my imaginary companion.
'Perhaps,' I say, 'they have heard
that drought has been declared.

'Of course, it's men they blame,
swimming while the park burns,
their plump green cheeks like silk.'

He smiles. We walk on
to the formal gardens. There
in flower-light, two lovers

have grown together like espaliered rose trees.
Slowly they turn to each other
and sink to the gold-haired verge,

into the gravity
of all that they desire.
A nest of differences

is closed with one winged shadow.
I cannot turn to my imaginary friend;
I have made him disappear.

4 *Reckoning*

At dusk, the May park is suddenly occupied
by hungry lovers. Their hips swing together,

dog-like along the dim paths.
The chestnut trees flick little white embryos

at their feet, their feet burn them brown.
Life is always on the verge of a massacre.

Look where the tulips have been pitched
headless, their rigid figures

starved and blade-like, red
smatterings of their flesh

stuck to the earth. Look where the daffodils leaned
to be photographed, each one

convinced it was the star.
They died as they were loved –

en masse, a whole generation
of perfectly creamed complexions

rubbished and outstripped
by nature's great law of green.

Now the sky glows the colour of lampshades
in a bistro, the trees are black,

crowding big-shouldered like waiters,
priests, aunts, pall-bearers.

Our flustered, red-faced lovers
can't get beyond the *hors d'œuvres*. They dip their fingers,

while the chestnut-blossom ticks,
ticks with the sound of a pen-nib totting numbers.

5 *Mediocracy*

Nothing here is sad or complicated.
The Open Air Theatre will perform
the same three comedies again this year.

The dolphin-boy is a legendary confection,
the drinking fountain, a folly.
The Bandmaster sticks to the light classics,

his shiny regiment buzzing around Sousa,
as if Schoenberg, after all,
had chosen a sensible trade.

Et in Arcadia ice cream
and billowing deckchairs.
Each grassy lap is nurtured by the state gardeners,

and picnicked on by the masses.
It's an English Utopian's dream
where the laws (against walking

on certain banks, and fishing
the duckponds) are so pointless,
everybody obeys them.

A quiet, shared happiness bathes
like a sunset, each limited choice,
and only the very few

are tortured by mediocrity.
They are, of course, free to leave
at once by the Golden Gates.

6 *Nothing*

Your absent presence spoke
softly across the summer
with your haunting absence.

I was between the two,
a child whose timid look,
swinging from eye to eye,

is a metronome of dread,
knows nothing, nothing, nothing
but his guilt-ridden innocence.

So shifts this sea of grass
beneath the wind, until
the sun burns it to stillness

and gold. But what is kept?
The daylight turns its back,
slips the transfigured quilt.

7 *Civilisation*

This is the made world.
The geraniums are so perfect
they could be plastic

except for their peppery smell,
pure red. The grass has been trimmed
to within an inch of its life.

The roses are better fed
than most of India.
The lake is piano-shaped.

Here are some children, shrunken
in chairs offensively tall.
Manhandled, staked like dahlias

and pushed towards the light,
they sit in on events of movement
with watchful tearless eyes.

The old nod their heads,
their death-colours suddenly split
by pasteurised smiles, sheer white.

8 *Tulips*

The tulips parade for May Day –
Galata, Golden Nephites,

Rosy Wings, Abbu Hassan –
all the glorious fighting units,

polished, drilled, not one
man short, happy as sunlight.

They glow like a great flag spread
over a nation's dead.

We admire them; we can't quite love them.
Their faces are hot and closed

as if they had seen torture.
At any minute, we know,

they could twirl in the dandified ballet
of the firing-squad, to face us.

And yet, it must be admitted,
they're a clean, well-balanced lot.

At night they sleep like the guns
of good fascists. Nobody plans

suicide, gets drunk,
falls in and out of desire.

Serene, they have finished with self.
No, we can't love them. But sometimes,

deep in our dreams, they call us
to name our freedom, and then

pepper us not with bullets,
but with bright medallions of laughter.

9 *To Construct a Rainbow*

Tulips, footsteps, history
unwind long ribbons through the forgetful green.

The trees rain petals – *da mi basia mille.*
The sky is playing at war.

The forces of darkness ride out.
But the sun, great pacifist,

turns a cloud-cheek, shows us
the long bruise of a promise.

I step into the boat;
it rocks on its packed fathoms.

God sends the rainbow love
springing from heart to heart

just once in a while; not for long
may the dull beasts float in such gladness.

10 *Phaedrus*

The souls of lovers, said Socrates
to his young companion,

can complete their wings only
by embracing Philosophy.

The way hard, these friends
paddled the stream, arousing

a bright complication of water.
Through the hot midday

their silvery dialectic
shimmered below plane-leaves.

Summer wings stirring the air,
love talked itself to oblivion.

They parted not with a kiss
but a prayer, honouring wisdom.

11 *Dark Path*

Beneath this unlucky white May tree,
we found all we could understand of love.

So we went deeper and deeper down the green path
whose stems grow thickly together like a great friendship,

as if we were dreamed by some old nature-god,
and bound and garlanded with children's hands.

Darker and steeper the green path plunges still,
but now I've lost you; it's late.

Gnats play like little lights above the ghost crowds
of Queen Anne's lace, the lake seems made of dead rain.

What if all that has happened which we named
desire cries suddenly to be renamed?

Here come my two black swans, desultory.
They snap their beaks in the water and complain.

One always in tow to the other, through the seasons
they float their listless epithalamium.

Better, they'd say, an unadoring pair
than one in deep love, alone.

12 *Numen Non In Est*

The city's ravishing make-up
is all over the sky
in teary streaks;

the sky is hurrying out.
The frightened flowers have sunk
their last coins into moonlight.

A runner heralds himself
with the gasps of crushed leaves.
The breath he unstintingly pours

is kept by the wraith trees;
now they're as lost as he is.
In the clearings are temples,

their pitch roofs low
as frowns. They are dedicated
only to shade.

All winter they'll stand empty
for the dark god has escaped;
his love is everywhere.

13 *The Rain and Time*

It was the rain, not time,
that drove us from our seat:
rain's fresh, abrupt and sweet

hilaritas, teasing us
with the bookish smell of dust,
the brightened traffic swishing

beyond that iron goodbye –
the gate – which suddenly
had become impassable.

We rushed from tree to tree,
caught not in time but the rain.
All night it stroked the dark,

and this was happiness –
not to care whom you held
while the flickering, whispering threads

held us. And somewhere still
on these dry, forgettable days,
perhaps it is stitched for us

dancingly, in minutes,
our life between-lives as it runs
caught both in time and the rain.

14 *Fallen*

The sky is leaning and leaning
towards the park, grey breast
suffusing the green with shadow.

The light is crushed between them.
They exchange slow breaths
in heart-to-heart dumbness.

I touch, deep in my pocket,
horse-chestnuts found for the children
and never given.

Dressed in their creamy caps,
they glistened like brushed colts,
silkenly sat in the grass –

creatures of the dew
and a moment's lending;
impossible, but I took them.

Now there's no need to look.
I can feel how the light has gone,
how the tree is dead in them.

They are museum pieces –
old conscience money, carved men
for a game of imagining.

15 *Appearances*

How like a branch a man
who stands in a high tree.

Blackly he bends on the bending
bough in the blind light.

Smoke rising towards him,
he patiently saws, diminishing

his own margin of safety,
He'd fall with his branch, of course,

in the next frame of the comic,
pursuing to its limit

this art of camouflage
now gathering its echoes –

a moorhen's weed-green legs –
the absurdly familiar smiles

of two who have just met
and share by chance their seat.

16 *Clouds*

The park flattens.
its perspectives simplify

to a statement of loss.
The flower-lights in their casements,

the lattices, the dark dells
have been drawn upwards, kept

by fat-lipped angels.
Mere blanks remain, an earth

too dumb for questioning
whether life or death enthrals it.

We all wear coats now –
gardeners, bulbs, the sky.

Forgetful snow will fall soon,
blue shadows thicken upon

the burial place, the closed book;
a story told for one.

The Sea Lover

You can't write down what the sea is,
if you've only streets for paper,
printed with city dust.
Though you keep the sea in your heart,
you know it's the pocket version only –
a kind of religion,
and won't do for real love,
that edge, those streaming salts.
So, in the end, you give up
and shamefully travel the coast-road.
Even before you arrive
a ripple of cold is born,
and you think without delusion
how the true sea runs to your hand
only to steal and betray;
how it mimes the desolate, heavy
roll of a loveless marriage
that could still resolve you to blindness.
By dusk you stand in the wind,
gazing, your face a prayer.
For the sea will always be more
than you remembered it;
a far, grey animal ranging
gravity's restless cage,
getting ready to come to you, sidling.
You will give it first the dead skin
of your city, the lighted streets,
the bridges, walls and windows.
You will give it your two curved footprints
and your curtain of sooty rain.

Then, with a quick glance back,
because it is hungry still,
you will give it, with love, the sand,
the marram grass and the steps
up the cliff and the road at the top
where tail-lights race like blood-spots.
And, because it is hungry still,
you will throw it your words. With a gasp
the last one whitens, sinks,
What pours through your horrified skull
isn't love or the sea, but the knowledge
of the long, washed throats of the sewers.

Yes, you've spoiled everything,
and everything always was spoiled
but this: you feel it at last
on the tip of your tongue – a silence
welling unstoppably,
cold to its brim – the sea.

Siren

Your children are your innocence, you prize them
greedily, three pink fingers dipped in honey.
At night, three souls slide in their perfect skins
into a rippling length of light. You bend,
damp-curled, still marvelling at the little bud
of abandonment, each tiny, cracked omphalos,
how it is almost an opening that you
might slip into, ticklish, precipitous,
a hair's breadth widening from tenderness
to pain. Sleeked as if by recent birth,
hair cleaves to each small skull, neat as your hand
to well-soaped limbs. So you relinquish power
to babble and disport with the loopy tongues
of child-talk. You have three faces now
with three clean smiles for the mother goddess.
I stand apart, waving a small goodbye,
and noticing that my innocence too has drifted
off with your limpid fleet, just out of reach,
leaving me pure sex, a dangerous pulsing,
a light that sings and warns on the bare ledge of self.

Cherchez l'ail

London that night was held by golden ropes
    Fraying through the river's black.
The 'Queen of Spain' with all her costly lives
Sat tight, as we sat, formal in our hopes,
The bottle on its ice-bed leaning back.
We touched the cloth with bright, impatient knives.

Tides turn, the damaged love-boat drifts away;
   The marriage-teasers walk
The plank, and one in torment almost screams,
But smiles instead. I sniffed my hands next day
To light those flames that stroked our ice-chink talk,
To meet you on the garlic breath of dreams.

Quadrangular

How to unfold the forbidden, scholarly gardens
was a trick I learned today
beside you. I practise it
alone, and a flat wall blossoms
perspective; a lawn,
stone backdrop and domesticated sky,
as astounding as if some tiny
sun-peeled door had disclosed
a casual stretch of marble,
a single fountain twirling
her white taffeta for no one.

To be in the garden at last
is to feel almost faint
with relief, like the right-sized Alice.
The lines drawn between
two classes that smile at each other
only through magic boxes
chained to the edges of rooms
dissolve in the merry lattice of our fingers.
While tourists are lectured, we
show each other round.
We'd like the walls to guess
which of us was never young here –
as if they didn't know.
I think they're scared by our mingling
of awe and disrespect
like some lost art of rhetoric,
the tight little problem we set them
by the plus-sign between us.

Afterwards, the light
blooms soft and yellow, forgiving.
On stones ripply-haired
as Pre-Raphaelites, our feet
dutifully part,
and only the page is left.
Here is the miniature plot
where I've laid fresh turves and paving,
opened a quad of words
with solemn, churchy shadows
for you to wave across.

Suicide Fantasy on Carfax Tower

The fivepenny bit wouldn't work the telescope.
It bobbed and swung hopelessly.

I was the captain of some failed spacecraft,
a black hole over one eye like a pirate.

How my silence hurt me
in this soft-stoned, many-leafed city,

so talkative and holy,
even the four o'clock bell

with more to say than I
on the important topic of dying.

Like targets in a video
war-game, the tiny shoppers jerked below

...But I was no Kamikaze:
I would time my obscurity

not to kill, but to astonish;
aim for the shifting

dot of the pavement,
not even brush anyone's coat.

How coldly and fluently
the swift air would disown me

but what wild running and ringing
would greet the stones springing

into brain-flowers of white and scarlet
like a medieval manuscript.

Cambridge

I am always distrustful of those places
I've never seen in the rain – too much blue sky,
and gilded stone, and young grass for one city,
I envied the legitimate – tourists, students,
structuralists, even the bored wives –
but wrote my subtext with a scared finger
over the moving sky until it blushed.
Advancing at 100 mph,
the narrative of stern diesel held sway,
and sleeplessness, unemotional
and strangely clear as the aftermath of mourning,
was all I arrived with on that cold station.
I could believe that even midnight here
is sunlit, and that the feasted birds sustain
their small night-music through the month of June.
The hitch-hiker made enquiries about breakfast.
I walked myself in and out of decisions
through soaked grass, thinking *none of this exists*
unless I'm here, then nothing else exists.
It is gathered in one room, its atoms swirling –
biochemistry, ethics, politics
(you know the terms, and that they're never easy).
Bathed and showered in visionary definitions,
I was only ever a traveller back,
glimpsing a lake's smashed sparkles, bright as granite...
but then, I am distrustful of possession.
What I have best is always what I lack.

Writing the City

Rhymes, like two different hands joining,
are those slightly archaic correspondences
I look for when in trouble. It's so easy
to start panicking in cities.

All roads lead to each other, sharing slick
anecdotes of combustion. They sell
tin lollipops, barren islands
and the one-way look for city faces.

Things happen and unhappen; cars, like eyelids,
blink time away. I'm due for demolition...
That's why I stand so long in the Poetry Section,
and buy apples just to slice them into cradles.

Double Exposure
(for David Rumens)

Come into my room now your better half
has floated off from you a little; don't
mock, don't make a noise, don't spill the coffee.
I'm playing house here, but it's tree-top-frail,
so leave your gales and lightnings at the door
and come and give me your blessing – what else
are the latest-model modern husbands for?

You could play, too. Why not become a student
chemist, crash out on the sisal floor
of an obscure first-year philosopher?
Show her some snaps – not of your holidays
or chess triumphs, but the future – two giant babies
who come alive and roam about the room,
eating cake and groaning as you kiss her?
The bed looks comfy, but won't give you shelter.
You'll have to pick a quieter afternoon
to marvel at the virgin you'd uncover –
double-exposed with baby-scrawls of silver.

Here, where our past and present planes bisect,
it seems quite natural, after dark, to find
the window holds a city and a room,
exchanging surfaces on blue-black film.
Look how the Post Office Tower wears my wardrobe.
A train, hurrying out of Euston, glides
its amber wishes through me every night,
until I pinch the curtains close, decide
it's time for old techniques of black on white.

Above the single bed I've tacked a 'Klimt'.
It's called *Fulfilment*. If you'd noticed it,
you might have found it raised a few light questions.
A joke, as bitter as its after-taste?
A profound statement on the spiritual
rewards of celibacy? A sly confession
or just a wish, perhaps? You might have seen
more intersections than at Clapham Junction,
had you looked up, and traced
the flow of gilded dressing-gowns, their scrolls
converging on a decadent embrace.

'Time will say nothing but I told you so' –
Is that our rubric? Janis, ten years dead,
still howls her living anger through my head.
'Freedom's just another word for nothing
left to lose.' What can an expert say –
that freedom's not like being sent a cheque,
nor working after midnight on a high,
nor walking miles, just for the hell of it?
That mine, at least, brims with the luxury
we thought we didn't have, and every lack.
An unmade past is like an unmade bed
at three a.m. Since you arrived, these walls
haven't stopped flickering with the lantern-show,
Fulfilment, all its tricks and vérité.

On a night that's Mediterranean-warm and dusty,
we drift to where the space-invaders flash,
and street-wise reflexes are newly honed
by the imminent loss of ready cash.
The Camden of stripped pine and harebell-shades
on bent, brass stems, has locked itself away
for dinner, *en famille*. Greek music braids
a brightened, scabby tenement, marked For Sale.

The plum-haired sons and daughters of tavernas
gesture like figures on an ancient frieze
though words and clothes declare them Londoners.

I leave you video-gazing, leave you winning.
Small faces lift for kisses, nonchalant.
I'm clumsy at this *weekend-parenting*
but no one cries or argues. Back indoors,
I add another bookshelf (just a brick
at each end, and a plank across) and stack
the comics and Sunday papers that you've left
and that I'll never read – one more sad sifting
of true from new. And then it's time for bed –
earlier than I'd planned, since, in the dark
it's harder to see double, hard to see
a thing, in fact. Freedom's just floorboards, walls,
a bit of glass. And yet it felt like home
till you arrived and showed me where I am.

Skins

There are those that time will carelessly perfect:
Leather, wood and brick fall derelict
As if aware they charmed us as they slip;
This deal table, strung like a harp
With a silky glissando of dark grain
Blooms like a lover from the hands it's known.
Scrawlings of knife and bottle, child and guest
Have warmed its heart, a rough autumnal feast
Spilled into soil, becoming nutriment;
The wood's more deeply wood because of it.
But there are others, the most loved and rare,
Time told them once, of which the years despair.
Laughter has scribbled not itself but pain.
Each face is fallen on hard times of bone.
Money will court them first, and then deride them.
There are no masks but sorry stones to hide them.
Yet to the end they haunt disgusted mirrors,
As close as love, and steal with snow-lipped fingers
From little, lying, scented jars each night,
Skins that are pillow-shadows by first light.

Lullaby for a First Child

This timid gift I nurse
as the one clear thing I can do.
I am new and history-less
as the name on your wrist, as you.
But flesh has stored a deep kindness
ready to welcome you.
Take it, a little silver
into your small purse.
There it will gather interest –
the warm, bright weight of you.

The Carpet Sweeper
(for Kay Lumley)

Mother, last week I met
that old Ewbank we had
when I was three or four,
standing outside a junk-shop
in Bridge Street. I was sure
it was the one because
it knew me straight away.
At first, we were both glad.
We looked each other over.
I think it felt the sharp
impulse of my pity;
it made no comment, however,
and I was too polite
to mention its homeless state.
Mother, the wooden case
was burnished still, and stout.
Its wheels were scooter-sized,
and, just as in the old days,
slyly it urged my feet
aboard to jiggle a ride.
I drew myself up a little
(I'd borrowed your scolding face)
and it apologised.
Ashamed, I turned to other
subjects, praised its lion

trademark, proud though worn;
spoke of the rubber mouldings
that had saved the shins of our chairs
when savagery and housework
boiled in your heart. Mother,
I'm sure it spoke your name.
The sighs of all women
whose days are shaped by rooms
played over it like shadows.
What could I do or say?
I turned, it became small
on the dusty pavement, trying
perhaps to recall the smell
of our floors, the cosy tying
of loose ends, scattered wishes
in its spinning brushes...

Israelites

*In a Jewish tradition God was called The Place because
all places were referred to Him but He was not in any place.*
                CHARLES WILLIAMS,
                He Came Down From Heaven

When you opened your eyes and gazed from antiquity
onto the new room, the half-born day,

I saw the god of no-place
and the ark of my skull became heavy.

Your eyelashes were little darknesses
distantly flying the broad skies of your vision.

I caught them in a kiss. Your smiles were mine.
For that moment they were mine.

Wake beside me again! I'll stay
in exile till you do,

dragging my years over the midnight desert,
the light I've kept too pitiless to see by.

FROM
DIRECT DIALLING
(1985)

A Prague Dusk, August 21st 1983

About a subjugated plain,
Among its desperate and slain,
The Ogre stalks with hands on hips,
While drivel gushes from his lips.
                    W.H. AUDEN

1

When his broad shoulders turn
in their leaf-coloured uniform
and square up to a doorway
on Revolucni Street,
he might be any soldier
and the bar, any girl,
its response no more than a certain
heightened inattention.
He orders beer and seems
as innocent as his thirst,
straining his young white throat
to greet the last drop,
but the pearl of Mitteleuropa
has dimmed behind him;
shadows slide unchecked
from the medallioned buildings
scaffolded up to the waist,
numb veterans who have learned
how short the life of honour.

He smiles, provincial, brash,
half-tame. The careful hands
that have served his purposes
slink off and busy themselves
with rows of glasses, small
change. Eyes follow him out,
each glint of hate a coin
with its own private value.

2

That he could not master speech
no longer seems important.
Perhaps only a poet
word-trafficking in the free-
market economy
of Oxford or New York
would have thought it a fatal weakness.

155

One blast of his breath was enough
to seal the twelve bridges.
With a few phrasebook phrases
he is armed for years to surprise
and amuse the populace,
his weight sunk in its silence.
Impassioned flattery
on the cut of his Westerner jeans
is not expected when,
naked as his fists,
he strides down Vaclavski Namesti
with his shuffling train of echoes:
what happens, happens without us.
We forget only the present.
It is the glue of memory
that hardens round the nerves
of the empty August city.

3

Going home on the metro
the children chatter
but the mother is almost asleep.
Some sweet, unscripted dream
wanders across her face,
follows the droop of her arm
to the grasses that nod in her lap.
It's already dark
on the staircase where she hushes
and stumbles; light from outside
shines on the two pairs of shoes
placed at each nuptial doorway,
intimate and exhausted,
moored like little boats
in an ocean of drudgery.
When she too, at last,
is sitting in stockinged feet
and the children asleep,
she will recall each detail
of the picnic: how the country
they walked through never changed,
monotonous and tender
as the afternoons of motherhood;
how tall the grass became
when they lay down to rest
and the stalks rose silvery miles
and whispered to the sky.

A Soviet Army Tenor

The Russian voice, it's said
has risen a whole tone since the nineteen-hundreds,

pushed up by nervous insincerities,
but the song that flickers high off the cassette

was earthed before the censor's chalk screamed
on the clean slate, or irony bit its lip.

And the choir, gathering leisurely reinforcements,
is only a windswept platoon of firs,

a chained sigh, an unhonoured
show of strength in the field of robbed time.

Medals burn in the studio-lights. But listen
to the soft, irregular, excited breathing

of the only animal said to have a soul.
He can silence his own kind

in multiples, blindly obeying his hands,
yet, when the mood takes him,

he remembers his disproven soul, and wishes
that every army could become a choir,

and the battleships dip their turrets
in shame at having borne the names of men.

Outside Oswiecim

1

Let me tell you the story of days, handsomely printed
in dawn and darkness, in sleep
and in burnt-eyed longing for sleep.

2

It puzzles the secular light, this polyphony
of dim cries. I wasn't there, I heard nothing,
but the air fills, and forces breath to sing them.

3

When the train banged to a stop and whispered 'where?',
then they began. Some rose, some fell. *The sky
rushed in like sea, we opened our mouths, it drank us.*

4

The hardest hope to lose is the last and smallest.
Those words on the gate, some dreamed of them, and loved
to walk in their shade, suck out the iron of their promise.

5

In the night, the light; in the light, the wire;
in the wire, the heart; in the heart, the world;
in the world, Oswiecim.

6

Dumb narrative curiosity keeps you from the wire
how many times? You watch yourself, amazed,
whipped to a panting run past outstretched arms.

7

It was Erev Shabbat, evil was fallible.
A shaved girl smiled in the sun. An angel had murmured
'Amen' before he saw the gesturing dead.

8

And what if his lord had heard that some of them
were raging animals, and still sent daybreak, still
sent no one to stroke them with their names?

9

No, no, the question is obsolete.
Nothing sees nothing. Mercy was up to us.
Our mouths bit down on nothing.

10

Emblem, exhibit, witness – Husserl's suitcase
flanked the rust-brown pile. The cold twine of its handle
I touch, then grasp for a faceless, weightless stanza.

11

Child, enchanted at gun-point, whose child are you?
Come here, take off your cap, don't cry.
How is it possible I can make no difference?

12

Oh they crowd in, death's kindergarten. Small grazes
scared them once. Their eyes are always yours.
I'd take their pain, here, where your absence is.

13

I loved in you, yes, what made you strangest.
The desert gave you its shadows. I'd watch for ever
the poise of your smile, its mocking tenderness.

14

Another race is only an other, strolling
on the far side of our skin, badged with his weather.
In love or hate we cast looks, hooks; get it wrong.

15

How shall I bear your indifference without hate?
It stirs in the dust, a length of hose. If I burn
how shall I not flex my whip near your eyes?

16

No, come away, bury yourself in the pit
of tears, be ash and stone, your stare
like his, a star.

17

They beckoned, they turned their limbs this way and that,
they whispered, you tried to get near enough to hear,
but the heat roared at you – *take your eyes, run.*

18

Not 'the six million', not 'the holocaust',
not words that mass-produce, but names. One name;
Husserl's, perhaps. His favourite food, his new watch.

19

Chosen to illustrate the Shibboleth's Tale;
An illumination from the Book of Fire,
Sand and Next Year; chosen to be most mortal,

Our pyramid swam and sank through the nitrogen
Fog as starving crystals ate our air.
Christ, to whom the soldier said 'Go on,
Call down your god if he's got ears and brains',
You would have understood our short-breathed terror.
Poor rebel son, you shared our tribal chains
That day, but now we wipe you from our mirror.

So we died for the last unforgeable scrap –
Our land. Got free for being something harder
Than walking zoo-meat. Fought like the Crusader
To nail our resurrection to the map.

Northern Woods

Small enterprises line the exit roads
out of London...then the bankruptcies...
and the long haunting of her absence begins
in a delirium whitened by birch trees.
They sidle past, existentialist poseurs,
with a soft slippery shine that is barely a shine –
what light is there in the world for them to borrow?
Go on, they say, dissolve into drugs and tears;
we are her trees, we are your memories
blank with all she could not bear to tell you.
But I never cry. I just keep driving, staring.
When I left her for the last time, our hopes
the sea-smashed continent, my flight-bag heavy
as a new tongue, I learned to swallow fire.
Now the colourless bottle leaves me sober
as a vision of birch woods, growing colder
and cloudier as they get to Pietarsaari.

Sixteen Dancers

1

One night in our first week of marriage
you asked me to meet you in your favourite square.
It's easy, you said. I was to look for the postcard
you'd sent me once in Prague.
I remembered the small, feminine fountains,
how I had stared into their silvery weather
and tried to taste the sea.
Now my feet crunched pigeon-food, gravel, wet ice.
And there was the lion you'd climbed, jeans slithering
on the cold bronze, ten years ago, to shout
for Ho Chi Minh. You were late. Traffic snarled
in circles; I waited at the centre.
How small it was, after all, this famous square.
I looked down at my coat, my shoes, my handbag.
Gifts. Yours. London's. Not mine.
And then that English snow I'd refused to believe in
came feathering into the wind, little iron tongues
licking my face. My shoulders had turned to salt
as I stared east, towards home.

2

The tournament hall was like school,
with tables, and a ticklish, whispering silence.
I wasn't scared, I always did well at school.
I decided not to look at my opponent.
He was bigger than me, and we both knew he'd lose.
Parents, opponents, boyfriends, the state –
I laughed at all of them, I was never scared.
My mother dragged my hair back, plaiting it
cruelly, tugging my brains into three.
I snipped the plait off whole,
and pegged it on the kitchen line; she screamed.
I revelled in such private enterprise,
the thrust of Machiavellian knights and cut-throat
bishops; power flickering like black magic
from palace to proletariat and back.
It was a picture-book I'd never tire of,
and each new story always began the same:
once upon a time there were two great kings.
One lived in the east, and one the west.
And they were enemies though they were brothers.
Each knew the other king like his own face.

161

3

Some heads had been guillotined from the family album.
No one seemed to know why.
Poor faceless ones, I searched for evidence
of wickedness in watch-chains
or the grey folds of skirts where wrists lay broken.
At last their wounded innocence burned through,
silencing my childish accusations,
like the starry cherry-flowers on Namesti Miru.
They murmured: The Russians are here!
I was fifteen. It was thrilling, like the first taste
of melon each year, or plunging into the water
at Marienbad. The walls burst into posters,
the wind chased leaflets, hands flew everywhere.
The soldiers lounged and smiled like elder brothers.
Then the holiday was over,
the grown-ups silent as suitcases.
Our leader bowed his head, got into the Chaika.
The chairs stood back, as one by one,
my friends, no longer thirsty, left the singing.
They were like the people in the photograph
changing colour as I lay the page
on wood first, then my hand.
I sulked. My mother cried. My face grew thin.
I moved my wooden men to win, to win.

4

When they teach you your past is a lie,
they extinguish your future.
When the party-machine drives words into your mouth,
starvation becomes acute.
When friends disappear, the door of your heart bursts open
merely to reveal another door.
When the spotless spring parade shines on the trees,
you blink, and brush the petals from your eyes.

5

You were the reigning British Champion,
your suit like a blue coffin, your hair like leaves.
Beneath the fire-weeping chandelier,
sat Timman, neatly torturing Polugayevsky.
The hall was emptying. I'd won my game.
Yours was adjourned. A small crowd had gathered
at the smell of blood.
We stood together, held our breath and watched.
In the silence I felt your concentration lapse.

You touched my arm, and we walked softly out,
linking smiles in a world of foregone conclusions.

6

You courted me smartly, eloquent, careerist,
but perfect-mannered, versatile at checkpoints,
customs, hotel-desks. Our sweet receptions
bloomed among the low-line teak veneer
like an elaborate, creamy, high rococo,
tumbled out of nowhere, out of time.
And this, like time, was always quite beyond us –
a liberty we took, and couldn't take,
the morning after, homing to our boards
and clocks, the slow, meticulous invasions;
nationality seeping back, the silver cups
spreading their wings, the draped flags, the speeches,
the return ticket, and the correct papers.

7

Architects, accountants, friends from Oxford,
arrived at eight in the flat you called the cupboard,
and I, the manor.
Your eyes challenged them with a lovely fire,
as if you'd risked your neck to bring me here.
(The builders had only just left,
taking the earthquakes and the thunder-storms
but leaving the rainbows, as you bad commanded.)
The flat was floured and trembling like a geisha.
Your friends pushed everywhere,
coughing a little, spilling drinks, at home.
One, I remember, spoke Czech:
and I, on my third vodka, told the joke
with the ice-and-lemon punch-line: what are the Russian
troops doing in Prague? They are looking
for those who invited them.

8

Sticky Fingers, Soldier Blue, Rough Trade:
I walk, take taxis, walk. My carrier-bags
multiply. It rains. The pavements darken,
the dust smells antique. My feet get wet.
I don't care, my shoes have turned to knives
in spite of hours of choice and wads of plastic.
I'm in the wrong element. As for marriage,
it cost me a country. Once, I queued
all day for a chrome teapot, dumb with hope.

I never dreamed of flight as now I dream –
in *samizdat*, my thoughts fluttering
always towards my murderer, my accomplice,
whose fingers check me, who looks up and smiles.

9

You know how it is with us.
Living out of suitcases, we fly
from game to game, from story to story,
new faces on the loose change in our pockets.
You know how lonely it is –
the faint taste of a different language,
and the hotels, always the same yet not quite,
and the smiles at the opening dinner, the same, but not...
and nothing ever quite real.
You know what it is to win,
and how the rules change then,
or how we think the rules change then.

10

Marriage as an inventory:
mine, the Bohemia crystal;
yours, the Chinese rug;
mine, the silver fox,
the dolls, the rosewood box
of marbles, the kitchenware, its brave colours.
Yours, most of the books,
and all but one of the war–games.
Mine, the thirst;
yours the cup.
Mine, the fault;
yours, the freedom from guilt.
Mine, the manor, ruined.
Yours, the cupboard, empty.

11

The radio, left till last
because we can't decide,
squats on the floor and mutters to itself.
We would orphan it if we could.
Instead, we try and listen to its news.
Someone should be making tea;
someone should be quietly crying.
But everywhere it talks about is far away.
There is no mention of our fallen city.

12

Postcards telling jokes or lies –
I could write home on any of them,
send them from nowhere, never to arrive.
The stones of Prague, the sharpness of your eyes
I shall never see clearly again.
Ten years on, what do I know about you?
That you have a wife. Her name.
That her star is Virgo and she is virtuous.
That she has fair hair and is fully-armed.
And what do you know about me?
That my victories are few. That I defect
regularly from those dictatorships
my lovers make of passion. That I claim
more freedom than there is in any world,
except the world of men.
Still I'd go down your winter streets again
to break a glass for one last toast. Bright-lipped
with sweet liqueur, we'd kiss and drink to life –
the life no kisses ever made less bitter.

13

How impassively they face each other,
the fighting men, before the players arrive.
A woman in overalls hoovers round the tables
indulgently. The fighting men exchange
the wan smiles of platoons on Christmas morning,
remembering cigarettes and oranges,
and what they still have left of being human.
The woman slides her hoover
noisily into the passage.
Dust twinkles in a sun-shaft, breakfast smells
seep from the kitchens. It is quiet, domestic.
The fighting men seem to have chosen peace
before the players arrive.

14

One eye on the clock, one ear on silence,
we take our sixteen paths into the darkness.
Outside, the universe of moves is flowering.
We have some choice. It dwindles. Who or what
chooses how we chose need not be asked.
It is enough to see that acreage
shine at our feet: first, the unharvested
squares of sun and shade; later, what's left
in the democracy of broken hopes –
this we call freedom, I and my sixteen dancers.

Blockade

Europe has been broken:
a panacea of banks,
steel cladding, the black
fugue of Berlin.

Oh Linden Tree, oh Linden
I cannot breathe
without your small hands, your great shade.

Aubade

Light as a rose
he sleeps beside
his first cradle,

intent on stillness
but breathing firmly
as if breath would always

give itself back.
He has travelled far
to be in his flesh,

to learn what happens
and to forget.
His existential

smile is perfect.
It tells me how
he will offer himself

when the time comes.
But for now he will keep
his excellent secrets –

the glossy function
of heart and lungs,
arms and legs,

the legend of his mouth.
His voice sleeps,
his sex sleeps.

In the faint shine
of morning when
flesh can be chilled,

I draw up the sheet
and cover him
to save us both.

Circe

Now we are nothing. It is as you wished
when we last held each other.
I saw you boyish, crass, forgivable
and mythic with departure –
but it was something that you'd come at all.
Surely your presence underwrote return
and surely all the brightness in your eyes
belied the casual phrase
by which you cut adrift our misty future.

Oh yes, I had your warm life by the neck,
yet somehow washed you in oblivion
like Lethe, for you went from my bed
that afternoon forgetting everything.
What is between us now? No conversation
or kindness – merely waves
that roll pig-grey, rinsing the silent cables.
Each night I try and drink my way across –
a moth-like weaving
to find the chancy formula, the voice.
Sometimes I drag it to the telephone.
My finger slips, I've been too long alone.
I could do an aria or a speech
perhaps, but how make small-talk of so much?

I think of you in sunlight
your body dark, local drugs on your lips,
god of the vines, banal as an advert
but for the greedy shining in your gaze.

167

It falls upon Penelope, betrayed
that afternoon, so unimportantly;
you take her now because she's there, and simple.
She has no song but offers you her mouth.
You give her all your kisses,
nicknames, money, whims (she loves you child-like
among the brilliant in the best hotels).

The breeze at sun-fall flares
suddenly and shakes your salt-stuck hair.
The fig trees start their soft, accustomed screaming.
Our northern dusk is slower,
a schmaltzy, dim, blue church for sick abeyance,
with love and pleasure always somewhere else –
Eden, Jerusalem, Arcadia.
The sirens can be moral – if you care.
Remember me, my faithful touch, my shape
before I aged, became entirely graceless,
all envy, all desire, all lack of hope,
condemned to sail upon a self-wept sea
each year-long night, Odysseus, of your absence.

Vocation

Is it poetry I'm after at those moments when
I must clothe your hands in mine or comfort your shoulders –
so bare and neglected sometimes when we wake –
or press your mouth to taste its uncurling flower?
Is that which seems so fleshly and truthful merely
a twisted track into words, a way to leave you
for your image? Art is tempting, a colourful
infidelity with the self, and doubly feigning
when what is repossessed secretly by one
was made by two. And I wish I could pour a poetry-vodka
into twin glasses we'd gulp unanimously
('I poison myself for your health' the appropriate toast)
but only a poet would have acquired the taste
for such a strange distillation; you'd never warm
to heavy-petting dactyls, the squeak and creak
from locked, suburban stanzas. And so my fingers,
dancing alone, are less than content. They perceive
how they have clung to moral adolescence.

Their vocation now could be simply to talk to your skin,
to take you at kissing-time; later, to close your eyes
by stroking the lashes lightly over cheekbones
flushed with some high, bright, childish fever, and so
write the poem in the touch-shapes of darkness
and let it end there...They are on the tip of trusting
this silent, greyish room, its astonishing view
fading from metaphor to the life with you.

In the Cloud of Unknowing

Goodbye, bright creature.
I would have had you
somewhere on solid earth,
wings clipped to pale

shoulder-blades,
and your fleecy head
a chrysanthemum, darkly
grown from my pillow.

I would have kept my tongue
for what salt weepings
it could tease from your finest
silences.

But it was written
into your book of life
that I should be brief.
Forbidden to count

the ways, denied
et cetera,
I worshipped the stone
from your supper-time plum,

the little hairs gleaned
in tears from the sheet.
Metaphysical desire
was all they would bear,

a bandage of art
for the low sob
of the vernacular,
a condition of prayer.

Now when I wake
and the dawn light names
your perfect absence,
I am at home,

lapped again
in my earliest language,
the vocatives tense
with desire and distance:

'Thou who art called
the Paraclete';
'After this our exile';
'Oh Sacred Heart!'

Dear iconoclast
forgive these texts
their cloudy haloes.
The intent pen burns

its slow path through
the slant rain of Greek,
the stars of Hebrew
...to touch your hem?

No, it was never
possible.
The old mystics knew
as they closed the book

on the dancing colours,
worn out with words
never made flesh
and with flesh that fought

their long abstraction.
They listened a moment;
the breath-soft footstep
in the cloisters faded

as always to sighs;
the cold congress of leaves
in darkening autumn;
the wind's dissolution.

Pavane for the Lost Children

When you rest in my arms and your heart
quietens against mine
I think of a midnight kitchen,
the kettle muttering on the lowest gas,
and the baby forgetting to feed,
lips plumped like a little mollusc
that is almost losing its grip.
They could not relinquish survival,
those lips; I knew what they dreamed of
would keep arousing them
to fits of greedy, absent-minded tugging.
So I sat on, enthralled
by thirst, by plenitude.

This, too, is our grown-up devotion
when fatigue is most pressing:
to pretend we will never put each other down
and drift singly away on
sleep's disappointing persuasions;
such lowly forms of life, so deeply marine,
we cannot move apart, or know what time is,
but are turned like bivalves on the lifting wave
that has promised us to the sand.

Time Trouble

I know all about these German wrist-watches.
They try to wake you with tinny, insect-like tunes
as the digits flip over on your bedside table
and my old-fashioned minute-hand
flies to your neck and whispers nervously
with that little pad of fat where your head is thrown back
because you're still in an ecstasy of sleep,
and your suitcase not yet packed.

Once upon a time
they'd take me to admire the German clock
in the museum. There were wooden figures inside it:

Jesus at wooden supper
with his twelve wooden apostles.
And when it struck three, they said,
the apostles filed out
and all bowed woodenly to Jesus
except Judas, who swung round the wrong way.

I never stayed to see this remarkable dumbshow.
By a minute to three, I was going to be sick;
I turned my back on the clock, the crowd
fell apart with a hiss.
As I race down the shadowless aisles,
though the horrible whirring has not yet begun,
I can see it all perfectly –
mad Jesus, his nodding guests,
and Judas, the simple materialist,
turning on his clockwork,
showing us his chalk-white face.

Revolutionary Women

Nechayev, dreaming of Tsar-death,
wrote about three categories of women,
and how they could be harnessed to the cause.
The first he dismissed as painted, empty.
You could twist them, break them, toss them away.
The second were good comrades, passionate
idealists, willing workers,
but dangerous finally, and disappointing –
their values weren't political at all:
they too must be discarded or reformed.
The third kind were the true revolutionaries;
deft with gun-oil, bullets, high explosive.
They'd take a lover only for his secrets,
milk him fast and leave him in his blood.

I know I'm with the second sort, cherishing
nothing better than a just cause,
except perhaps the man who'd die for it;
who grows entranced, watching allegiance crumble
and rebuild itself in curious gothic snow
like candles at the hovering hour of sleep.

Turning soup into a bowl I've started
at a white face in the china, both yours,
Nechayev, and that of any bourgeois
gazing up in naked appetite.
This is what causes the strong hand to falter.
Armies, official and unofficial, learn
that what they kill aren't men, or are only men.
But we, that regiment of the starry-eyed
you need and fear and try to educate,
who type your manifestoes through the night,
may still in the morning be discovered,
the counter-revolution breathing gently
beside us on the pillow, while the Tsar
goes to breakfast, and his men to torture.
In our loose night-gowns warm and obvious,
too slippery to cement a single brick
of the just state, even the state of marriage –
Nechayev, you'd be right to gun us down.

Winter

It begins in secret
with mist, a dazed bee
in the lavender-bushes
and radiators mild
as human skin.
This would be May
to your serious habitat,
the iron-black river
that is its heart-line,
wobbly as a frontier,
untrammelling itself
in endless dissatisfaction.
I think of the Burlaki
trussed in rope
like performing bears,
who trudged the plashing weight
of their servitude
to the rhythm of the thaw.
You bow your head,
fists on the table,
chest-notes swelling,

and silence the room
with their empire of grievance.
In your perilous climate
the wind has already fastened
stiff white grave-clothes
on the auburn water.
It settles everything
like the hand of a lover.
So the winter river
accepts its birth-right
calmly, as you must –
the massive silences,
the gift of utter cold –
locked in its own
solid crystal, surveyed
by a few tethered craft
hungry for a new trade
of skins and revolution.

Escape from White

Here, people's eyes, like the cities of this country
Are large and clear; never does the soul's tumult
Move the pupil with an extraordinary glance;
Never does desolation cloud them over long.
                    ADAM MICKIEWICZ,
                    'Forefathers' Eve'

Slowly, the bruise of afternoon lavender deepens
to bilberry, and slowly it seems to withdraw
from my approach, the sea-coloured coastline of sleep.
An edge of chalky moon appears, gets cloud-lost;
the book in my hand thins to another window.
Where in this walled city shall I go, where shall
I turn in the almost-white June night, and evade my need of you?

The cathedral swims like a whisper out of the sweat
of coppery lights. What nerve it takes to retrace
our descent into heavenly ordinariness when we roamed,
camera-hung tourists, hand-in-hand through St Stephen's
on a midsummer morning quiet as ourselves;
when, moved by your extraordinary glances,
I saw you admire the parochial, upright, lawn-trimming,
France-hating, surly soul of this dreariest county.

I was busy observing you with my old affection
for the edges of maps, that breath of the East you bring,
irresistible as the anecdotes once told me
by the milliner's girl, my Kentish grandmother,
whose hair as she swanned by the Medway glistened so black
the sailors sang at her 'Japalady!' If only
you'd naturalise me to your strangeness, I too might gaze
on this cabbage-patch with tender, sea-grey eyes.

Idiomatic now, you perfect your tongue
with irony and bad grammar. Who would guess
from your study of gardens, supermarkets, cars
and American-English, that your true pursuit
is a moral example; how, in secret anguish,
you whisper to the child that dares not hear you
'But look how well this other one tries to behave!
Why can't you do the same?' And you almost pray
for the end of that damaged life, abandoned now
to the crocodile technicians of survival.

Each day abroad takes you curiously closer
to the narrow, silent, intimate hospital-bed
where the flesh is kept alive but whitely blank,
and you stare into eyes that cannot sleep or see,
their last wild doubt fixed in a glaze of sedation,
until the lavender dusk, the cathedral and my hands
with their foolish island behaviour of grasping and closing,
fade into the sombre night of your pilgrimage.

From the moment of touchdown you were free to fly,
and, at the first embrace of an *inostrantsa*,
to enter the terrible candour of homesickness.
Sometimes its waves swell to such a height,
I fear for your life; sometimes I think your heart breaks
whenever I say your name. If love exists,
is there more love in it than truth in *pravda*?
What can it do but take from you this gift
of night and bear the mourning it permits?

A Jewish Cemetery

1

At dawn they are one great shadow, whispering.
They are warning their children:
don't break the backs of your books.
Sunset. The shadow multiplies;
the backs break.

2

Among the swaying sighs
and the candlestubs, gothic with catarrh,
wanders the upright citizen. He is bored
and uneasy. He shoves the broken bits
of alphabet with his illiterate boot.
What else, these days, can you do with the past?

3

The closed books.
East looks West and sees East.
West looks East and sees West.
The apocalypse rides both ways.

4

Names must often be silences
in this city, in this world.
His block of flats is dark
and hollow like a chimney.
I climb it twice a day,
doubling my heartbeat
as I touch the bell that bears
his faded, biblical name.
My hope spirals up
and falls back, levelling
with my lack of hope,
a conversation of kinds
between the flame and the ash,
between the name and its silence
in this city, in this world.

Direct Dialling

To trade in bliss
alone would never
be permitted us;
I understood this
from the start, although,
girlish enough,
I bought the dress,
and fed the scene
to my moment-adoring
Polaroid;
a little window
of flower-dotted green
that trembled in
your attentive hand.

But our faces, sad,
already told us
of time and the state –
their thirsty methods:
the prisoner reading,
heart-in-mouth
a thumb-stained letter
three winters old;
his wife bringing
his yearly half-hour,
like a wound they must both
stroke to bleeding.
Our kindlier pain
is simply this
rinsed teapot packed
in a cardboard box
with your cook's knives.

Where the law can't reach
mischance has set
his ancient looms;
he doesn't forget.

We faced across
the empty table;
could no more touch
than if watched. You,
silently smoking,

re-read the airmail,
its soldierly lines
of refusal shaky,
barbed like wire.
'What can I say
to your invitation?
Do you suggest
I betray my country?'
Then, later on,
'All my friends are dying.
I'm old and alone.'

Letters, phone-calls –
those vanishing sparks
in the great places
of absence and
fidelity;
the summer nights
ringed by ice.
Prometheus,
you wake each day
in your distant city,
stung in the ribs
by the acid spear
of prison-food;
and when you sleep
it's a kind of flight,
desperate, intense,
and, you say, dreamless.

We stand in line
to snatch a moment.
Our conversations,
furtive, hoarse,
hang by a thread
at midnight. Where
could we build our house,
by what dispensation
secure the loose sands,
the iron winds –
and our sturdy, late,
bilingual child
scatter, regather
the brightened stones
of all your loves?

Greetings from Düsseldorf

A cobbled yard, an impatient bronze colt
fenced in by spears, a livid spire or two:
I've learnt to pick these charming fragments out
from the money-boxes thick in every crater,
and make up a camera-fib, a street in filter,
that saw the Emperor once, or a hurrying Jew.

Admiring a sleek old fräulein's haute couture
(if you must be old, be tall, I always say)
over a mineral water in Königsallee,
I woo the big names like an editor:
Schumann stumbles outside the head office
of Mannesmann (the looped double-M's
a gas-blue cross-stitch fallen from the stars)
and claws cadenzas in the laundered grass:
Heine on Bolkerstrasse slowly climbs
to his mattress grave above the Schwinken Grill,
praising God he's lost his sense of smell –
but these are my ghosts, not the bürgermeister's.
The roads are young, the young wear pink or white
with their tans. Midnight's rush-hour, every door
a jumping rainbow. You, in love, post-war,
would rate this city of stylish appetite.

Digging

(for Seamus Heaney, from Surrey)

In this subculture of gardens
one who avoids weedkiller
might well be hung from the tallest
ornamental cherry:

but, if I'm hooked, it's simply
a lei flung over my shoulders
to welcome and shame me
as I home to my graveyard patch.

I knew if I looked too long
I'd fall in love with flowers.
Their tender vividness,
helplessly self-parading,

catches my breath as if
they were my own daughters
pursing their lips to paint
the sharp little shadows and brighteners

into too-candid glances.
I bow towards the soil,
and unshawl the first damp babies –
lobelia, kitten-faced pansies.

I don't understand what they want
or what they silently know.
Are my fingers making them cry?
All afternoon I'm at sea

in photosynthesis.
I tell the time wrong
by the unusual sun.
Half my life has passed;

I should be digging elsewhere.
Yet still my hand, obsessed,
grips the blunter tool,
says: I'll write with it.

ICONS, WAVES

(1986)

Icons, Waves

The scalding gulp that almost clears the glass,
love rushes to the human eye, and lends it
illusions of a focus so exact,
a driver might lurch out, steer straight to death.
But we, late diners who've got tired of dining
and turned to iconography, believe
inaccuracy is also revelation.
Under the broad lamp with its singing bulb,
we stare into each other's brightest stares,
unselfed with curiosity, archaic,
and paint each other in a universe
where nothing's lost by lying in perspective:
I have the details – red formica table,
rinsed baked bean tin with its clutch of spoons,
your flatmate's skinny plant, the sallow glitter
of our once quickly filled and emptied glasses.

                    *

It was a dangerous ship we put to sea in;
over-freighted, dressed in Baltic ice,
crewed by the breath-clouds that had been your story.
Burning hope like kerosene, it suffered
the magnets of exile, every wave.
And though we raised our glasses, splashed our beer
with the sly diminutive brewed for thirty degrees
of ideology and new-year frost,
our toast was the old harbour of Atlantis.
I'd come aboard for word-trade, narrative,
warm money in my hand. You silenced me,
and it was then I felt the monster turn
his armoured intricacies under the waves,
and follow us like whispers, like ice.

                    *

So we'll be ageless, therefore timeless; so
we'll leave our heavy, fascinating shadows
on the doorstep; so, I said, we'll simply trace
in unobtrusive strokes what we are now.
You cracked the mystery fish, peeled the caul
from the red crayon of roe – which you gave me.
What part of taste, what part of time is this?
The bathrobe keeps slipping from my shoulders,
but we've been married silver years and gold –
a bare breast would neither shock nor rouse you.
Tell me their names – this fish, this salty planet,
so like and unlike earth, its bright omphalos
a kitchen table. Minutes ago we were strangers,
hours before that, lovers. It's two o'clock
I said in the new language; that's nothing, you said,
your mouth full of scales, that's children's time.

*

We slip into the darkest colour – stillness.
A half-sleep floats like tempera across
our pillows and our limbs, sunk on each other,
and in the dream that blooms from our alignment,
we wake into the rosy corner where
an icon flickers, wake into the icon.
On crimson cloth, the twenty chosen fingers
enact their imperfective verbs of touch.
The child's left hand clasps the maphorion
as it would a twist of hair; his mother's cheek
touches his, and one hand curves a cradle
for the small, uncertain spine; the other, raised,
hushes the infant universe. Dissolving
into one drowse of gold, these chosen heads,
these twenty fingers, can never say enough,
though laden with the silences of art.

*

The sun was like a diamond. Sleepily
while you worked nearby I tried to hold it
between my eyelids. All the birds were singing
to the sky's cold lavender. I slept again
letting you float – I trusted you to float
not far away. Such brightness trellised us
as if the iconographer had worked
in silver foil and gold, in pearl and turquoise.
The Virgin of the Don, like a czarina
in tear-drop gems and furry velvels, parted
the sky to smile. This was the world of money,
of purchasable grace. I woke and saw
your turned back, the diagrams spread out,
the lamp dipped as an aid to concentration
on slightly displaced, slightly obsolete fact.
Your small hand fetched the ruler in its mouth,
precise and happy as a little dog.
You squinted down and drew a swift straight line.

*

But space is curved, and all who sail in her –
plasmid, bacterium, foetus, curly brain,
the sea. Deep in each other's laps we slept,
well-matched for cradling. One shall never move
without the other, that's the law of nights.
The law of days is – one shall always move
while the other grasps, writhes up, sinks back,
sick as a sturgeon ripped from its spawing-ground
and flung in pouring silver on the heaped
and blushing deck. Only the sturgeon is luckier... –
it makes a single mistake.
We live to lift the glass again, to chase
the flying stillnesses, the mortal icons.

*

In the window lay blue light and other windows;
then there was only the print of this room
on glossy black, with a bare, sickle moon
that seemed to pierce me; now beyond the faint
kitchen glints as far as I can see
there is only black. I could be persuaded
that no moon exists, no trees, no windows
rooted in the round earth, no hope of daylight.
Patience, patience, say the little hearth-gods
smug on your hooks and shelves, unafraid of fire
or servitude – despair is simply one
point of view. And so I try again.
I imagine you travelling beneath the moon
I cannot see, I imagine you moving slowly
into this narrow frame. A greenish dawn
follows you, then the trees, the houses, daylight.
I imagine hope, and hope's redundancy,
our dark silhouette of reunion
an endless still that vanishes behind
the kissing curtains and the piecemeal snowfall –
after which there is nothing ever after.

*

She waited too; dawn did not bring you home.
Letters were sealed in tears, and crossed. One pleaded.
the other said – impossible. She froze...
The iron echo rings – impossible.
Something she'd read was happening to her:
a train pounding over the wooden bridge
over the frozen lake, and then its windows
slithering like a deck of yellowed cards
down through crashing struts, flames, slopes of ice.
The doors of the water closed. Your letters crossed,
sealed in freezing tears. Everything froze.
She stares up from the bottom of the lake.
The ice has healed smooth as lies, white-faced
as history. Impossible... yet you,
when I look down again, are lying there too.

*

This was my dream. You stood in the doorway
turning the dimmer-switch to a dark glow.
I saw the smiling boy, his butterfly-pause
in the shiny perspex trap, the matted gold
curtain-weave, the junk-shop paperbacks;
then, by the bed, your blue-bound Russian-English
slovar – a daring marriage
of words solemnly trying to mean each other,
telling their secrets in each other's arms.
I woke to the old standing-pool of dawn,
seeing only myself. The light changed,
shook with a breaking tremor...
You were beside me. So it's possible
to be happy, I said, and, in my dream,
I took your warm, lost body to my heart
and nursed my happiness to sleep again.

*

Minutes ago we were strangers... Now,
expecting my surprise, you fetch the *vobla*.
Have you forgotten the first taste you fed me?
Our tongues were stiffer, salt was sweeter, then.
You gesture doubtfully, intent on stripping
the fish to a few details of its life:
the papery, jointed pod of the swim-bladder
still tenderly inflated, twisting free,
and now the roe, delicately male
and seaweed-brown, not red as I'd imagined.
What part of light, what part of time is this?
Age, weariness, iconoclasm
watch us for our living salts, our rich
human skins...we swallow the drouth
till nothing's left beyond our lips but scales.
You wouldn't eat them, though I said so once,
wanting the pun, and your dear, careful mouth.

*

The boy, so harshly combed and tightly buttoned
into his miniature pin-stripes, looks up
with sparkling gaze and vague, milk-tooth smile,
all-trusting, though a tiny flinch betrays
his sudden, bright, important loneliness.
Somewhere off-camera you are watching him,
moving farther away but watching, watching,
till your eyes bleed with their attempt at filming.
Twenty years later, and you telephone
a birthday greeting, straining to receive
across a shower of crackling stars his tall
uncertain image, and to hear him smile.

*

There was another child, a child of wishes.
Long shadows had fallen, it was late,
but I saw him playing down by shallow water,
his language yours, diminutive, rinsed new.
For a moment, I thought you watched him too,
and the brightness in our eyes was double bright.

*

I am not the one.
Your fingertips understand it when they blindly
trace my short hair to a little below
the nape of my neck, no further.
I am not the one.
Still they trail onwards, smudging adored soft ghosts.
Dark were they, or light, or in-between?
Ringlets, or straight strands?
Your finger-tips could say, but so much knowledge
cannot translate to our shadow-language, thin
as the paper I write on. Without a past
we'll die to each other, ghost to ghost...
Your fingers mark the stony place.
They are human enough, they search for comfort,
but go on whispering: this is not the one.

*

Into the snowy east of consciousness
your dreams pull sledges, and your eyes are sealed
to keep the future from your wintering heart.
What's sourer than the after-taste of hope,
the nightly vodka at the wrong table,
the wrong attentive gaze? I think of those
who paid their one-way fare in useful lies,
the state turning a crass, wolfish cheek
on which a frail tear announced motherhood.
Is it freedom to forget the life you had,
or to carry it with you like necessity?
The west too is full of snow and whispers,
and if it were a woman it would say:
I had no choice but to disappoint you,
to become the cancelled myth, the ashamed silence,
a word that simply isn't in your language,
a foreign country, even to myself.

*

It was forbidden to destroy an icon.
Although, in time, the jewelled saints fell homesick
and dwindled smokily in mass ascensions,
their charisma remained, and only God,
sighing his aimlessness in moving water,
might wash and wash the remnant to pure nothing.

*

We too have left the life we dared not lose
on the vague strand where history runs in,
cold, innocent, light-fingered. *Goodbye
until the next world,* Zhivago sighed
heroically to his mistress, but we lack
such cheerful metaphysics. Time is all
we ever had: you scarcely treasure it,
and I can only lock it like the ghost
of the present-tense, into these antique rooms.
Better not to have tried to love at all,
perhaps, if this is the only world to love in,
and kinder never to have roused the child
we settled all those years ago to sleep,
if we did so merely to abandon it.

POEMS 1974-86 FROM

SELECTED POEMS

(1987)

Waiting for the First Boat Train

An iron sky heats pinkly at its edge.
Chimneys are cold still, blue stones of dreams

in windows. It's as if we were at sea
already, floating on our platform-raft

out to the glinting swathe of rails, the dead
islands of sheds and padlocked offices.

One by one small figures dot the track,
their capes orange lamps, the small glow

of bed and kitchen slowly dampening
inside them as they file past our feet.

Daylight is waiting in its usual siding,
stacked in clean new metals. Their job

is to tap it down to rust and dark again,
building the years as signals click on silence.

Today, we are the light that floods their tunnel,
their moment of dazed forgetfulness,

bound for the sea, our schedules wide as hope,
our losses barely felt, like the weight of back-packs.

May 1976

That May when flowering chestnuts spilled not light
but words, black riddles printed on silk white,
in the green book of the park I read about
       a feast, a rout.

Two shadows wandered under towering trees.
Then one was gone. The other, in a blaze
of dread, lay down, perhaps it was in prayer
       to grass or air.

190

The names on streets, the names on playbills shone.
My bare arms earthed the sun. All that could burn
was you, in dreams more live than anything –
    my child, my ring.

The Advanced Set

My three mysterious uncles
were my father's elder brothers,
but not like him at all.

Arranged in steps, by age,
their three small portraits frowned
above the tea-time doilies.

They didn't frown at me,
but as if they sensed
each other's eyes, too close.

My grandma, sawing bread,
glanced back at them before telling
how they took care not to speak

when, by an oversight,
they were in the house together.
They ate in relays.

What did they do next?
They went to war. One
got taken prisoner.

(His tortured shadow lurked
dark-yellowish in the damp-stain
behind the print of Mount Fuji.)

One lived by the sea.
He had asthma and a mistress.
The other drank port-wine,

alone and grand in Tonbridge,
officer-class to the end.
Without a word they slipped

past my childhood gaze,
having never patted my head
or spun me a sixpence.

Those three Advanced Level uncles –
complex as love affairs,
far as the Burma Road –

might have talked to me in the end
but had the wit to die
before I grew tall enough

to sweep the brown photos down,
laugh at them, dance on them,
sigh, 'But you're ordinary.'

A Postcard from Brighton, 1980

One man's whelk is another's cornucopia.
JEREMY TREGLOWN

Now there's nothing –
only a mad blue wall
building and toppling itself
hopelessly, over and over,
in the cage it can't understand.
We sit down suddenly like babies,
and stare at our cuttlefish shins.
Everything ends here –
the Victorian wrought-iron
descending in pastel-green waves,
the sound of feet munching
the land's dish of leftovers;
the railway, and the pink tickets
always nearly lost –
even London ends here,
signing itself off
in dots of panicky neon.
We are locked in the mad blue present,
an instamatic snap
from the eye of some child, a king.
His palace, a harem of curves,
glitters behind us; his artists
are now at work on the sky.
The real children have bought
a beach-scene to send home,

saying Don't you wish you were here?
They scan the polished crescent
of *pointilliste* sunbathers,
and readily pick themselves out,
so confident are they
that their particular gladness,
shadelessly gold and blue,
finds its true place in this.

Letter from South London

Tonight I have no fixed abode, and write to you
sadly from the bus number 159,
where I brim my head like a child's sea-dipped bucket,
with swarmings of the city that I call mine.

The river's its usual brown, the sky dawn-misty:
across the jetty the summering crowd strays
lured by the pleasure-boats to their salt-free sample
of leaving home, and the leisurely water sways

between drab shores, much like the state of mind
induced by sniffing rich diesel
and swinging round too many corners. Just now we passed
a souvenir clock's pretence at a cathedral.

No time for that big, pale, V-signed face to calm us.
The slender candle-light of democracy
has flickered out in a gloom of broken doorways
where tramp-schools study meths-economy.

Lives are still piled into blocks of flats, but now
the architects think lengthwise, thus decreasing
the incidence of suicide-by-leaping.
Tonight it's almost Elizabethan how

the low balconies are encircling us with faces.
But they're already bored with watching us
languidly watching back from the stalled bus –
there's no reason why we couldn't change places.

This, after all, is metamorphosis country:
the dead cinema comes back as a Bingo Hall;
there's a Doner Kebab where Uncle's three satellites glowed;
nailed boards where the tears of Polish salami fell.

What does home mean? Money can smell of childhood;
work to the worker is his motherland.
It's an odd fact, though the jobless can believe it,
that the easiest way to belong is to be owned.

Nothing like that for us – no leases signed:
we occupied each other for a day,
and then took off, being children of the world.
Forgive me if for a moment I've lost my way,

a compass-needle shivering sickly round,
finding no North to settle for; a tongue
saying too much in a language not its own;
a blistered heel, a newly ringless hand.

Yes, though I'm local, that's the state I'm in,
while you, strange as the desert, make it clear
as an arrow on a street-map – you are here.
No, you can't judge a sausage by its skin

as granny says – and who cares where the pig was born?
Identity's what we tell ourselves in private.
It flows with language, rivers, streets – or someone
hands it to you, free. Or snatches it.

Love's windrush flight makes all folk émigré:
we wake in the oddest places, call them home,
refuse to leave, though there's no claiming them:
they may not want us. Where we're wanted may

hurt us too much. I won't find out while I
keep moving. practising the city's fine
art of survival, freely recommended
by escalators and the thin blue line.

In Brixton now, to illustrate my point,
a boy in dreadlocks races down the streets
that are both his and Babylon's, doesn't notice
his unlatched rucksack spilling tape-cassettes.

They clatter onto the pavement. The queue shouts 'Oi!'
He turns: a flash of panic, the he whips
back, picks up the tapes, and is off again,
earthed in a single, effortless round-trip.

He gets his bus, which roars like a ghetto-blaster,
reggae-ing down the dusty old A23 –
a road joined, as the signpost reminds us, to Brighton
though Streatham Hill has never seen the sea.

April in February
(for Becky)

At four, the afternoon's baby eye
is opened still – a miracle. The blue
fades slowly in my bare, west-facing window.
Its lingering is as sweet and new as April –
when folk still long to go on pilgrimages
through the old dust of houses, marriages –
your month. You wailed in that municipal
ward, in your pollen-coloured Babygro...
Birth tunes us sharp and makes us fall in love.
Then we must live with it. These days, you change
faster than the year, or seem unchanged,
depending on my light. Think of the downs –
still in their thick, tucked, winter pelt of mud:
small birds, circling on the air's lasso,
over and over each black, thorny crown,
find nothing creeping or unfurling there.
Yet if we walked towards them now, I believe
the hills would be all softly green and scattered
with those faint suns, those small, tremendous wishes –
primroses of April, of your month.

Weeds

In gardens, it's the unwanted
babies that grow best and biggest,
swarming our beds of frail
legitimate darlings with roots
like wire and crude, bright flower-heads.

They seem oblivious
of the fury of steel prongs
earthquaking around them.
If they fall today, tomorrow
they'll stand all the greener.

Too soon, the beautiful lives
we've trembled over with sprays
of pesticide, friendly stakes,
and watering-cans at sunset,
give in, leaving us helpless.

195

The weeds, the unfavoured ones,
stare at us hungrily,
and since it is hard to live
empty of love, we try
to smile; we learn to forgive them.

Virgil for the Plebs

The child in front of the television set
bends half her mind to a dead language.

Its italics hook her down
between linenboard bent and scarred by generations.

Some progress has been made,
a teacher might say, reporting on the centuries –

a girl, and no patrician,
let loose among the big imperial words;

yet, lacking that substance of self-love
called class, tricked into myth

by special-offer potions for bright hair,
soft-focus studies in the art of kissing,

she's lost her heart for books,
says it's better to marry than learn.

The Trojans and Greeks were fighting over Helen.
Their ships and spears and shields

litter the page, stout but expendable.
Tanks nose across the screen.

Because the wars are in our living-rooms
we think them literature.

We can adjust them, strand the President
in silence, wipe off blood

in the twinking of a switch.
Child-like we gather round for the old stories

of passionate nominatives and accusatives,
or, suddenly quiet, turn up the news to discover

the verb that waits for us
at the end of our sentence.

Two Women

Daily to a profession – paid thinking
and clean hands – she rises,
unquestioning. It's second nature now.
The hours, though they're all of daylight, suit her.
The desk, typewriter, carpets, pleasantries
are a kind of civilisation, built on money,
of course, but money, now she sees, is human.
She has learned giving from her first chequebook,
intimacy from absence. Coming home
long after dark to the jugular torrent
of family life, her smile
cool as the skin of supermarket apples,
she's half the story. There's another woman
who bears her name, a silent, background face
that's always flushed with effort.
The true wife, she picks up scattered laundry,
and sets the table with warmed plates to feed
the clean-handed woman. They've not met.
If they were made to touch, they'd scald each other.

Up Lines, Down Lines

1

A winter waiting-room where the gas-fire mutters –
scarce tremor of blue filaments, scarce heat

thinning towards benched walls – those benches hard
as the Ragged School – floor, walls and air one dense

matting of nicotine, loud loose-boned doors.
Outside, a wisp of trees, a North Downs valley

tarred for the greater work force. It's a small
drift of the casual or managerial

that settles here to an embattled leisure
tented by *Telegraph*s and *Sun*s. The clock

pursues its cautious policy of perfect
accuracy twice a day. There's time

for the nine-thirteen to enter Merstham tunnel
at twenty past, time to get six across,

or watch the vast statistics of collapse
blur and devalue in a yawn. There's time.

A favourite cartoonist's simple moral,
a centre-page of packed bikini, hold

dereliction at arm's length from the heart.
Cigar butts star the chill subsistence air.

2

Know that you'll see nothing beautiful on this journey,
but, swayed between a window and a book,

let landscape hold you. Parse its rougher grammar
of scrapyards and sidings, house-fronts smirched

by their seven-decade dialogue with the railway.
Against patched, flap-skin windows, mouldering steps,

the sagging ropes of wet-bright washing argue
that lives are somehow made, and hold together

inside, that crumbled plaster, spores of wet
will dazzle to a symmetry of roses

over beds where children lie. Read on towards
the common, and a man hunched on a seat,

your train his book and window. Read the river
in slack-necked cranes like damaged birds, dank wharves,

their last transactions closed. Study the tracks
of slippery light that write your future clear

through the gathered shadows of the terminus.
It is your story. Enter, with proud steps

along a well-swept platform, that last freedom –
to jostle at the gate. To take your wages.

3

Dodging their overseers – typewriters, Xeroxes,
phones – those battering tongues of retribution,

from platform seventeen the year's first tourists
chase flight down flickering rails. Beyond the station,

the airport; beyond grey sea, the world;
but the world is only a place of other stations

and other airports, doors that hoard no power
(though the sun silvers them) of greater worlds,

as they swing towards curved tracks, the flight-path home.
Cheated and tired on the same trajectory,

I wait, watching the smashed pane of a warehouse
open a wound-black map the shape of Ireland.

Rain spits its beaded strings, skylights the rails.
We fly through hidden colonies, feel the breath

of threats nail-packed and wired in attics, taste
our own blood on the pitched-back stones of insult.

These travel with us. But tonight we're hauled
clear to safekeeping. Streamlets plait each gutter

as, hunched through the mild artillery of rain,
I run for a porchway, quickly step inside.

Tides

The other night I slept in a red-roofed village
that was trying not to topple off the land.
Outside the Seamen's Mission a rusty-scaled
cod gasped for coins, standing tip-tailed,
but I turned in at the sign of the Dolphin, where
the landlord drank like a ghost at his own bar,
and his dog barked 'time' in the small hours.
I escaped at dawn to clear my head with the wind
that bounded out across the turfy clay
where at last the moor slipped into the arms of the bay.

Three hundred miles from the pinpoint of a chance
of meeting you, I was perfectly cool.
I watched the sea drag its malevolent, gleaming
tons away from the land it had just darkened,
and was glad I would be cosily south before
it hurtled back to boil at the sea-wall
and unveil a winter, the streets white or streaming,
the mouth of the mission-cod encrusted with ice,
and no one stooping on the pooly sand
to weigh the small cold of a starfish in a warm hand.

When I took the little creature from my pocket
later, I found it had changed shape, as if
in some last, inching retreat from life,
it had been reborn. I placed it in a glass,
freshly filled, with some salt from the breakfast table –
but it didn't stir again. I suppose I'd thought
it might unfurl like a Japanese water-flower,
brimmed with its element. So the foolish hope for
resurrection, or at least the kind of death
that brightens corn-rot to alcohol, driftwood to jet.

All that remained now was a valediction
to tender doubt, and the backward-racing lines
of the railway, sepia after a night of rain,
since I had to come home, leaving the dead starfish
for the landlady, leaving the village
to its history of cod and non-conformist virtue,
and the helpless plunge of its streets to their salty source,
leaving the chastened tourists clambering still
towards the mysteries of some clouded hill;
since I had to trade the rich North Sea for stone;
talk with you, touch you, let the tide turn.

False Wings

The house with its many windows drew the dawn
into itself, and light touched open shapes
and colours – a yellow quilt, our human darkness.
Pillow-grass flowered in all its varieties –
your lashes, soft as charrings, the crisp maze
curling along each forearm,
tiny needles of midnight in your jaw.
By the day's slow brightening,
I discovered the clairvoyance of your eyelids.
They flickered up, even before my lips
had found your sleeping face.
I loved your look of happiness, its pure welcome.
You touched me like your first-born, with a marvelling
sweetness that inventoried each part
and found me whole; yet you touched my heart
most when, climbing our tumult, you took its peak
with a child's candour, and I saw my name
flying into the sun, amazed by falling.

Lines

Remembering our lunch, alone and later,
what I get is a vision of a coat-sleeve,
black and creased, my own, complete with arm.
What was I doing, wasting so much time
        lost in the dark of myself,
        looking away from your face?

And that black sleeve swims before me like space
dotted with tiny stars of refracted light.
Your presence always had a curious grace
for disturbing the self-confidence of matter
        while dashing hope through the slip
        betwixt a cup and a lip.

Lost in that hour where flesh resurfaces,
we fed each other questions –
what we had done with the past, what we had kept
of each other, and lost;
        where we were now – the one
        that interested us most.

We were quick and brilliant cartographers,
penning our continent on the tiny scale
required for a plate to go from full to empty,
and a tablecloth to become the North Pole –
    bare, but for two glasses
    that might be our lost souls.

'Time's nothing,' you said, and as I smiled,
ready to doubt, I felt the furious slam
of lightning and its big immediate echo;
Suddenly I was in flames
    like a stripped tree.
    Your words were earthed in me.

How often, quivering between mind and gland,
imagination seems no more than the thread
from a child's hunger-wet mouth to his playful hand,
frail as the caterpillar's shaken guy-rope –
    yet this is what tugs and saves us
    as we climb; this is time's hope.

If, when we are distant points upon
an arctic blankness, tented and alone,
I can still drop you a line,
send it through dark, not fearing to be thrown
    on your mercy, this will be to live
    with stars sprinkling my sleeve.

And that delicate poise between what happens
and what's imagined will become our art
as long as we obey the simple lesson
of a meal and a wineglass, still assert
    the importance of common air
    to walkers on the moon.

Here is my rope-trick, then, requiring one
volunteer. Let's move towards each other,
not looking down, each word's taut centimetre
nearer the possible. Pursue these lines
    dear questioner, to the end
    and we will touch again.

Writing at Night

Light on the page, the shadow of a hand
slow as a carver's, leaving intricate trails
of cuts, the whiteness bleeding into black.
Notation of what we are, our heart-beats, hormones,
the chemical lights of the brain. The soft tick
of dotted i's, then the imitative rain
outside on claws. A little wind-animal
beats the back of the gas-fire where it's caught
in faint, metal shudders. The hand continues
over the page, gathering the massed night
which slowly reduces to a single line
joining our two rooms, our two lit selves
lost in the drama of their alphabets,
freeing the sentenced lives. I glance out at the dark,
and there's your face, written in shining drops.

Simple Poem

Why didn't the room say
how long your absence would be,
that night when you climbed the stairs
in your quick, expectant way
and sat across from me?
No word from the lamp or the chair
though they've both been around a bit
and ought to have guessed, not a sign
from the much-used willow plate.
It watched you laugh and eat
and did not seem to care,
as lost in desire as I –
and now you're not here.

And now you're not here, why
must there still be a room
with surfaces that mime
the slow life of the sky,
and a clock to strike off time?
Like an implacable heart
the blind swings open, shut,
on leafy blue, on grey.

203

Darkness refuses to stay,
and always the numb dawn light
shows a chair, raggedly turned,
and a small lamp that once burned
all through the summer night.
Oh, how the light loved then
all the white length of your spine.
My pillow was dark with your hair.
Why doesn't everything die
now you're not here?

The Last Day of March

The elms are darkened by rain.
On the small, park-sized hills
Sigh the ruined daffodils
As if they shared my refrain –
That when I leave here, I lose
All reason to see you again.

What's finishing was so small,
I never mentioned it.
My time, like yours, was full,
And I would have blushed to admit
How shallow the rest could seem;
How so little could be all.

The Usual

It is a clear midsummer night:
They glow upon the cooling light,
The Traceys, Lisas, Janes and Dawns,
Barbaric and composed as swans,
For whom the world has yet to happen.
All day they've drowsed on close-clipped lawns,
Feeling their youth and colour deepen.

And now in chalky blue the moon
Melts like a tablet; lights go on;
In small front-rooms the power-packed boxes

Blaze into apocalypses,
Or storm the disillusioned street;
Plumped mini-skirts out-sex the maxis –
It's Sixties Night at Les Élites.

Life is the old deceiver who'll
Take every daughter off the pill.
They're after him in leaps and bounds;
He's got the stuff, he'll buy the rounds.
They laugh and jeer: we know your kind!
But, after all, they like his pose;
Ravenous, thirsty, rightly blind,
They shrug: what have we got to lose?

A Small Inequality

When a man loses desire
it's no joke
either for himself or his partner.
Their mortification gives work
to the sober psychiatrist
who may also enlist
the Marriage Guidance Counsellor
or the Hypnotherapist:
money will be no object.
All his house will cry woe
till dreams or drugs re-erect
the master's libido.

But when a similar fate
befalls a woman
it may simply amuse her mate.
Such 'moods' are common;
he cites the eternal
headache and all
the 'no's' that really meant
'If you must'. And of course she still
can please him if she tries.
This show will run and run
as long as he ignores (most can)
the glazed look in her eyes.

Academic Perks

Stumbling round Heathrow,
peering at hazy flight-times,
your hand-baggage pitiless
with heavy reading –
including parts one and two
of *Serbo-Croat for Beginners* –
you're the perfect prototype
of the travelling intellectual.

That despicable English habit
of letting down the hair
in foreign climates
has never crossed your mind.

You cover your face
with your *Historical Guide*
when the plane unwisely begins
to get serious with the air.

'There are six republics.
There are five nations.
There are four languages.
There are three religions.
There are two alphabets.
There is only one desire: independence.'

At thirty thousand feet
what can you do but munch
half-frozen salami,
and silently repeat
such terrestrial certainties?

Shuddering, you touch down
not far from the workers' flats
and the new ring-road,
on whose wrong side
you will soon be travelling
towards the tallest hotel
in the many-windowed capital
(THERE, TO YOUR LEFT
THE FAMOUS SUGAR-BEET FACTORY
HEROICALLY OUTSTRIPPING
LAST MONTH'S PRODUCTION NORMS).

In your bedroom the first night,
trying to take in
the latest publication
of one of your learned colleagues,
that moon of a lampshade
drives you almost spare.
Its schmaltzy red glow
reminds you of a bar,
which in turn reminds you
how alone you are.

You pick the screws out
and watch it fall apart.

...But later, so much has happened,
your journal has turned pale
in the middle of Saturday,
and refuses to say any more.

And the last night you appear
to be a different person.
Somewhat dishevelled,
sporting the peasant-blouse
no peasant has worn
since the revolution,
you hum that famous
Serbian folksong:
'Let the lamp be as dim as it likes.'

In the Craft Museum

Some nations lock up their poets. Ours have the key
To a high, clean room labelled Sensibility.

They have sat there now for a very long time,
And are clearly no threat to a democratic regime.

They are old, of course, but remarkably unspoiled;
Their edges still cut, their moving parts are oiled.

Of course, they're permitted to go down to the street,
And the street may visit them, if it wipes its feet.

Here comes the guide now, telling the solemn young faces
That, yes, the poets still work, but don't touch the glass cases.

Ballad of the Morning After

Take back the festive midnight,
Take back the sad-eyed dawn:
Wind up that old work ethic.
Oh, let me be unborn.

After a night of travelling,
How can it come to pass
That there's the same tongue in my mouth
The same face in my glass,

Same light on the curtain,
Same thirst in the cup,
Same ridiculous notion
Of never getting up?

Cars stream above the city;
The subway throbs below,
Whirling a million faces
Like shapeless scraps of snow,

And all these melting faces
Flying below and above
Think they are loved especially
Think they especially love.

This is a free country.
The jails are for the bad:
The only British dissidents
Are either poor or mad.

I put my classless jeans on,
Open my lockless door;
I breathe the air of freedom
And know I'm mad and poor.

Love is the creed I grew by,
Love is the liberal's drug –
Not Agape but Eros
With his Utopian hug

And in the *close, supportive*
Environment of the bed,
He is liberty, equality,
Fraternity and bread.

That is the supposition –
But I say love's a joke,
A here-today-and-gone-tomorrow
Childish pinch-and-poke.

Perhaps I'll believe in something
Like God or Politics;
I'd build those temples wider
But there are no more bricks.

Some women believe in Sisterhood;
They've rowed the Master's ship
Across the lustful silver sea
On his last ego-trip,

And some believe in Housework,
And a few believe in Men.
There's only one man that I want,
And I want him again and again.

He sat down at my table.
He finished all the wine.
'You're nothing, dear, to me,' he said,
But his body covered mine,

And stoked the fiery sickness
That's done me to a turn –
The fool that chose to marry
And also chose to burn.

Burning burning burning
I came to self-abuse,
Hoping I'd go blind, but no,
It wasn't any use.

I see a mother and her child
Both turn with starving face.
And that's the story of our lives,
The whole damned human race.

My conscience is a hangover,
My sex-life, chemistry;
My values are statistics,
My opinions, PMT.

Beside my rented window
I listen to the rain.
Yes, love's a ball of iron,
And time, its short, sharp chain.

The middle-aged say life's too brief.
The old and young say 'wrong'.
I'll tell you, if you don't like life,
It's every day too long.

Carpet Weavers, Morocco

The children are at the loom of another world.
Their braids are oiled and black, their dresses bright.
Their assorted heights would make a melodious chime.

They watch their flickering knots like television.
As the garden of Islam grows, the bench will be raised.
Then they will lace the dark-rose veins of the tree-tops.

The carpet will travel in the merchant's truck.
It will be spread by the servants of the mosque.
Deep and soft, it will give when heaped with prayer.

The children are hard at work in the school of days.
From their fingers the colours of all-that-will-be fly
and freeze into the frame of all-that-was.

Passing a Statue of Our Lady in Derry

She appears tired, though dressed in fresh, white stone,
And bows the bandaged snowdrop of her head
Pleadingly to the bus – which hurries on
And leaves her stranded in my childhood,

Mother of small contritions, great hopes
And the lyric boredom of the rosary
When miracles seemed at our fingertips:
She is much younger now than formerly,

And in her narrow, girlish hands, she weighs
Not holiness, but a frail, human idea
That might accomplish anything – dismiss
An army – or, like childhood, disappear.

A Dream of South Africa

Trafalgar Square is only a pigeon-sea,
but he could hear the waves sigh up and fall
as he passed the sooty door-stones of Pall Mall.
The men in their navy suits were sailors, he
a brisk cadet. He marched behind, in step,
towards the lighted windows of his ship.

An office job! It didn't seem like work,
so I painted it in childish, Admiral colours.
My mother laughed, fought off the social climbers...
In fact, he was a shipbroker's clerk,
the fourth, last, disappointing son,
sea-feverish since the age of seventeen.

Cathay Pacific, Cunard, Peninsular House –
one night not long ago I followed him –
saw where he boozed – the Travellers', the Reform.
The wind hustled his stumpy, pin-striped ghost,
practised now, and as managerial,
almost, as if he'd been an admiral.

He stayed becalmed in these local pools,
drawn by the whisky siren's easy mood.
'South Africa,' she whispered, and he glowed,
imagining that palm-green, palm-court cruise,
a charming old imperialist of the fleet,
who'd crunch the diamonds under hard, white feet.

If he had doubts, he didn't ever say,
although he sometimes talked about retirement.
Once, he brought home from the Embassy
a pamphlet – boring, but it sounded decent.
It offered 'separate development for the Bantu'.
'Apartheid' tripped my tongue; a long word, new.

I've never understood what happened later.
My mother grumbled: no directorship,
no retirement cruise, no Africa.
Age moves so fast, the young just can't keep up...
The liners that slid, shining, down the Thames
had sailed without him. Or he'd sailed without them.

Cathay Pacific, Cunard, Peninsular House:
I listed them, as he must have done
with boyish love, before he veered off-course –
wrong man, wrong job – but kept his head down,
having a wife and daughter to support,
until the lights went out on his horizon.

Ashqelon

At Ashqelon, I searched
a diaspora of sea-shells
for the perfect affinities
of size and patterning
that make a couple.

Little hinged bivalves,
they were unpartnered now.
Marked out for loneliness
as faces are,
each knew its sad uniqueness.

The sea had never valued
their delicate compacts.
It had plunged them into war,
then dragged them, fighting and broken,
and beaten them into the shore.

There they lay, one nation,
bathed in a flickering dream
which every sleeper read
from his own eyelids.
And, as I gazed at them,

it was as if the sea
scattered them still, or the wind,
and whirled their coloured rain
to the ends of Ashqelon,
and to shores that have no end.

A New Song

(for Naim Attallah)

Silences of old Europe
Not even the shofar
Can utter: Maidenek,
Mauthausen, Babi Yar –

Death of the innocent being
Our speciality
Let us add Lebanon's breaking
Sob to the litany.

So many now to mourn for,
Where can the psalmist start?
Only from where his home is,
And his untidy heart.

We pluck our first allegiance
With a curled baby-hand,
Peering between its fingers
To see our promised land;

Yours on a hillside, clouded
With olives; mine a cot
In a London postal district,
Its trees long spilled as soot.

The war was all but over:
It seems my newborn cry
Was somehow implicated
In yells of victory.

But it's the quieter voices
That keep on trying to rhyme,
Telling me almost nothing,
But filling me with shame:

Germany in the thirties
And half my family tree
Bent to an SS microscope's
Mock genealogy.

Duly pronounced untainted
For his Aryan bride,
My uncle says it's proven –
There are no Jews on our side.

Ancient, unsummoned, shameless,
The burdens of prejudice:
All through my London childhood,
Adults with kindly eyes

Muttered the mild opinions
So innocently obscene
(Hitler was not 'all stupid',
and 'not all Jews are mean').

Later, the flickering movie;
Greyish, diaphanous
Horrors that stared and questioned:
Has God forgotten us?

Oh, if our unborn children
Must go like us to flame,
Will you consent in silence,
Or gasp and burn with them?

It is so late in the century
And still the favourite beast
Whines in the concrete bunker
And still the trucks roll east

And east and east through whited
Snowfields of the mind
Towards the dark encampment;
Still the Siberian wind

Blows across Prague and Warsaw,
The voices in our head
Baying for a scapegoat:
Historians gone mad;

Thugs on a street corner,
The righteous gentile who
Pins Lebanon like a yellow star
To the coat of every Jew.

Silences of old Europe
Be broken; let us seek
The judgement of the silenced,
And ask how they would speak.

Then let the street musician
Crouched in the cruel sun
Play for each passing, stateless
Child of Babylon,

Conciliatory harmonies
Against the human grain,
A slow psalm of two nations
Mourning a common pain –

Hebrew and Arabic mingling
Their single-rooted vine;
Olives and roses falling
To sweeten Palestine.

At Kibbutz Amiad

These are the solid texts –
houses in white lanes
scribbled with jacaranda.
But it's in the margins

we'll find our poems
said footloose Mandelstam.
I weigh this as you sleep
and all the kibbutzim

of the Upper Galilee
grow moody with children
escaping vaguely home,
tired as the khamsin.

Quarrels, piano practice –
nothing is lonelier
in this story of families
than our marginalia.

We keep ourselves to ourselves
in a flower-shadowed house
with an empty second bedroom
that cannot fathom us.

Camouflage

Hot Rhine-Valley days, the misty odours
of pollution and Late Romanticism;
hubris on a meagre city beach
where I am burning my base self to gold,
shifting with the sun as it slyly escapes
at an odd, foreign angle, never overhead,
thinking it something like our conversations
in the tongue we cannot share, haunting, oblique:

twilights that whirr with home-flying bicycles
and a perennial, anxious excitement
in case the night should betray its incredible promise –
for we are moody and unverifiable
chameleons of a thousand joys and troubles;
parted by so much daylight, we might arrive
at our violet-skied, electric meeting-place
as strangers who must touch each other's skin
over and over, and still not quite remember:

night, and the reading is from Dostoyevsky.
Your new voice, fiery, rough, argumentative,
astounds the room, I dare not look at your face,
until at last the flare of language dies,
dies back to the dark garden
of breath and watching. Sunlight glares from my skin
like a confession, but my secrets are white.
You comment on my 'distinctive markings'
as I home towards you through the branching shadows,
fierce and intent, in perfect camouflage.

Eclipses

Midday. The earth holds its breath,
the shadows can't move an inch.
Only the sky seems to be rushing away.
It vanishes into the blue of its furthest blue,
dropping a little curled handful of sun-smeared iris
onto the world for us.

The poppies are clear glass bowls of some inky night-cap,
the grass, an amazement of light.
And you and I, what are we,
our soft, random collision
eclipsing us in this garden,
this room? Pass your hand
quickly over the sun's brow and invent
a glowing midday dusk
where I shall undress to my ear-studs
and you, to nothing. Where the exotic, slow,
brachiating animal we evolve,
time-lapsed, will have no name,
and I'll press my lips by mistake to my own skin.

Laboratory Visions
(for Peter Meades)

A suspiciously light, bright room,
it had surely been planned
for advanced psychological torture.
There were interrogation-cells,
where the subjects faced the wall,
rows of turntables
and slender miles of tape
packed around miniature cart-wheels
whose fast, fluttering spin
took my breath away – almost my fingers.
Dry-lipped, I sat down;
preparing a full confession,
ducked into the headset.
It fitted like a migraine,
the two black pockets
crackly as lightning.
When it spoke, I marvelled
the voice was human.
I became human too.
Among the towering words,
I was a stranger, still
gripping with both hands
th eluggage of my local grammar,
but getting acclimatised
simply by breathing the air.

And then the room I was in
was an ordinary kitchen,
cramped high above Moscow.
Smiling uncertainly,
a woman turned from the stove.
She greeted me. I answered.
Zdrasvutye. Kak vas zavut?
Hello. What is your name?
For a moment our languages were mirrors,
and I thought I was in heaven.

Wire Baskets

Real-fruit yoghurts whose nutritional benefits
are said to be vast, but which will be spooned with a fearful
delectation that never exceeds half a carton;
baked beans with their modified starch, sugar, water,
cheerful as Belisha beacons, civilising
the most unrefined slice of toast; stout, country burgers
70% pure beef; bright young Grannies
from police-states, gleaming as our teeth should gleam,
gleaming as if waxed by the ardent housewife
I never was: these I remember. I believed
I was structuring my children's bones like crystal
palaces, cheaply but strongly and beautifully,
just as the state, which offered free education
in those days, was fitting out their immortal minds.
My own was a supermarket of clichés, e.g.
every child has an inborn right to vitamins
and scholarship, whatever the parents' net income
...It isn't true of course. They have no rights
which the law can't take away and we had no right
to conceive them in such innocence, rosily tumbling
like shabby storks out of the sixties sunset
into the broken-classroomed eighties, beaks
and wings ripped off by the weight of our wire baskets.

West Berlin Pastoral

Hans's country retreat
was a few minutes drive from Head Office,
but country, nevertheless.

If we weren't quite at ease,
neither was our taciturn host,
born on that side of the Wall

where nobody would splash graffiti
to make themselves immortal.
There were too many tongues, adrift

and tipsy with cross-currents,
for one simple picnic;
but the grass befriended us,

and the thick gooseberry hedge
that marked the boundary
between the woods, birch-misted,

and our luminous clearing, dropped
its sweets into our palms.
Someone began 'Kalinka',

and Hans joined in, loudly
word-perfect, commandeering
the drama of its *tempo rubato*.

The sweat broke on his brow
like raw grain; we could tell
he had learned success

at the knees of the Komsomol.
When the small fire-roses
had faded in the charcoal,

and the flats and sandy shallows
of a mildly remarkable sunset
flooded darkly over,

he lit the hurricane lamps
ranged along the privy roof,
and ordered us to dance.

Then, with a slight sigh,
he sat back watching us,
his feet in their triple-striped

yellow Adidas jumping
on the overturned beer-crate
like two insane bees.

We were babbling nightingales now,
paired and cradled and brilliant
with impromptu history.

Drunk, we knew every language,
and that every language was touch,
every wall, a gooseberry bush.

The Compass Plant

Ya skuchayu pa tebye.

'I am bored without you'
is Russian for 'I miss you',
but somehow weightier:
east of the Brandenburg Gate,

boredom can be very black.
It gets a whole mouthful of sounds
with a cruel twist at the end
like something Fate might do.

It resembles 'escutcheon' –
a bat-like museum-piece,
solid, medieval, filthy
with a coat-of-arms we can't read,

declaring the thickness of blood.
Bored as a sentry I've taken
to vodka and dictionaries.
I guzzle words like a fly-trap,

but am really a compass plant,
my leaves tracking the sun
with blades perpendicular
to the incoming light,

220

irreversibly orientated
to you, your tongue, your absence.
If I seem to be asleep,
my senses are open wide;

I am highly photoperceptive,
and geared to the trembliest rumour.
All future-tense, I dream
bored into borders, opened.

Lovers in Westgate Gardens

When I passed them, tucked away
On a bench cut deep into the privet,

I observed two masculine hands at urgent play
On a small, cotton-clad, feminine ribcage,

Which seemed content to lie there and accept
The attention, snug and close as a bird in its plumage.

At once your absence swept me, fiery-cold,
And common envy, spiteful, mean and dull,

Froze to my skin. I thought how, when we loved,
I could do something better than lie still.

Then a sharp rustling shook the dark-leafed bower;
The lovers faded, you sat quietly waiting

For me to notice you, to sense you'd spoken.
'In love, the one pleased has no less power

Than the one who pleases. To accept with grace
Is also to give.' And then, it seemed, you opened

Your arms towards me so consentingly,
I was enfolded in that mystery.

Second Lives

Wedging himself by degrees
through the unlatched door,
the foundling tomcat

with his double set of neuroses
looks at the woman in bed,
decides he needn't leave.

They listen to the plug
knuckling the wall's far side,
then the granular buzz

of coffee-beans spinning
into fragments of themselves,
truer than themselves.

Around her stand the dead,
risen as usual,
encumberings of teak

veneer, uncut moquette,
thin brass and sprigged plastic
glooming in the dawn

of her second life.
The man who left that crumpled
space on her right,

chose them carefully.
She knows in which junk-shops
and at what price.

He was by himself,
breathing in the strong essence
of private ownership,

tongue-tied and stateless
as the tense face that dodged him
from mirror to speckled mirror.

This is his second country;
she, his lost wives;
she is twenty, thirty, forty

as she waits for him to bring
the Oxfam tray
with its dusty wicker plait

and scribble of poppies.
He'll set it gently down
on the quilt's collapsing flesh,

and, stepping back to watch
her childish pleasure, taste
the day's first sip with her.

Dark Harvest

They shine like tiny apples, black,
Scented with gin and loneliness,
The easiest fruit, perhaps, to pick
But firm against my tongue's duress
As I interrogate their skin
Kindly, tactfully, knowing that soon
They'll have to break, confess their lies
Of ripeness till my whole mouth cries.

A bush of fruit-lamps burns as clear
In Harrow as in Chistopol.
It brings the life you fled so near
I'm dizzy with its taste and smell.
I wade breast-deep, the whispering bush
Opening up, against my wish,
Those glints and lights I least can bear –
The darkest eyes, the softest hair.

They have survived their altered state,
Your exiled loves. They stir their tea
With teaspoon-clouds of summer fruit,
And test the sweetness patiently.
Your absence falls as light as dust,
Now, on the lives. They're almost used
To swallowing what's dull and cruel:
I think they almost wish you well.

Christmas Dinner Borscht

Don't look for spies or angels in our kitchen.
We're Christmas-ing far from all religions.
Utopia doesn't mean a thing to us,
And we've forgotten how to talk to children.

Eating, though, continues. And ever since
I dipped my spoon into this wavy, scarlet
Winter sun, lifted its cap of beet-leaves,
I've felt as festive as a wedding taxi

Climbing in clouds of exhaust, frost, ribbons,
With a bride who'll simply giggle and take snaps.
The sandy, pointed beard, implacably growthless
In its mausoleum, needn't expect a visit.

Don't look for revolution. In our kitchen
We know religions all get cooked and eaten.
And artists catch only the incarnation,
Its living wonder, kissed from Rheims to Kiev.

Cooks, too, like colour. Look, our beetroot angels
Were here before us, bowed towards our plates.
They've left their traces, though the soup has vanished:
For each of us, one rose-gold halo print!

FROM

THE GREENING OF
THE SNOW BEACH

(1988)

Foreign Affairs by Phone

They used to make me cry –
your hushy consonants
and the forms of the vocative,
intimate as fingertips –
ti, tvoi, tvoyar –
you finally confessed,
the handset warming
in your attentive grip.
In fact, I never ceased
to hear a declarative
and reverberating sigh
touching a small ear, tensed
and eager and not far away –
even when I'd advanced
sufficiently to divine
that the probable topic was pig-farming
or the new Astrakhan gas pipeline.

Due Back
A Leningrad-born émigré visits the Russian library, ULU

The Senate House, an ark devoid of graces,
Is lofty enough, at least, to vaporise
A memory of your city's more precise
And elevated *ports de bras* and *glissées*.

The afternoon glows plushly like a breath-cloud
Hung by a skier on an empty run.
You trudge the edge of crisping emerald lawn:
The cold clings to your scarfless throat, a death-shroud.

You disappear. The hungry, clustered trees
Stare with a burning, stoical compassion
And wait. Even the sun goes down with caution.
A little light is saved for your release.

Your polar dialect thaws at minus one.
You creep between the stacks on sibilant parquet,
Quick-eyed, entranced, and hear the date-stamp marking
Time, your tongue pressed to your heart, on loan.

Russian Lessons

(including the theme music of *Dr Zhivago*)

1

This is a revolutionary song
but they are singing it in the émigrés' cafés:
how good we are to cut the bourgeoisie's necks!
They are changing this words, of course.

2

At first, didn't you know,
during this revolution
they have some private enterprise
so a woman is selling bublyechki.
For this
Bublyechki
Give me roublyechki!

Bublyechki are like doughnuts
but more dense.

3

Why do you look like this for?
You think it is banal
for your European taste?
The picture, of course, is quite rubbish
but, I am afraid, for the tune
he took something from my soul.

Welcome to the Club

Soviet Film Season foyer: birch trees, slogans
And sickles drowning in the day-for-night
Illumination, nosed by grooming shoals
Of your fellow islanders, across whose polite

Post-imperial blah you catch the skirling
Rushy current of your native prose.
Your eyes slide at once to a hopeful angle,
Although already wise enough to suppose

The foreigner will not proclaim himself
By his shopping bag or his sentimental ways.
Even his premature ageing will have slowed
To the local rate; he will not look victimised.

Having defined one voice, you discover more
And more, emerging from the undergrowth
Like mushrooms, their fine threads spooling back
To a Urals cart-track

Or a Moscow park, but equally at home.
And you think of all the other loosened tongues
Convening for their particular celluloid dawn
Ritual beside the grey, incurious Thames –

A silent frieze of semaphors unfurled
Across the blank sheet of the metropolis
To an audience of kids who've seen the world,
And know it speaks English.

You move away, silent and self-contained,
To float somewhere among the subtitles.
The highlighted bas-relief of vowels
Gleams on the guilty air like the Elgin marbles.

The birch tree has become an endangered species,
Scarred horizontally with wounded eyes
And dried-up lips that must reserve their judgement –
Even their lies.

You've ceased to understand, you've ceased to listen.
You're left with culture and a weightless smile.
Don't be afraid. At least you're the man with the tickets
Not the girl in the overall.

A West Country Twin Town

In the new year of our new life together
        When, dreamy, diffident
As stuttering English snow, we stole each other
        From history's Janus-glare,
And then, to cure our failure of intent,
        Glanced at a map, drove west

Towards the refuge of that kindest city –
    Fathered by Rome, but a true Hellenist,
Whose naiad waters, glorying in their own
    Warm, emerald climate, try to wash the frown
From marble rectitude: in that new year

A birch tree sidled up to welcome us
    Plaintively, a skinny city peasant
    Sighing the forest wasn't what it was,
And we, lounging in bed at noon, could count
    Through snow-dim glass a row
Of colonnades or pan-pipes, not convinced,
But happily suspecting that the pleasant
    Angel of English fantasy had swished
    Her wing across our view:
So we were held until the room went dark,
And vision sank to a shady glow of flesh...
    But midnight, scathing as a Bolshevik
Of love's imperial privacies, burst in
    And flung us out to public life again.

By one o'clock the city was a mess,
    Silent and slumped after the ritual shrieks
To *auld lang syne*, and dangerously chilled:
Even her dreams were limestone, moist and cold.

In that new year that wasn't a new start,
    Simply its shadow which, when lost,
Might still seem solider than all the rest,
    We watched grey water shrug itself along
In ruffled furs, and the mosquito snow
    Hugged by a ring of lamplight as it danced.
So deeply cold the sleeping city grew
    Each night that I believed her comatose,
Deaf to her naiads, fatally entranced.
    Even the Renault seemed about to die;
Curled like a mercury-ball, a frozen mouse,
It could not raise a spark, but coughed
    With wincing shoulders, frail, tubercular,
While, from your rag-bound thumb, a hot, red tear
    Was futile, like all human sacrifice.

I was prepared never to get away:
    Now that you'd told me where we might have been,
I'd come to think that it was where we were,
    And every street could float off into sea.

Your 'most-premeditated' city, scarved
   In tremulous rivers, numberless bloodstreams,
   And yet unable to escape its dreams,
Had locked us into one stern homesickness,
   So even when we freed ourselves, our roads
   Would always take us north, and Bath appear
In memory's closing window like the ghost
   Of Petersburg at the start of each new year.

The Difference

My first time abroad,
I was nineteen or so
and crossing the laid-back pastures
of Normandy in a train,
my forehead bumping the window.
When distant cows appeared
I knew at once they were different.
French, I whispered, *French*,
wishing I could hear them
moo the Norman way.
And my first time in Moscow,
only the other month,
I was crossing Herzen Street
in a shower of piano scales
when, before I could stop myself,
Russian pianos, I thought
wildly, *played by Russians!*
And the world streamed out again
into an opened vista.
Whatever it was, that difference,
unfathomable, possessed me;
my forehead jumped on the glass,
as if I were still as abroad,
as foreign as nineteen.

The Flood of Silence

What killed Pushkin was not D'Anthes' bullet;
what killed him was lack of air.
    BLOK

What a Devil's Trick that I should be born
with a soul and talent in Russia.
    PUSHKIN

On London nights, Decemberish, icy,
When streets and sky and Thames are all
One shimmering bale, gold-sequinned, pricey;
When the wind hardens to a wall
On corners where theatres glitter,
And words are tossed away like litter
While golden eggs lay pizza-chains
And burger-bars and video-games,
I think of you in Tsarskoye Selo
Writing your Ode to Liberty;
Bliss was it in that dawn to be
A dreamy, radical young fellow
Saved from Yakutsk, if not from court
By exile of a milder sort.

I think how silence spreads its rivers
Over unstable, swampy banks;
Even the bronze-wrapped horseman shivers
As bridges float away in planks.
A wave shins up a lamp-post's rigging;
First doors, then balconies are swigging
The muddy water, then the chimes
Of plump St Isaac's; on it climbs...
Miraculously, we can hear you
Still, as if you were a bird –
Art with an olive-sprig – absurd
Image that surely fails to cheer you
As you gaze out of Leningrad,
Your mausoleum, huge and sad.

You built your ark, although the rising
Flood was almost at your throat –
A speedy, shapely, un-capsizing
Twentieth-century language-boat;
But still the future's uncreated
And writers with an elevated
Sense of buoyancy tend to drown

In deaths as airless as your own.
Brave actor, forced to play the gallant
When, in that proud, possessive place,
Adultery giggled in your face,
You died, having bemoaned your talent,
In shallow rivers of your blood –
Though you survive the greater flood.

The Duchess and the Assassin

The Grand Duchess Yelizaveta
Worried about the troops in Manchuria
While Sergei went on crushing the Revolution
In his silk-lined German carriage.

That afternoon of the palace sewing-bee
She was thinking about men's shirts,
Not of the bodies that might break in them,
Proving her perfect seams incontinent.

She watched the lazy bouncing
Of vulturish wrists, and knew it was for the best
That her mind should simply float...
She had drawn out the needle again –

The cotton had the strong pull of sunlight –
When the day went up like the Tsar's fleet at Tsushima.
She flung down the shirt and ran
Straight for the flushed smoke-cloud: silk and skin.

She picked up what she recognised
As the Governor-General, thinking: 'not my husband.'
Her apron sagged with the enormity...
The blood on her thighs screamed like birth-blood.

Clothes, after that, were water; even flesh
Showed her its inmost threading.
She sat, untouchable, by the opened curtains,
Burning her eyes on a lifetime of unpicking.

At last she came to the prison,
To the windowless cell, the stink of certainty.
She wanted to know why.
Even terrorists had their reasons.

He was nervous, and tried to sneer.
She felt her power. She wanted to lift her finger
To singe the skin of his cheek.
You don't understand. Forgiveness

Is the last thing I need, he said.
So you'll hang, Iván, she said.
His smile cleared: but the cause will outlive us both!
And she thought of the ripped halves

Of a shirt, stitched together
In stringy blood – two deaths,
Seamless, that Russia would wear
When it came to bury her.

How the Tsar Tried to Restore Law and Order in Revolutionary Petrograd

A General Remembers

Martial Law Declared
By Order of the Council.
It was Golitsyn's last stand
In feathering pencil.

I rushed to the City Print-works,
Thrust a dumb cadet's
Nose at the signature:
He ran off fifty sheets.

Glue? I'd stopped a Gendarme.
Not for any honey-cakes!
There hadn't been a dribble
In Petrograd for weeks!

No glue, no soap, no strings
For fiddles. *Them Red Guards*
Must have been liberating
The knackers' yards.

After I'd rinsed his words
In a depthless glass, I hit
The streets, and met my Conscience
Again, looking like shit.

233

Paste, it muttered, *Flour*
And water. Flour? I said:
People are starving here.
My Conscience sank, half-dead.

Midnight. Sleet. Mud.
A smouldering police-station
Lit Sadovaya weirdly.
I was viewing my situation

As both historical
And unfortunate, when
The glinting tines of a railing –
Like a streetgirl's grin –

Leered at me from the gloom.
I was enticed, undone.
I spiked the Proclamations –
All fifty, one by one.

I strolled back to HQ
Thinking – What a devil
You are, Comrade Khabalov –
A secret rebel –

And how those paper wings
Would battle till they tore
Free and rode the wind!
So much for Martial Law –

Trampled and drowned in mud
And sweat and blood and sleet.
Like February, I'd washed
My dirty hands of it.

Conversation Piece
(loosely based on a sketch from
Fragments of My Diary by Maxim Gorki)

Petrograd, 1918.
They stroll in the Summer Garden
Discussing whether the masses
Deserve an education –

One believer, one doubter
From the poles of the social classes,
Bound by the fond condescension
That writer reserves for writer.

They sit down under a tree;
The masses are swarming about –
Soldiers and shop-girls and sailors
Where the Romanovs walked on glass.

Only the gardener's unchanged,
Impassively slaying the grass
In the haemophiliac rosebeds
While the little Tsarevich stares,

Turning paler, paler, paler.
Gorki gets out his pipe.
Blok crushes a lozenge of sunlight
With an apocalyptic boot

And denounces, as is his habit,
The Intelligentsia's rôle.
Gorki the guttersnipe
Instantly loses his cool:

'The Intelligentsia drives
The engine of Progress. Your
Aristocratic contempt
Deserves a sock in the jaw!'

His cheeks shine tubercular red.
Blok looks at him strangely. The leaves
Of the ash tree scrape in his head
With a sound of puppet-strings, knives.

The smile of a passing laundress
Somehow changes the mood.
'Do you think there's a hope, old chap,
Of eternal life?' Blok mutters.

Cries Gorki: 'Of course it's eternal.
It's bloody miraculous
But everything's being recycled
Including the human race!'

'Listen. One late summer evening
Ten million evenings from this,
A shabby old pair of hacks,
Who should have something better to do,

Will be puffing out smoke and hot air
And explaining the Universe
As they sit on a bench and gaze
At a washer-girl's twinkling hips.'

Blok wrinkles his nose. 'You mean us?'
'Who else?' chortles Maxim, 'Who?'
Blok turns pale, he jumps up
In a fury of terror. 'You

Westernised heathen!' he shrieks.
'Thinking's the curse of the Slavs
And so I curse you and your granny!'
(Blok never does things by halves.)

Gorki sits calmly on,
Feeling sad for his fellow writer.
The young moon rises and glows
White as a peeled onion

And the stars shine brighter and brighter.
'Revolution! Eternity!
Mankind!' whispers Gorki. The gardener
Goes home for a glass of tea.

Death of an Elder Brother

Stern-eyed Sasha, midnight reader,
Student of the worm,
Connoisseur of annelida,
How could he do harm?

Sasha spared his soily wrigglers,
Shunned the hook and knife.
But, said Sasha, Tsars are different
Lower forms of life.

There's a cause I'd gladly die for
Yes, and kill for too.
It's not natural, it's not moral
But what else to do?

Stern-eyed Sasha walks in leg-irons,
Clanking down the bight.
Ladoga laps, a workman taps
Out in the yard all night.

Sasha, Sasha, best Ulyanov,
Sobbed his brother, why
If you tried to save the people
Did you have to die?

In the young May dawn a broken
Life droops from a beam;
But the hempen rope binds stoutly
Dream to brother's dream.

Stern-eyed Sasha, midnight reader,
Student of the worm,
Connoisseur of annelida –
How could he do harm?

A Moscow Wife, Waiting

Husbands wait sometimes, too:
But when I think of waiting,
I think only of you,

As if you were the true
Symbol of all waiting
And all who wait are you,

Larissa. And I see
The blackish lumps of snow
Surging to your dark porchway,

The flats in rows, the stairs
In hundreds, and I climb
Praying you'll be there,

Praying you won't be there.
I hear the clattered chains –
It's like a prison-door.

You peep an inch. I'm scared
I've scared you – and just scared.
But then – I've stepped inside.

You sit and listen, pale
Distracted. You look ill.
The message falters. No,

It isn't much. I can't
Say much. And there's a word
Which you repeat and which

Baffles me. That it means
The most important thing
For you is all I know.

'I'm sorry.' I bring out
My pocket dictionary.
The word is *amnesty.*

You said 'I think there's hope.'
You didn't smile. I said
'I'm glad.' The words seemed small.

I took your hand, I went
Into the sleety cold.
And now I learn that hope

Was simply one more way
Of torturing you: they've sent
Your husband back to camp.

And yes, he's waiting, too;
But when I think of waiting
Somehow I think of you

As if you were the true
Symbol of all waiting,
And all who wait are you.

The Fire-fighter's Widow
on her First Memorial Day Outing

We ride in the hired coach
North through April grey.
Spinneys of frail birch
Stagger up through the snow
Still rucked along the highway
As it rolls towards endless Moscow –
Nothing much else. We try
To lose ourselves in the view;
Pressed to our own faces,
We watch them travel with us,
Sickly, shut-out, like ghosts.
It was twelve months ago
That day our air was lit
Hugely and blown apart,
And still some people say –
Though they're not supposed to know –
Death hasn't gone away.

We're far, far north of green.
I'm glad to be so far,
Though they say the crops are clear
And plentiful this year,
I don't want to go near
Whatever our lives were then,
Between the rushing Pripyat
And the lake which never froze.
How warm and clean it was,
That water as it lapped
The broad towers of the plant –
Water that swept and cooled
The sun-packed rods, and kept
A little of their gold.
We fished (the fish were fat,
Sun-lazy), swam and dreamed.
Uranium was our friend
Until we forgot to fear it.
That was the night it turned.
The lake shrank in its heat;
Above the towers the air
Poured in savage plumes
As if the sun had been thrown
Earthwards. *His* grave is there.

He was a hero. We,
Therefore, are hero wives,
Trudging through burnt-out lives
And finding less and less,
However patiently
We stir the ash.
Pensioned, re-housed, redressed
By this Memorial Day
We wipe our eyes to say
None of it means a thing.
Surely our country's smashed
More heroes than it's worth?
I hate its giant hand
Which gathers men like clay
And moulds them into masses
To build red victories with.
They should have counted ten
Before they dashed away
And rose above the furnace,
Thinking they had to fling
Their lives down with the sand
In order to be men.

A Western scientist, one
Of those who built the Bomb,
In later life admitted
'I didn't think. I did
Experiments.' He's dust,
Now, in a Christian tomb,
And small as his regrets,
But if there was a God
Perhaps he'd be hauled back
Somehow across the years,
And made to ride with us.
He'd see what hope still is:
Our children, picnics, tears,
Our cheap new dresses, black:
He'd see the white graves
That now gleam into view,
Cleaner than any snow –
And leave the rest undone.

No other cemetery
Is quite as new as this –
The unplanted burial-ground
Of a spaced-out century.
There's no eternal flame
(As if they thought a glimpse
Of flame could drive us mad),
Only carnations, red
And dark as the burrowing
Roots of the meltdown.
Uniforms guide us through
Our public sorrowing.
Speeches drip their vowels
Through the muddy afternoon
Like ruined icicles.
We are praised, and shepherded.

Under us lie the dead
Heroes we used to know.
We watched them as they changed
Inside their unmarked skin –
Their useless, shivering courage,
Their shame as they vomited.
In a tangle of thick vines
All the good essences –
Saline, bone-marrow, blood –
Streamed down to rescue them
But sank in the rotting web

Of burning they'd become.
We touched them through our gloves,
Felt nothing. When they died
We were relieved. And then
Relief seemed out of date –
Like happiness, an echo
From life-times ago
When death was still a child,
Before it learned to breed.

We are the heroes' wives.
We are decaying too.
Some kneel beside the graves
Forgetting what they know –
That the world is a carelessness,
A chance in a universe.
Some weep. I'm not like these.
I simply walk away
And walk away, and then
The circle seems to close,
I'm back where I began,
Looking down in dismay
At the grass, the flowers, my shoes.

Leningrad Romance

1 *A Window Cut by Jealousy*

Not far from the estuary's grey window
They lit cigarettes and talked. Water kept meeting stone,
Lips kept sticking to paper, time kept burning.
The lilacs were burning down to the colour of stone.
She said, I was born here, I've lived here always.
Stone kept moving in water, time kept burning,
Smoke became palaces, palaces faded and faded.
My home's in Moscow, he said, my wife and children...
Perhaps they are just the white ash-fall of night,
Perhaps they are stone. Stone kept looking at shadows,
Shadows died in the white ash-fall of night.
Water kept playing with windows, time kept burning,
Fingers played with the burning dust of the lilacs,
The palaces faded and faded. I've lived here always,

She said, I've friends in Moscow. Thoughts became palaces,
Time went out, hands became estuaries,
The estuary was the colour of dying lilac.
They talked and lit cigarettes. Shadows flowed over the table.
They fingered them, but they didn't notice mine,
Not far from the estuary's grey window.

2 *Safe Period*

He will unlock the four-hooked gate of her bra,
Not noticing a kremlin of patched cotton,
With darkening scorch-marks where her arms press kisses.
She will pull back her arms, disturbing drifts
Of shallow, babyish hair, and let him drink,
Breathless, the heavy spirit smell, retreating
At length with a shy glance to grasp the chair-back,
And, slightly stooped, tug out the darker bandage.
Her cupped palm will glow as she carries it
Quickly to the sink, like something burning.
He sees the bright beard on each inner thigh,
Carnations curling, ribboning in the bowl.
Her hands make soapy love. The laundered rag
Weeps swift pink tears from the washing-string.
He's stiffened with a shocked assent. She breathes
Against him, damp as a glass. A glass of red vodka.

Finding the Sun

On Vasilievsky Island, brown and rumpled
With tramlines, stone in all its dreamed canals,
And plots still whispering through its plywood walls
I thought of the sun which Mandelstam had buried
In Petersburg, in the *velvet Soviet night*
And knew it lived, under the people's feet.

Wherever they trod, damp walkway planks or cobbles,
The crowds in their furry earflaps were trampling a thaw.
Rocks of soiled water loosened themselves
From the lips of drainpipes; soon, they'd dash for the river.
Spring's muddy pools would flower and the people know
That the time was ripe for exposing fragile earlobes.

In the meantime they went about hugged to themselves.
I thought of boats, their iron skirts swarming down
To the harbour-bed, lodging an iceberg's depth
Against a rusting anchor's mud-sunk sickle.
Dogged, they dreamed in queues, or butted the wind
Over bridges and through the arcades of Gostiny Dvor.

Darkness softly wrapped the great, flowing rush-hour
And still they were dawning and homing, those platoons,
Surging on their inscrutable manoeuvres.
They poured up from the burial pit of the metro
Like pyramid-builders, yoked by necessity.
Yet I saw how some had a secret happiness:

The militiaman in his heavy, mossy coat
Held a box of Napoleon pastry by its string
Daintily as a child's hand; a grey-faced woman
Lulled with her breath an armful of red carnations.
And in all the palaces rackety lifts crept up
Into night and the gleam of doors, bright-medalled with locks.

I sniffed a dialect, then, of *savoury pies,*
Pancakes, the evening samovar, soft sighs
And warm shawls and a hot stove to sleep on:
And the speeches lengthened, irremediable
In the lonely, jarring light of television –
But everyone wedged a chair in at the table.

Measured vistas, the seamless welding of Rome
And Byzantium in gold as thin as skimmed milk,
Cannot contain the skyline of their hope.
It sinks and flickers, looking for depth, for stone,
And this is the point it rests at. Vasilievsky –
Where the poets will meet again and find the sun.

A Blockade Memorial

There were platoons of tents: not one was closed.
Inside, in each wound's dark, we knew there'd be
Pale puzzles like ourselves: a flawed yorick

At last conversant with his mess of props.
But when we dared to peep, the ossuary
Held simply straw, the light dormition of roses.

*

Since graves were everywhere, we couldn't see them.
The walkways bore them off to a last farewell –
A frayed red hand, waving up from the ground.

We trod on oak-leaves, stars – the splashed confetti
Of giant brides. The verb 'to die' is vast –
A city. But 'to die for the motherland'

Has no visible end, works in all tenses,
State-like, and makes them present: there are always
Live feet going over and over the dead.

*

An east wind, solid with processional ghosts
Carrying brands that first lit glowingly,
Then blanched, the faces of the crowd, swept through us

And drove us to the gates, the sheltering temples.
They frowned in pity, gathering the shades
Into their smaller, denser, human forms.

*

Here stood a country looking for itself.
First, it would find a baby's fist of bread –
The daily ration for 900 days –

And then, a diary. If the power-lines ceased
Their faintest song, and tyre-tracks, slithering,
Curved, for whatever reason, into silence,

If dry tongues ached against walls and shoe-leather –
How could a diary speak?
Somewhere there are girls who still know how.

*

She was called Tanya. Round her once had lived
Her family. True to girlhood courtesy,
She dipped her pen, listlessly, carefully;

As each one died, redeemed their gravelessness,
Making a loss-shape from the name and date
Until she had exhausted all her time

And reached her final name,
A child brought up to wait politely, take
The last turn in the complex grown-up game:

Everyone's died. Only Tanya's left.

*

Past the necropolis the earth lay snow-stilled
And empty, free to grieve in her own way –
Northerly, reticent. A concealed flood.

In moments we were tearless and absurd.
High-kicking, floundering through the half-whisked whites,
To storm the silver woods, our boot-tops foaming.

*

We found a pool. Dark water shivered thinly.
The adolescent birch trees seemed to step
Suddenly back, not liking to admit

How passionately they'd dwelt on their reflections.
Such slippages and slynesses and rumours!
We heard them, then: the ice-locks liquidly

Yielding, the wind more westerly
With each gust. But the lost weight of the starving
Still drifted from the camps: who'd cup its grains?

Distant, triumphal chords kept touching us
Like old soldiers vaguely fingering
Their medals, asking why there's so much dust

On swept and watered stones. And spring, too young
To hear them, stoops to the tents with a light breath:
She wakes the roses, snips the bandages.

Green Windows

Antarctica. Great plasterwork of gales.
The beach tumbled and whorled dull shades of white.
The surf a distant, quartzy heap of shale.

One step would crush the illusion. Underfoot
The relieved snow sank and fainted gushily.
More windows, glassy green, were breaking out

Each moment to the right and left of me –
For this was marsh, or would be, soon, a rippling
Of languid mosses mirroring the sea.

I became strangely homesick for the coupling.
I longed to breathe its salts across the warm
Midsummer midnight's pale, circadian riddle.

Instead, I would be guided dully home
By the same trail that brought me here, and plod
My own deep, swampy prints – the paradigm

Of the tourist trapped in ever-widening odds
Against a revelation. In that slow
Defeat, I paused and stared. A rain of buds

I'd missed before shone round me: pussy willow –
In any sky or language, Proserpina,
Eyes starred with sleep, and mellowing as a rainbow.

And now her promise soothed a hemisphere,
Carefree of borders, seeping, roaming, greening:
A wash of flowers left at an English door.

A Memo About the Green Oranges

They sat like a disarmament proposal
On our table in the hotel dining-room,
Looking less and less negotiable.
Even the vegetarians flinched from them.

The Talks beside the lake weren't going well.
Neither was the turnover in these
Miniature ballistic atrocities –
Which now began to occur at every meal.

Oranges Are Orange. Grass Is Green –
Like policemen's greatcoats. Never Trust A Red.
(It's better to be dead than dyed that shade.)
You Can't Tell A *Sosiska* By Its Skin...

But what about an orange? Feeling less
Hopeful than thirsty on Sadóvaya Street
One day, I bought a mossy half-a-kilo.

The Geneva Talks stand just as still, or stiller,
And this is simply a memo, a PS,
To say those green-skinned oranges are sweet.

'Night: a street...'
(Aleksandr Blok)

Night: a street, a lamp, a chemist's;
Dreary, thought-erasing light.
Live another quarter-century –
Nothing's different. No way out.

Everything begins again,
Bearing the same old rubber-stamp:
Night: the freezing-cold canal,
The chemist's shop, the street, the lamp.

The Admiralty
(Osip Mandelstam)

In the Northern capital moulders a dusty poplar,
Its leaves entangling a clock's translucency,
And through the green darkness a frigate, an akropol,
Brother to water and sky, shines distantly.

An aerial boat with a mast like a touch-me-not flower,
A slide rule for Peter's children, it declares
That Beauty's no whim from a demi-god's leisure-hour,
But a homespun carpenter's predatory stares.

We honour the five reigning elements of creation:
Now a fifth, thanks to human freedom, has found its place –
An ark of such design it asserts the negation
Of the tyranny of three-dimensional space.

Bad-tempered medusas jostle, exchanging their poison;
The abandoned ploughs of the anchors are tumbling to rust.
But look how the three dimensions burst from their prison
And the seas of the world lie open to us at last!

No, not the moon
(Osip Mandelstam)

No, not the moon, a clock; its homely face
Pouring down brightness. Am I in disgrace
For saying the stars are weak and watery?

Now Bátushkov – his was the real crime.
When people mildly asked him: 'What's the time?'
The crushing answer boomed: 'Infinity!'

Kolya's Poem

I'm lucky. Russian-born, I think in Russian.
I eat my soup with bread instead of meat –
The Russian way. I dream and drink in Russian,
I even know the 'mother' oaths by heart,

Although I can't recall my actual mother.
I'm lucky. I've no friends. I feel no sadness
For anything on earth. I'm no one's lover.
I never fret about my circumstances.

If life is just, why should I start complaining?
What should I plead for if our needs are met?
Why should I sit behind the window, pining?
My day will come, the last and brightest yet.

Yes, it will come, that final, shining day
But, in the meantime, knuckle down, square up
And do the job. I'm lucky, certainly.
I wish my enemies this kind of luck.

Persephone in Armenia

The snow was a blue lake in Pushkin Square,
A twist of streams down Tsar Alexander Boulevard.
Buds split against the greenish
Luminous sky, rare as Cuban dates.
It was warm, it was burning, it was spring!
The girl moved swiftly with her blood-fall.
She tore off her coat,
Laced on her chilly sandals.
We didn't have time to stop her.
She was racing up the hill
Where snowstorms were massing again,
Her bare legs white with winter,
Plaits sparkling like iced wheat.

FROM

FROM BERLIN TO HEAVEN

(1989)

From Berlin to Heaven

1 *Long Weekend*

Wasn't it called the 'Arosa' –
With a whiff of the kitsch South,
A touch of the cuckoo-clock –
Somewhere in the design?
The shutters, painted black,
Though not for some time,
Stood prettily ajar.
Geraniums bubbled over
The flaking sills –
But why was the terrace bar
Permanently closed?
Night after night the chairs
Leaned their hot foreheads
Against the tables.
Songs and laughter rippled
From the other hotels.
Why such silence, afloat
In the city without bedtimes?

We had a last resort –
An inexhaustible
Fridge that shuddered
At its own miracle.
Rows of sleepy bottles
Pointed like little guns –
Whenever we opened it
They wanted us.
You gave yourself up to a beer.

Mine was something darker,
Oily as plumskins.
I thought of Anna Karenina,
Displaced for love,
And that love died
For want of place,
Whatever was done behind
A gilded room-number
With the passion of grand opera.
Could anything happen next?
The sun was going down
So we let it in,
Small, shy and naked,

And watched the afternoon
Turn pale with marriage.

We ride into our sunset,
Anonymous as exhaust,
Or a chainstore nightie,
Its wishful furbelows
Crushed, forgotten
Under the feather pillow
That won't be mine again.
But the postcards fly
In hot pursuit of us –
The borscht, so red
It ought not to be eaten;
A waiter who speaks Russian
Macedonian-style;
His following eyes,
Jealous as mine will be
When, drunk, you call him
Your brother Slav;
The flatly urban
Subjects you photograph
For sending home:
A used-car sale,
A hedge of scaffolding,
An entrance to the U-Bahn.
So what was there to see
At the border zone?
The defeated foliage?
The unimpressive watch-tower
Anyone could climb?
I lean from the platform
Trying to discover
From a gutted tenement
How you used to live
While you read a guidebook
In one of the mobile toilets
And occasionally groan.

Here I should modulate
To a distant key,
Surprise the hidden, grey
Sweetness of Unter den Linden
Satirise the two
Basilisks that stamp
Around the Gate.
There is a tour, of course,

But no earthly train
Driving into the iron
Teeth of that river
With the practised whoop
Of a border cavalier,
Could tear from it a promise
To give you back,
And I'm afraid
Some treacherous loneliness
Would wake in each of us
Were I to claim my privilege
And leave without you.

I take your hand instead
And in the spoiling air
Of mythic decay
Still breathed as liberty,
Still bought with blood,
We enter ritual
Like honeymooners
Swaying east
To watch the dawn break
Over Torremolinos.

It might indeed have been
Simply a wall –
Some usual, useless,
Surly, inner-city
Lump of municipal shit
The young had tried to claim.
I studied the slogans,
The painted names.
Now all I remember
Is 'We have smoked here',
The crimson Cyrillic
Rising clear out of all
That artful, artless writing
On our side of it.

2 *Munich*

Utopia – nowhere
I ever knew
Until that morning.
We had left the sleeper
Blackly streaming

South like an *anschluss*,
A riderless nightmare.
I was still wishing
Vienna, Vienna,
As her breath touched me.
She was pure city
And her brightening forth
In the moment between
Waking and blinking
The heavy gold-dust
Out of my surmise
Was familiar as only
A constant hope is.
We called her 'München',
Tender with surprise.

A sixties child
In a fire-touched brocade,
She curtseyed across
The Marian sky.
If she had willed
Her forgetfulness,
We couldn't blame her.
We too were wide-eyed,
We too, faintly poisoned.
As the day withdrew,
She possessed us differently.
Her shadow found you
And the catch in her voice
Was the buried grace-note
Of the Slav.

She turned and turned
Her Russian face
And I heard her whisper –
Extinguishing, enchanting –
Of divorce and marriage
It is divorce
Cuts the deeper heartline:
There can be no future
That is not his past.

Bound to this course,
One night we sat
In futurist Odeonplatz.
Islanded, water-dazzled
Lorelei,

We softly murdered
A song of the people.
Our thin strophes
Were the circles where
A mail-coach butterflied
With its snow-faced driver.
As the storm encrystalled
His upturned room
And kneeling horses
To the arched, brilliant silence
Of a polar tomb,
He dreamed a letter home
And his blood-sugar, sinking
Slowly to zero,
Saw him through
To the death-drowsy, solemn,
Last 'I kiss you'.

Perhaps the blur, stinging
Our eyes, was him.
Beyond us, too,
Lay distances,
Blanked by longing,
And, beyond these,
Expectantly
Fading towards us,
The radiance of footprints
We had each called 'family',
And betrayed.
And then I thought
Of a place too small
Even to spell,
A broken star
Where the map creased.
It blazed in the glare
Of an island's crime
Against her continent.
But we went on singing
Until history fell
In easy shadows
At the city's feet
And *peace in our time,*
Our breath said, peace
In our time.

3 *Democracy at the Burgerbraukeller, 1926, 1984*

We just walked in
And found the moment where
Enormous amber waves
Run beautifully over
The map of soiled empties
And history's remade.
Apprentice Hitler
Jumps on a table,
Trenchcoat-belt frisking
Like a clawed, clumsy tail.
He shoots the ceiling –
A Michelangelo
From the heavy suburbs
Where art is caricature.
Stage dandruff sifts
Onto uniforms, suits.
The patrons still don't know
Whether salvation dances
In such smeared boots.
They study surfaces
Especially those that wink
And brim their glasses –
Worth ninety Marks a sip.
When the order comes
To carry on drinking,
Up go a thousand suns.
The chairs scratch and clap
The floorboards' backs,
And full throats roar
How they will always be
For hops and barley
Whoever's yelling 'Time'
At the pantheon
From below an aproned lip.
He shrinks a little now.
He's almost Chaplinesque
But not incredible
(And not quite charmless) –
His glance could quickly pierce
Us where we sit.

There was a youth curled up
On the balcony below ours
One morning.
A scarlet thread
Ran from the resting side
Of the light-haired skull
To the small, exactly-placed
(As it would prove to be) drain.
Neighbours slid from their doors
And took to the public landings,
Darting their eyes to show how
A contretemps had occurred
In the early hours.
The widow had since disappeared
On brassy stilettos
And a puff of Eau de Cologne.

Some dangerous precedent
Had been let loose,
We all knew it,
And, as the morning brightened,
I knew it wanted me.

I waited for it to phone.
Already I could hear
The urgent clicking, through
The wall of atmosphere,
The banked-up heat.
No bell shrilled. But I saw
Its breath condense
In blackmailer's dew
On the grid of the earpiece.

After scrubbing everything
I set off for Holland,
Pedalled flat out
By the unswerving river
That could swallow me and not tell.
I ran into a gatepost,
Thinking about death,
And in my nostrils travelled
The iron smell of blood,
However many bridges
Opened their wings to me,
Flew close, flew past.

I'd known false love could kill –
Could true love, too?
Confused now, I turn
Through the lilac rush-hour.
I think I know what I am.
It is unavoidable.
I shall wait for my victim
Outside where the ghost-shirts
Waft pheromones not his,
And are his enemies,
My weapon six tired words:
I can't go back to you.

But as I plunge it home
The wrong heart will be there
And I will be alone.
I shall sit out the night,
Tense as a filled glass,
Noticing distantly
That someone or other's tears
Have again lacquered the stars
In the narrow reclamation
Of muscatel city-sky
Where tortured balconies
Try to step upwards, fly.

5 *David*

His home was in Tel Aviv
But he didn't mind Berlin.
Some leisurely Department
Of Guilt, perhaps, or Cleansing,
Had lately appointed him
Writer in Residence.
He wasn't writing.
He showed us, instead,
The new watercolours,
Rainy, soft, Northern.
His poems had translated
To something brighter-lit.

Though we never quite said
The words he wished to hear
He treated us for dinner
At the *Grosse Mauer*.

Service was ponderous
As a Brahms adagio
Carved with a chopstick
In Chinese granite.
We sat like our starched napkins –
You, depressed and shy
Because you thought us closer
Than was the case –
We, platitudinous
In the scoured EFL
We felt we had to use,
Both far too courteous
To meet. To live.
He wrote in Hebrew, dreamed
(He said) in Yiddish,
Got by in German,
Remembered Polish,
But now he was worn out
And best at silence.
He feared the path of words
In any forest.
Too many branches threw
Deranging darkness there.

The other day I found
An early book of his,
Opened it at this:
When they call my name
With a Slav accent
It's as if my mother were calling me
To the Sabbath meal.
And I stood still,
Dismayed that we had missed
Something so simple,
Needing only your voice
At its most artless
To tender and release
The familiar shadow,
Spread it at his feet,
Pale with the bloom of snow.
First he would pause and then
See the window change,
The moving, dark mass,
Sheened by candle-light,
Turning into a face –
Young, unmarked, long-dead
That laughed, that let him in.

6 *Jerusalem*

From our window on the third floor
We look down through glass
Into the wakeful restaurant,
Its roof thinly strewn
With rushes, soldier dolls
Pressing their olive knees
Together under the tables,
The tables streaming outwards,
Meeting the competition,
Dissolving in it.
So God diversifies
Into many fields
And some are bloodless.
He can be worshipped here
By sitting stunned and bright
As a shekel in the glare
Of the rival videos.
Their howling close-ups swim
The blue desert night,
Box-office Ayatollahs
Irresistible as sex
And disappointment.

But they are not our drama.
I move from the window
To see how far you've travelled,
To touch the thread
That drew you tense and sinking
Into the clotted weave
Of snow, birch-forest, blood,
And, severed, drifts you back
To your first estranging.
We've slouched, letting our fingers
Creep in each other's pockets
On the Via Dolorosa,
And drunk pure alcohol,
Obtainable all over Zion
From any mirage.
Perhaps that's why you seem
So far from me, so small.
Above the double bed
The air shakes violently,
Becoming water.
As the fan turns its face
First to one, then to the other,

I ask for the last time
The impure but essential question
'Who did you love the most?'
And this is Jerusalem
And so you have to answer
And so the word is made flesh
That will stare at us all summer.

7 *Masada*

There was one god
Too huge to bury.
We crawl in his frown.
Its lumps and pleats
Ache against
A small, cruel sun.
If sacrifice
Is necessity
And we honour those
Whose blood was teased out
Like a tress of crimson
River from rock,
Should we admire
A truck or plane
That assumes the form
Of a burning bush?

Our cable-car
Shivers, sinks.
Better to say
We're in god's hands
Though his fingers are nothing
But wings and prayers.
We're looking down
On an aftermath:
The sleepy lips
Of the dunes parting
Over steel thumbs:
Transfiguration's
Eye-blink, then
An ash of visions
Where the sky touched Gehenna,
Where we were human
For the last time.

The earth is sweet
But a tar path
Sends us in scalded
Leaps to the sea
And that grainy chair
Is comfortless
As Jordan's arm
Round Israel's shoulder.
Seraphim walk,
Piercing, careless,
All over us.
We hang and hear
The tablets gasp
As a flung bottle
Bursts with commandments:
To be soul
To be salt
To be sky
To be skin –
To be stripped of it.

8 *Religion*

Most days you strolled
The piazzas in shorts,
Baring your knees
Like rosy scarabs
To ward off the Church.
I'd look for the door.
You'd sun yourself
Of find a bar.
I began to get curt,
Felt it a crucial
Impediment,
When carefully you missed
The Maria Assunta.

She rose in her dimmed lamé
Above Torcello
As if she tiptoed
With a mute but piercing cry,
Uncivic, eternal,
On the ashen rim
That was once the world.
You'd have known by what blades
She had been cut

From the craftsmen's hearts
(*And after this our exile*) –
How the tears became dryness,
How the mind shone,
And how the child's weight
Can never be put down.

As for the pantheon
Of the swarming mainland –
Perhaps you were right:
Faith had clutched so warmly
The inscriptive hand,
It died before it knew
And rose as cliché.
I too asked where
The Inquisitor stood
In all this
And saw the air
In canvassed chancels
Dull with used blood.

We sought asylum then
In decomposition.
Refused all icons,
Lapsed. A charred pizza
Smelt somehow of kindness.
Religion was simply
Corn-coloured masses
Of hand-cemented stone,
Flaking into shifty
Waterlights, sunlights
And dust that unremembered
Women swept
And men trod home.

9 *The Stars, or a Tree on Rhodes*

Perhaps we like the myths
Because they rarely claim
To be authentic:
They are simply rooms
To play *perhaps* in. Take
The myth of Helen and Paris.
There are three possibilities.
One, she was seduced.
Two, she seduced him.

264

Three, only her form
Ran off with him anyway,
Leaving her soul at home
To embarrass Menelaus
Who had no idea what to do
In bed with a woman's soul.
Of these three Helens, two
Are caked in a fine dust
Of masculine prejudice.
Seduced, divided Helen
Is Anywoman, lost.
The bright, grape-bunch curls,
Slant eyes, brown waist,
Fade into wispy shorthand
As a jar full of sorrows,
Hunching its shoulders, stares
Deep down into itself,
Into the pores of tradition.
The Helen that remains
Is less negotiable.
She perfumed her wrists
But didn't forget to squeeze
The poisoned tamp against
Her swimming cervix.
Diving between the teeth
Of her beautiful stranger,
She mothered a war
And launched herself.
As Sappho reminded us,
She forgot about everyone,
That most believable Helen –
Even her own children.
So what shall we do with her
Now the jar's alive,
The fire bursting out of the clay
And sprouting into tears?
She's ripe for one last legend –
To be hung with the Dioscuri
Among the brightest stars,
Or hounded out of Sparta
And simply hanged –
According to which Helen,
Which moral, you prefer.

Guiltlessly loitering
On what may well be the site
Of a future excavation –
Easy to date
By the pale, immortal,
Wave-buckled bleach-bottle,
And the shadow that was us –
It's good to face south,
An ice-age drizzling
To bronze in the tumbler
With its ghost-kiss of a mouth
From the age of refrigeration.
A roof is vital for this –
One, perhaps, which hums
With beetle-work
And a young vine's distillation
In radiant leaves and topplings
Of cloudless, skin-tight bubbles.
It must be knitted well
With shady minuses
To cool a skull too thinly
Served for its own yolk.
Then, after the blandishments
Of the zinc-top table,
The Asian jig, jangled
On a microchip's pinhead,
And the last, clean rock-fall,
There must be sea.
Superlative exile
From star-nests more remote
Than Copernicus,
Teasing the absolute
We wish on her,
She dissembles mildly
As a picnic cloth, stained
By immortal feasting,
With deeps and wind-plains
Of every conceivable turquoise.
From such a posting,
Hallucinatory
Beyond the captioned glow
We first reclined in,
We can detect the sun
At his daily confidence trick,

The elegant, coasting
Style that suggests progress
But is closer to suspension –
Busy, myopic
As any firing mind.
In the tangible sphere
Long thought inferior,
Earth's patient wash-day,
Hand over hand beneath
The hilly froth,
Is visibly everything
We're boiling down to –
With diminishing hope.
Zephyrs and Vespas,
Winking on the tongue
Of wine-dark bitumen
Waspishly ape
That losable art of horizons.
They surge and drown
In Procrustean silences.
The corpses too,
Chalky or rosy, matt
Or gloss, are mere burlesque,
A miniature send-up
Of high catastrophe.
They lay themselves out,
Thieved pinches of ozone
Scenting the orifices
Where, as the heart stills,
Life, with any luck,
Will open again
Its friendly, crawling eyes
In diamond multiples.
Though light's their element,
These simpler retinas
Are hooded now
With the horrible, peeled blindness
Of statues, approached
Too closely in peopled rooms.
But imagine how
Richly millennial
The stone imagination!
Ours is no different.
Peep-holes compressed
To their shivering fringes,
It gorges on blackness

And dappled fire-squalls,
While a beq more radiation
Than flesh can bear
Frisks the astonished cells
Of a naked marble breast.

11 *Hypothesis*

In Heaven, it's said, we meet
Our relatives. And so,
Love being the thickest, brightest
Of all the body fluids,
I must look forward to
My three handshakes with his past.
Leaving him ungreeted,
We'll take a step closer
To hold each other at arm's-length,
Utter the names we fear.
We'll add the dates and places
Of each attachment, sworn
To keep beyond time and place.
There will be competition
At first, manoeuvres.
But slowly we'll learn
How innocent we are.
Heaven has to exist
If only for people like us –
Haunted, ambiguous,
A veiled colony,
A broken sisterhood.
It is our one chance
To read beyond his eyes
From the mixed grain of our hair,
From the tiny stars of our skin,
To our complicity.
We shall launder our differences
In the strong river of tears
Whose end is sunlight.
And I shall let him go
To each one as she was
In all her young desire
When I was less to him
Than London on the blue
Globe he revolved
With slow-burning fingers
Away from the known world.

Our Early Days in Graveldene

Houses eat money, even council houses.
Ours was officially a *maisonette*.
It was first in a block of twelve, its shiplap coat
Still neat and almost white. We were 49.
Not far from a box of a pub, The Bunker's Knob –

Named for some veteran's clopping wooden leg.
Each cul-de-sac spoke rustic legends: Foxwood,
Broombank, The Grove. I worked on the inside
Where everything could change. I glossed the stairs
Orange. Orange for hope and happy children.

I had two friends in Graveldene, both *Elaines*.
Big Elaine moaned about her hips and her husbands.
As we queued for the bus, she'd shift their weight with sighs.
I used to sit in the summer with Little Elaine,
Drinking Coke on her rust-streaked balcony.

She looked too young to have children, and too small.
I was scared sick when her toddler swung the kitten.
He's killing it, I cried. She wasn't bothered.
She smiled with her own kitten-face, creamy, cruel.
I thought of battered babies, I couldn't help it.

There was Stell the single mother, Rose the widow –
Women who worked and were always dashing out
For cod and chips. There was the Rasta, Cyril,
Who slashed his throat that time the bailiffs came.
When they came to us we hid behind the door.

They pushed through a folded paper, promising us
Distraint of Property. Oh boy, we simply
Had to laugh. One mattress, several prams,
A high-chair for the eldest, a rush-mat
Half-way to Shredded Wheat, and the transistor.

'All you need is love,' sang the druggy Liverpool voices.
We knew by then they weren't singing for us
And that love ate money, just as houses did.
The sixties were dying, starved for LSD
In the mines and factories, on estates like ours.

We split up in the end. We've done all right.
Sometimes we meet. The other day he said,
'I drove round Graveldene just for a look,
And the door of 49 was off its hinges.
I went inside. I saw your orange stairs.'

Wealth

One Christmas we'd have said 'Rovaniemi'
And bounced in lightly on an Arctic tail-wind
To see the sleigh parked on the airport roof.

I would have steadied you on your first skis
Between the clotted fields, and sent you sailing,
Inarguable brightness overhead,
The clean, etched groove ice-hard in front of you.

Surrey

The birds did not bring leaves
To cover us as we slept
Under the purchased trees;

They were clapping their wings in fear
And we woke to find
We'd abandoned our own children.

We'd walked for a long time.
It was car drivers' country
And arrival, long postponed.

So many green vistas
That hugged their fences –
But we tried to appreciate it:

The glamour of leaded lights,
Hedges shady as trust funds,
As full of rich substance.

A boy stared as he cycled
Languidly down his lane,
Master of every pebble.

We found a bridleway
Choppy with hoofprints,
An ungrazed field where

The sweet, high, piercing larksong
Was a burglar alarm
In someone's Mercedes

Parked beyond the stile.
It was a place of signs,
White-lettered threats,

And sometimes less than that –
A skein of wire, strung
Almost self-mockingly,

Biting the leafy dust
Between two rotted posts.
We crossed without noticing

Into the shade-dappled clearing
And knew we'd found just the place
For feasts and happy cries.

A Geometry Lesson for the Children of England

1 *The Triangle*

You wanted the cymbals.
    A fat boy got those.

You wanted the side-drum.
    The prefect got that.

You wanted the tambourine.
    A pretty girl got that.

You wanted the maracas.
    A black girl got those.

You wanted to be the conductor.
    You got the triangle.

It's very important to count
    When you've got the triangle.

If you make a mistake
    It sings 'mistake'

In a tiny voice, shameless,
    Above the rest.

The conductor jabs her stick.
    The band lurches on

To the big crescendo.
    Light winks from the silver tubes.

Your chance was trembling towards you
    Why did you forget to count?

2 *A Lesson on the Uses of the Instruments*

What is the protractor?
    A boat no a half of melon
    Says the silly child's pencil

What is the set-square?
    A ski-slope whoosh here I go
    Says the silly child's pencil

What is the compass?
    A roundabout just for me
    Says the silly child's pencil

And when you've finished playing
    Says the teacher, snatching the compass
    A bayonet

3 *The Circle*

You choose the dissenting circle –
The one that fits your head
Exactly, and most of your heart.

How comfy to sit in a circle
So nice, your hands ring-a-rosy
With other, like-minded hands.

You chant the high principles
And the quiet rage of your circle
As if they were 'Three Blind Mice'.

Do you know what to sing next?
Do you always know what to sing next
When you sit in the right circle?

4 *More Triangles*

The isosceles triangle
Is lofty and refined
Like our democracy

The scalene triangle
Goes its own sweet way
Like our democracy

The equilateral triangle
Is fair as fair can be
Like our democracy

The obtuse triangle
Seems to have fallen asleep

A Lawn for the English Family

I did not invent this garden
though I put the children in it.
I was not its ruler. I wanted
only pity and beauty to rule it.

Fat dahlias rule it now
and small, flushed fish, strategic
in their twisted pool,
aiming their confidences.

All will be sucked back
into the light one day
and you'll see the eternal law,
the dictatorship of green.

No whisper will shield the rose
in her fevered return to nature,
nor the infant pimpernel
who foresees the weather.

Like an official broadcast
the untaught mouths
of convolvulus spatter white
on tangling wires.

There is a room in the corner
that has crawled out here to die
and the apple tree hugs its only
apple, its shrivelled soul.

Can you see them at last
swimming the leaves? They are children
who were thrown on the world's mercies,
who were unendurable.

Neither the state nor the state school
nor the solitary jungle-gym
purchased by mail order
could teach them the finished trick

of emergence and escape.
At first, though, they climb quickly.
Their sandals squeak on metal
warm from their hands and the sun.

For a while they can sit in the sky,
laughing at money, its blades
on all sides, slicing and scouring
the shapes of pity and beauty.

Jarrow

Nothing is left to dig, little to make.
Night has engulfed both firelit hall and sparrow.
Wind and car-noise pour across the Slake.
Nothing is left to dig, little to make
A stream of rust where a great ship might grow.
And where a union-man was hung for show
Nothing is left to dig, little to make.
Night has engulfed both firelit hall and sparrow.

Docklands Scenes

Where dirty bonfires
Dream of becoming
Large, clean clouds
And memories are stopped
Like the two stripes of rust
At a vanished gate,
Security fences
Lightly topped
With Docklands Development
Logos, announce
There is life. No death.
Further inland,
Sold and For Sale boards
Clap the sky
Proclaiming how
The City flows
Sweet as the Thames
In a buyer's market.

Somewhere in Bow,
Two men are climbing
The broad steps
Of a newly Sandtexed
Freehold terrace.
With a thin glance back
At the weather-stained
UNDER OFFER sign,
They thump the door
And can hardly wait

To force the lock,
Brutish and slick
As their sucked-in cheeks
And serviceable shoulders.
Rooms dark with mortgage
Hushingly
Permit them to print
The unhoovered carpet.

They move on their toes
Backwards and forwards,
Handling easily
What they knew they'd find –
The gleaming boxes
That wink and purr,
Finger-friendly,
At the heart of success.
But, having soon
Exhausted these,
Each comes out cradling
A chair, the wicker
Sapped and split,
Blond pigtails curling
Stiffly from the seats.
They toss them in the van
And seem content –
Let the yuppie bastards
Sit on the floor.

The van shoves off
With the chairs inside
Weightlessly joshing
The micro trash.
Justice has been done –
By somebody's lights.
The sun is awarding
Stardom to all
The little skipping flags
Of the new marina,
Its idle water
Salmon-skin blue,
And the narrow, high,
Uncleanable windows
Where Ayesha and Soraya
Bend their heads
To the millrace of cotton,
The jiggering needles.

Above Cuckmere Haven

(for John Burningham)

This is a reachable coast:
The cliff, though it unscrolls
The modest curve of a buttress,
Is no young Atlas
And doesn't presume to try
Shouldering up the sky –

And the sky itself,
Translucent as a harebell,
Pales, but will not disclose
The point at which it wavers,
Becomes an immortelle
Of gases, stars.

The forsaken pillboxes
Doze in their rust,
No patriotic gull
Wooingly calls
The farm-boys to enlist;
Though the air seems prodigal

With ghostly fires again,
These are the grandchildren
Who never went to the Somme,
Dunkerque or Spain,
But packed the silos dumb
With missile-grain.

Visions, like meadow-blues,
Are dust in the hand,
Seed where the grass thins
To light, and where the cliff
Perishes, chalk and sand:
This is a coast of bones.

What remains is a view:
The cliff, upswept from the beach
And the drying threads of the mere,
Lifting whitely two
Crumbling wings, on which
Other wings briefly appear.

Sharing a View

(to Leonid Borodin)

Stooped in our borrowed
London window,
Look up a little.
Follow the rowan's
Forking paths
To find a thrush
Vermilion-breasted,
Lit like the berries
Whose sprays she twists
And shivers with her need.
Look still higher –
The aerial bracken
Silvers and fades
Till there's only blue,
Wind-washed, familiar.
Call it Siberia;
Pardon these streets
For keeping you.

The First Strokes

Letter to a friend learning English

Before he died, my father drowned in silence.
I thought of him just now, writing to you
In my head about the sea – that medicinal light
I longed to rush to your city of rooms and deadlines,
Your lost July – since it was he who taught me
To swim. In any sea he was stylish, fluent.
He knew its idioms, loved its argument.
So, when my four-year-old, his adventuring grandchild,
Slipped her hold on a wet rock, dropped speechless
Into the swell, he plunged and rescued her.
She used to tell us how huge fish came leering,
Making eyes at her as she bubbled down;
Now what she likes to remember are the hands
That drove apart the soupy green, and calmly
Scattered her suitors, saved her for the sun.

278

It was soon after this I led him to the pool:
I made him teach me. And, in half an hour,
I had left his side, was lazily at home
In the deepest water, thinking I'd always known how.
It was as simple as doing what he told me –
An obedience I could never risk as a child.
By the time he lost language, I had almost learned
To talk to him. He studied dictionaries
At first with an embarrassed grin, then frowning,
And the deep words we could have plumbed together
Ran white. I thought of all this, writing a blue
Letter about the sea, wanting to coax you
Into the tongue you almost know, but fear,
Having come so late to its stories; wanting to say
That the strokes of an English sentence are easy, requiring
Only a little self-trust as you kick off
From the margin and glide towards me, sensing all round you
The solid, patient, unbreakable arm of the water.

After an Emigration

To cut free of the past is not very hard.
You must do it quickly, fall
Absolutely into the offered hand or city.
The past is light, the past is obedient.
It spins from its severed moorings into nowhere.
Only gradually from nowhere it returns.

First it's a dream, at length, a door, open.
Ironical, you appraise
From every angle that city or that person
Not, after all, so bright, free, fascinating
That you were spared the poignant recognitions.
A face floats back. It's yours. You become yourself.

You exist daily on the one thought:
Not that the past was any better than this
But that this is no better than the past.

You try the present again: it isn't yours.

You buy the rounds and abolish past and present.

When the future smiles you edge away: *don't touch me.*

279

Late Travellers

Your antiquarian friend
Shows you a perfect city
On its death-bed of water.

October smoke has stolen
Into the dying hair
Of my lover.

He never touches me now.
The curves of my body do not move him.
There is no language for this.

It weighs on me simply, like exhaustion.

Bheir mé o

The night, that traditional
Short cut, where friendly
Differences meet,
Roving instinctively
In the foot-hallowed places,
The air familiar
And dense and fragrant
As they push it gently nearer
Each other's faces,
Is overgrown by sea
And strangeness now,

A permanent travelling tide
Of long black shadows,
Bright-edged and cold,
Where we, with cancelled senses,
Timidly wade,
Not knowing whose lamp, if any,
Stretches its fingers
In hope or in mimicry
Of hope, from the other side.

The March of the Lance-Bombardier and his Children

The road is stopped with corners; darkness moves
All round us like a forest of blue soldiers.
To walk much farther needs a sense of purpose
Beyond the iron love of feet for world.
There are no villages, not a single cottage.
No lights. Yet everybody takes this road.

The mountains have been blinded and let loose
To wander where they like among the planets.
The waterfalls are only storms of ashes,
The loch a vast slate from the tumbled sky.
No headlamps stare, no burning stubs of cat's-eyes –
And that's why every driver heads this way.

We turned back for the only certain shelter
(Or so we thought) – the one we'd started out from
In flares of sodium, gassy as champagne,
To plunge into the flute-pure black of pine trees,
Our torch blanching the rain: yes, we turned back,
While you, with ghostly footsteps – you kept walking.

Was it good, sometimes, to march in uniform
In clouds of human breath between the mountains?
Perhaps it almost felt like solitude
With Ursa Major's posed, angular brilliance
Above your head, more pin-up than Great Bear
And other ranks and stragglers, melting nowhere?

You passed us miles ago, we merely saw you
Vanish. Now you must have turned all corners,
Silenced all waterfalls, and reached at last
The garrison town, to wait for further orders.
Something will happen; something always happens.
You steel yourself for the pitching sea-road: France.

Or else you're only dreaming of it all.
Men can nod off, you said, while on the march.
Their eyes close while their feet, on auto-pilot,
Cleave to the old rhythm of the road.
I didn't ask you if they dreamed as well;
But now I'm sure dreams are inevitable.

You lay your kit out by the barracks window;
You brasso every button till it burns
And waters into stars and leafy sunlight.
You swim the green Ardennes; float back, still sleeping;
Begin to darn your heavy marching sock.
The needle stumbles brightly, pricks your finger.

Your eyes jump up, salute the road again.
All round you is black Scotland, men and pine trees
Marching as they breathe. Without agreement
Or argument, they haul the sullen load,
And each turned corner pays out a new length
Of dark. Yet everybody takes this road.

Memorial

I know why you liked marigolds –
They're not afraid of blue.
They drink the sky neat
And toss away the dazzle
Like dogs shaking off a swim.
If you look close you can see
How each slim heart of a petal
Was snipped to the same design.
Their stalks are a rougher breed,
Leaves a thick, oiled salad,
Breath loamy, spiced, not sweet.
I know why you preferred them
To grand blooms gardeners choose.
They flourish on poor soil
And harbour few diseases.
Even at night their closed
Grates keep in a small fire.
They come back year after year.
From the couple of plants you gave me
Sprang this prodigal family,
This garden of lost borders.
It's a place where thoughts of you
Are cut and gilded, sped
On a breeze. The flowers would gladly
Give you themselves if they could
Now, instead of rose trees
Marching in wintry line
Through a park without children.

Embarrassment

Our parents knew about fear.
What we know is shuffling and lies
And staring down at our feet.
What we know is embarrassment.
And it happens again and again
Whenever we dare to lift
Our glance across Western seas,
We simply can't find our tongues
At the sight of our tired young armies
Who do not know even that.

Reconstruction

The Dietrich Bonhoeffer Kirke
had no name to me then
in nineteen-fifty.
A tall, meat-coloured ruin,
it was perpendicular
but dead-eyed, haemorrhaging
bricks and secret rainbows
in the thickening leafage.
My father told me
it would stand like this forever
to teach the Germans.
As we climbed the wooden bridge
over the railway
I kept looking round
more and more dizzily,
garbling the fact
of cloud with retribution
till a whole fleet glowed there
like cherubim,
each pilot forced to gaze
down through the smoky nimbus
of his last mistake.
Was there truly a pact
between God and ourselves
to hold them eternally

in the sky above Dacres Road
even as they burned
ashen with their planes?
Modest in victory,
I felt their shame, and turned
instead to watch the trains.

White Lego

We have the word Lego
We have the patent the moulds
The plastic. Only the dyes
Are difficult to obtain
In this part of the world.

What we manufacture
Is therefore Building Snow
We truck it in quantities
To our markets cloud-high
Like the top of the volcano

It is on special offer
Because of the rare lack of colour.
It is quite warm to the touch
And unlikely to melt

When your child unwraps it
On Christmas morning say
Immediately Don't cry
You can make a chalkpit
An igloo an ambulance
A cubist polar bear

Your child breathes rapidly
As if to demand
What is white what is Christmas
And you show him just like this

You build and build
Until he smiles
And takes the blocks from you

Don't say What are you making
You know, you are his mother
He is making a garden

It is quite astonishing
Colours are pouring
From his busy hand
Wonderful rare colours
Colours even the rainbow daren't imagine

If when you say to him
One day Look at the rainbow
And he says What rainbow
All I can see is a white curtain
And if one day you pour him
A glass of Cola
And he says My milk tastes funny

He will only be joking

It is good to make jokes
It is good to mnake gardens
Building Snow makes it possible
For your child to do both

A Meeting of Innocents
A Birthday Sequence

1

On the bus up the hill
She profiles her best side
With its dangling half-moon.

She wouldn't feel unhip
In Carnaby Street: not really.
Her tights said 'Snow-Flake'.

The fishnet holds her nicely:
Small knees, sharp ankles.
Her jacket's PVC.

Getting off on the hill
She's early for the doctor's.
Nufortes is all there is.

Jukebox, burgers, banter,
Manoeuvres. School's out –
But no one even sees her.

That's the only fun
Of being eight months gone.
It shows. You don't.

She crams herself between
Chair-and-table, both
Fixed to the floor, rigid

As the laws of fashion are,
But it's OK, she's in,
Leaning on plastic elbows

To kiss the cappuccino,
Forget the doctor's, feel
How it was to be young

Only a minute ago.

2

The rubber flag tightened
And tightened its clammy grip.
Her heart jumped into her arm

And hammered to get out.
She could almost see her blood
Pulsing round faster than lights

On a neon signboard.
Then the soft, easing sag
And another winding up

With a breathless huff-huff-huff
Like the second climax she'd read
She ought to be capable of.

3

She felt good, she felt perfect
But the needle touched the sky.
It said she was four seas over

And still swallowing –
The child, her toxin.
We'll have to induce. She caught

The name: Pitocin.
They took her in, they sent
A girl nurse to shave her

Without a smile but with
A certain cold finesse.
They frowned at the kitten claw-marks

Pimpling her legs,
Gave her a wooden commode
'To spend a penny in'.

She unclasped the earrings slowly
And lay, inert as her tongue
Over the tasteless drug.

It was the usual thing
After all, being too happy,
Being undone.

4

This was how home slipped through unlucky footsteps,
As the solitary cart of belongings
Tilted into the future by itself;

How the sunrise sank in the eye
Of some huge ocean mammal,
Trussed up and drowned on its back

On blazing boards, its mouth
A stretched, horrified vulva.
The comb of filmy tooth

Would be pliable as fingernails
And laced, she thought, with the green
Last meal of a species.

5

She's living in the novel
That was where she learned about birth
And revolution.

She's not the heroine:
Her ankles are tied
Too far, too wide.

She's got muscles, she must try
To grip the subtext.
She grabs some kind of a mike:

This is an outside broadcast,
I'm here, behind the weather,
The frantic jamming.

Eavesdropping, near to tears,
The poetry-writing doctor
Imagines what it's like.

To live your life
Is not so easy
As to cross a field.

She thinks of Niagara Falls,
Love's second disappointment.
She could scream: but so many

Acres – and in bare feet –
And the mud churning and shifting –
It's easier to live

Your life than to cross this field.
I'm not just crossing the field, I
Am the bloody field.

6

It was the crying hand
Thrust from the shawl, unannounced
As celandines in cold March grass.

It was the five little swimmers,
Waxed in each wrinkle and seam,
Bent at the waist, sea-wearied.

It was the stronghold they shut
Round her probing finger, the way
The crying shivered into stillness,

That made her think that the teeming
Shambles of it all was planned,
And the plan was matchless.

7

They brought her the baby
Every four hours for precisely
Five minutes on each breast.

But the child had travelled too far:
Its lips worked busily
Then slowed, slipped open

In the trance of a lost time-zone.
She could have waited all day,
Conversed with it haltingly

In handfuls of dreamy sucks.
No lover's mouth was exact
Like this, no head so neatly

At rest where her armskin was palest.
But they lifted the child away
And frowned over the scales.

She'll cry later on, they threatened.
Such a thin, inaudible, public
Lament, she thought. The lace cones

Of the nursing-bra turned yellow
And crusty with wastage.
Her arm felt cold. The child

Cried on, somewhere. She cried.
She thought: this is where money starts.
This is how candy's made.

8

She discharged herself politely.
Rode the tall white hospital bus
To her mother's house –

A popcorn maisonette,
Its walls bright-speckled,
Its windows glaring.

Her father came in,
Politely drunk. Withdrawn.
He didn't dislike children

But when, in the kitchen,
She began to unbutton her blouse,
He sent her to her room.

She went out, the high street
Made her dizzy.
She sat in the garden

Among the little rocks
While her husband's mince dinner
Dried out on gas mark three,

The white page in her hand,
On which nothing was written,
Translucent with sunlight.

Inflation

I stand on the edge of the place where I am expected to become invisible.
I ask if this is all there is.

The fog lifts slightly and I walk towards an area slowly creasing into
water. I look into the water and can just see a blur of grey. I do my hair,
combing it carefully over the place where my scalp shines through.

When I look up, a young ferryman is standing in the shallows. Once,
I would have caught him in my arms and pressed his body into mine: I
would have fingered obsessively the small curls on the nape of his neck
and pretended to read his soul. Now I feel nothing but hatred for him.

He grins mockingly and holds out his hand, making a deep bowl of
the palm.

I lie that I have no change, not even two obols. He doesn't understand,
or pretends he doesn't. His eyes still mock me.

When I have explained, he says he will not accept foreign coins. He
mentions a three-figure sum, and demands a cheque, made out in sterling.

And it turns out he doesn't even go all the way to the underworld.

Queen Bluebeard's Palace

Henna peroxide vitapoint hair gel block powder loose powder avocado neck-cream elberberry eye-cream – you won't catch me out, I'll never go into your prison. I may choose you for pleasure. Never from necessity.

But I still have to climb the stairs and go from room to room, decade to decade.

I peer round each of the doors. The women smile back. They always look young, even in the rooms at the end of the corridor.

But then I come to the last room. I open the door. An old hag frowns at herself in the mirror as she twists the rollers from the colourless, thin strands of her hair. She brushes the frizz out happily. Then she tries different-coloured scarves against her crumpled throat.

And suddenly I'm screaming like a brutally disappointed child – don't do it, don't say there's nothing else, why isn't there something else I want there to be something else.

Lacunae

Once more the name of the earth she stood on changed.
The pine tree's name changed.
The pebble's name changed.
The mud's name changed.
She tried to see them in the new language.
A child pointed at her. A uniformed man
Took her arm. She explained
The pine tree still speaks Pine Tree,
The pebble, Pebble, the mud, Mud.
She used the old words. The child giggled.
The man tightened his grip, her arm-bone sang
And the mud, the pebbles, the pine trees
Broke suddenly into recognisable pieces
That rushed into her face, and blinded her.

Perestroika

This is my sadness –
To have been the future
You thought you wanted.

This is your sadness –
That the most astonishing future
Began without you.

A Dialogue of Perestroishiks

Good riddance to that old eyesore, the Engine of Justice
Ah, but the Engine of Justice was theoretically beautiful
Ah, but the Engine of Justice was all bloody theory
Ah, but it went, the good old Engine of Justice
Ah, but it never ran on time, the Engine of Justice
Ah, but the Engine of Justice was greased lightning in its heyday, and it could
    sing 'How Great is Our Motherland' in four parts
Ah, but the Engine of Justice was ecologically unsound, and it stank to high
    heaven
Ah, but everyone on board the Engine of Justice had a job
Ah, but the Engine of Justice was a dictatorship
Ah, but the Engine of Justice was a dictatorship of the proletariat
Ah, but the Engine of Justice gave fat hand-outs to the bosses
Ah, but the Engine of Justice put potatoes in all the children
Ah, but the Engine of Justice knew nothing about female orgasm
Ah, but what d'you expect of an Engine of Justice?
Ah, but did you hear the one about the Engine of Justice?
Ah, but there have been some grand stories about the Engine of Justice
Ah, but the Engine of Justice was a fabulous all-time con
Ah, but the Engine of Justice only needed a new oil-can
Ah, but the Engine of Justice only needed a new definition of Justice
Ah, but who will build us a better Engine of Justice?
Ah, but each man should aim to be his own Engine of Justice, and each woman
    too, of course
Ah, but the Engine of Justice was for everyone
Ah, but was everyone for the Engine of Justice?
Ah, but anyway, I had a soft spot for the dear old Engine of Justice
Ah, but the dear old Engine of Justice eliminated people for having soft spots

Ah, but, excuse me, what have you got in your hand if it isn't the plans for a
        new Engine of justice?
Ah, but we're not calling it the Engine of Justice
Ah, but it looks very similar to
Ah, but it's not, so shut up
Ah, but
Ah but ah but?
Ah
Ah!

Rides

The enraged father,
His new romance on the skids,
Yells 'Get out of the car!'
The daughter stumbles out:

'I'm going, don't worry!'
But her fury dissolves quicker
Than his tail-lights can bleed
Away down the Mile End Road.

She's back to square zero.
She had her bag with her, packed.
She was happy. She was going home
And now she's not.

She sits against a door,
One elbow on the bag,
One tube of Tennent's in her hand.
She keeps telling herself to move on,

But only her mind moves...
Like this boy she vaguely knows,
Might pull in beside her.
'How you doing?' he says.

'Fancy a drive?'
They head for the motorway.
'I hate my dad,' she says.
'All I did was tell him

His girlfriend's mental.'
'North or West?' the boy asks.
'Alton Towers or Stonehenge?'
She chooses North. She sings

And now she's shrieking
Upside down and his arm's
Strong and the music's loud;
Even his armpit smells good.

This is all she needs to be happy...
But the Towers are closed, stupid
And they put a fence round the Stones
And stoned the hippies...

She wakes with the sharp dawn light
Trying to get through her eyelids,
Weaving jazzy black into red
Like something to cover a settee.

Trucks are lifting her hair
On their stream. Her body's pavement:
She's got to break each bit
To sit up, to find out

If she can walk. She feels robbed.
She could have been raped, so much
Is aching, so much is empty.
She's not got a dream left

About boys or cars or fun
Because all bloody England's wrapped up,
Fenced off, there's nowhere to go
And not be taken for a ride.

FROM

THINKING OF SKINS

(1993)

Until We Could Hardly See Them

It was the living who took offence
At our elegies, our desire
To find out, to make amends.
They called it appropriation.
They said we were the wrong race or religion.
Borders and ghettoes held like knots in their hearts
And shortened their memories.
They should have asked the dead before they judged us.

Whoever tries to imagine them
Comforts them, the dead,
Who have learned they are simply children,
So must one day be abandoned.
Now they cry from the middle of the road,
Stop, please, stop, take us with you.
We don't weigh much, we won't take up much room.
They are glad of any hand,
Even one whose flesh is scented with luck,
And any voice that names them –
Never mind our bad pronunciation –
Warms the great silence they bear.
They smile, they stretch their fingers
To touch our cheeks. They say we take after them.
They say we're their living image
And indeed we will be, that day
We ask nothing more of the future,
Only not to be left like shadows on the road
Where so many became no one.

St Petersburg, Reclaimed by Merchants

The wind was terrorising the simple river,
Smacking the wobbly flesh about its waist-band.
Pushkin, the tourists thought, looking tenderly down
At the curled green lip, the slurping meal.
The locals stared at a different kind of moral.
Flood was a long word in a poem they'd learned
At school. Now they were learning grown-up things:
How much to ask for a papier mâché icon

Stolen by someone's cousin, how not to be sold
Down the metaphorical river, and other secrets
Dark as the dark-eyed bride the match-maker brings.

A Prophet, Unhonoured
(for Jan Kavan)

Eloquence, irony and lying low –
These were your gifts, the gifts of opposition.
I hope they're proving useful to you now,
As when I learned the fine points of your mission
In London, back in '82 and '3.
Your neighbours, it turned out, were qualified
For jobs in Husak's State Security.
They asked me if I worked for you. I said
I was your girlfriend. (But I never was.)
They shopped you to the Council, all the same:
Your crime, running a business from your place
Of residence – a very English crime.
An investigator called. We buzzed him in
('The lift's gone wrong, you'll have to use the stairs!')
And flew about, got every damned machine
Bundled away, toys strewn, said a few prayers.
Your daughter's absence filled the room. He guessed
Perhaps, but chose to leave the signs unread.
We made a sort of family: Brits, obsessed
With 'freedom', Czechs, hard-boiled in Prague street-cred.
Arrests and disappearance, beatings, rape –
The bad news had its ways of twisting through.
You'd spell the names for me, place accents, keep
Them talking, simply telling what they knew.
You *lived in truth*, I think, but not in hate.
(Is this why some have struck you off their list?)
You thought it worthwhile, arguing with a state
Which might still earn its title, Socialist.
For that, we'd work the night away, my longhand
Struggling with obsolescence as you schemed
And sped the filthy era to its end.
Your passage home was earned, not merely dreamed.
So was the revolution 'velvet', new
And candle-soft? Or did it win its rough
First shape from the patient realists, like you,

Working with slipperier, more dangerous stuff –
Jan Palach's last handclasp, the ink-soaked type
In use before the new technology,
Back in the days when innocence, like sleep,
Was one more spurious foreign luxury?

Seascape and Single Figure

It isn't the seagulls, whitened
Lecterns of rock or wind,
Whose cries make the heart cry,
But those who scatter delinquent
Footprints, feathered with sand,
As the visible evidence that children fly.

My shadow, askance and pale,
Crosses the beach with me:
We sit on the spread towel,
Folded together complicatedly
As a marriage or Swiss Army knife.
So the shadow is one with the life.

Nearby, a village is settled
With windbreaks, push-chairs.
Children gather and build.
The candid embodiment of
The most popular version of love,
They are the day's, its flush, its goldening, theirs.

And disinheritance
Is the sea, burnt almost to nothing,
A chemical, austere,
Standoffish radiance
Sending a few thin waves, slow-lathering,
Choked, to encrust the shore.

What does it matter if less
Than a dazzled moment ago
I swam with the warmer flow?
Those choices, that lack of choice,
That enviable sorrow,
Are not renewable.

Bright as crayoned sunshine, still
The coast-train winds among
The drifted crowds, pouring them out like grain
From a summer which, for so long
Disguised as a miracle,
Empties only to fill and brim again.

Walking Out

Walking out on them would be like this,
She'd always known: the feeling of pretence
As she strolled on and on (she could go back
Any time, even now), the shore-lights drilling
Through scrambled pinks and blues the inky block
Of river (or she could jump in and drown),
The thrill of reading from a bland tin sign
She'd stepped across a border, changed her town
(But even so, she could go back). And then
The hunger, deepening till she called it hers.
She crossed towards a blare of infra-red
Announcing the Monster Burger, the Special Grill,
And took her place, and thanked the hand that fed.
There was another room, half in darkness:
She couldn't work out what was going on –
The disco sex-thud, squealing playground voices –
Until she saw the cake float by, frilled skirt
And seven shivering haloes. Then she cut
One more smashed mouthful, pushed away her plate.
This was how it was too, she might have known:
Whichever way you walked, their mugger's eyes
Shone at you. They didn't want your life.
They wanted everything you'd planned to give them
Before you knew you had no choice beyond
The choice that gave them birth. Birth was your crime,
And after that all innocence was gone.
At the till she waved a dirty five-pound note –
Not for the children's childhood, but her own.

Last of the Lays

Part One

At Ivalo's tyre-crazed crossroads, snow was the sphinx
And *Murmansk* was what she murmured. One night you got restless.

(The nights were long, alas. We weren't new lovers.
'Follow me. I am your Fate' wouldn't wash any more.)

I heard your foot-swords slicing the forest-fleece
With finality. Then from your breast swooped a brilliant birdman.

Choice, choice, choice gasped the wind as you gashed it.
In front of you, ghostly as lilacs, stood your live lungs.

Part Two

In Persil-white Ivalo the enemy was drink.
I had nothing to come to but a Finnish Cosmo

And nothing to read but a radioactive omelette.
My cutlery stuttered, my skis would begin any minute,

So I tacked outside into a mean minus-thirty,
And wound up at the Word, that high-lettered horror.

I turned as it told me. I plummeted and plodged
And became wildlife and expected instant extinction.

I lit on the luminous secret of synchronised movement
Momentarily, but omitted to take it with me.

I slept on my skis, and revolutionary roughnecks
Lobbed snow-lumps like one-off hand-jobs, and roamed the ice

Like spinning-tops wreathed in a frost of eye-water.

Part Three

Bang on the border, they'd opened a Super-Safeways,
Hit by recession, closed for the duration.

Some tanked-up gun-jabber jogged me: 'Nadezhda Krupskaya?'
'Crumbs!' I said. 'Wrong revolution. Julian Clary.'

Part Four

He didn't find that funny, which meant, as I'd feared,
History hadn't happened, it hadn't begun.

And though the ski-tracks still straggled under the *Push* sign
They were being disexisted at serious speed.

This was the hairiest I had ever imagined:
Me, on God's side, just about. You, back on the other:

The border, bristling. Remember those terrible games –
When the sound's switched off, there's got to be someone dancing,

And the grin's de rigueur, because English losers are laughers?
I hope, wherever you're harboured, you look like a natural –

Straight bck, heels tgthr, bm on chr –
I hope when it thaws and the home-thoughts unfreeze our faces,

Whoever I am I'll
                    author an honest tear.

The Muse of Argument

At first, no more than
   A fret of breeze that twists
The fossil bracken,
   Shyness and anger twin-
Leashed to a straining wrist:
   Then she is visible
And she embodies all
   Silence that steels itself
Under a woman's heartbeat
   And stammers to take aim.
I keep back my breath
   For her, but the dart has skimmered
Already, sealed its roost
   In disarray: the sky
Plunges, heels alight
   And tightly pressed.
Plaudits, abasements die
   At her feet, with clouded looks.
And still she seems to doubt
   Her own connection.
Her shoulders are a book,
   Caught naked, trying to close,
And her face has taken on
   The colour of a wound,
   Its deep, historic rose.

Dreams of Revolution

She's walking somewhere unresolved, sea-ravished,
Taking the flesh-tints of the facing sky
Among the stones, distributing them in water
Because there are no poor, now, in the village.

This is her lover's name-delighted class-room.
His finger prints a chalk-rose on her wrist
And leads her eyes to where a migrant shimmer
Of cursive vanishes on the rinsed slate.

He doesn't mind her townee misconceptions.
He scarcely knows the drift of his own arm –
Whether or not it lodges on her shoulder:
All her dear world's his habitat, and habit.

And this machine contracts them both, so perfect,
One stolen berry means a night of storms
And flight scattered next day in lumps and meltings
Of slashed upholstery, as if the sky

Had tried to move, and failed. Nothing moves freely
Here but the sea, old and unreconstructed.
It drowns the clover, mocks the poor, entices
Love's great protection-racket to its housing.

In the Season of Green Gowns

Summer will take from you everything I desire:
It will pluck at your sleeve, quietly undo
A handful of buttons, seeking no disclosure
That wasn't first fully consented to,
As you walked and turned in your mirror's candid gaze
And wouldn't be rushed. Summer, shyly approving,
Will lead you from chaste decision to easy living.

Summer will tell me what I could never enquire:
The pale length of your arm, sleeved in its years,
The freckled blush at the wrist. Summer confirms
The less-than-perfect as our most tender haunting.
It pours my desire into the depth of the mould
Like a conception. But, like a man or a child,
I simply can't tell if you are filled or wanting.

The Impenitent

The wife of the poet can't be innocent
Her eyes must be narrow
The wife of the poet can't be humble
She must lift her chin high
The wife of the poet won't be flattered
If he writes a poem in her blood
The wife of the poet knows the missing word
But she'll never tell him.

The husband of the poet can't be light-hearted
He must watch the pennies
The husband of the poet can't be clean
He must live in his dust
The husband of the poet can't be original
He must be, or obey, her muse
The husband of the poet knows the missing word
And that it's 'wife'.

The Last Wife's Consolation

When his body grew tired of hers, she knew there was no solution.
He had never seen her young, so he lacked that particular image
To gloss over her blemishes, to kiss in her unlit eyes.
She looked in the mirror, and nothing there entranced her:
On the other hand, she had never been honey and bright new milk –
And maybe his body's tiredness had nothing to do with her,
And maybe not even her youth could have been the beautiful cure.

The Colouring Age

Like a shower of red rain
   Blown across the wall
Of that suburban garden
   Where sense is made of all
That's rampant, archetypal,
   The hawthorn sails again
Into her colouring-age,
   Her knack is effortless
But might discourage
   Those for whom spring's good news
Is getting worse.
   Moans in the quiet night
Could equally be the dryad
   Bled by a vandal
To pulp, or the deferred
   Grief of the gardenless
Ex-suburbanite
   Acknowledging a loss.

Ghosts never cease to pull
   On a woman's wrists,
Beg to be carried, still,
   At twenty-plus.
They're all ventriloquists
   Hurtling their voices
From each secluded lawn;
   And she will always turn,
Being an expert on love,
   Burdened by sheer talent.
O trees, O pavement,
   O things that never move,
Tell her how to live
   With no doorstep to stand on.
Each doorbell lately pressed
   Had lost its tongue.
None that she ever kissed
   Could bear it for very long.

This flowering tree invites
   Her to go under,
Suffer the pains and lights
   That prove the wonder
Of modern physics which

Disprove the clock.
Forward is really back.
　There's no other to get-out
From the whole silly story
　But to unravel, stitch
By stitch the contrived plot,
　Downsliding all the way
To that beginning,
　That once-upon-a-time,
She'd pitched her life to swing
　A million miles from:

Home. And what is home
　But to be thirteen
And mocked, for ever,
　Your love, a crush; your dream,
A different mother?
　Nothing in your garden
Is quite inanimate
　And that deep-blushing tree
Your father slashes down
　With incomprehensible hate,
Has certainly been hurt.
　Hawthorn blossom's unlucky,
The wise folk say.
　You mount an artistic
Rescue-operation
　Boldly, any way,
Lift armfuls of it in,
　And scrape persistently
With crumbling pastels
　Until the paper's skin
Breaks into leaves again
　And the heat of petals,
Forgetting while you can
　That the dark grass outside
Had seemed to float in blood –
　And that blood, your own.

Prelapsarian

Glassy spittle shot all over our windscreen
As we arrived, but the bevy of hook-shaped birds
Swaying towards us, bluer than any storm-cloud,
Was a different proposition, an augury
That seemed benevolent. The donkeys watched
From sly, archaic eyes, but we were careful,
Treading the frosted ladder to our high
Loft, and I was careful every morning.
Though always thrilled with the first splash of flight
That drenched the trees in blue, I came down slowly,
Forcing both my hands round the scalding rails.
There would be mountains to climb, the hips and noses
Of lightly-sleeping giants, and Christmas Eve
We would remember the distant births of children:
Otherwise, though naked, we seemed blameless.

When we held out dark jewels of Christmas pudding
The jostle of beaks scarcely pricked our palms.
The donkeys wore old velvet, hung their heads
In an extreme of patience, almost satire.
Knowing the world is paddock grass, that apples
Don't grow on trees, they let us offer them
Our cores. Their soft black-tulip mouths were smiling.

Green Love

To watch you is to watch some other species
Going about its life, a graceful expert,
Unaltered by the passion of my study.
For how much longer? How can I be withheld?

Can I, by taking thought, subtract one image
That made these eyes confederates of your heaven,
Find the small place where wings became leaf-mould, where
A god might shed his last human resemblance,
File away love's name in the catalogue
Of skins and brittle forests: let you live?

England to Her Maker

Hephaestus we tried to tell you
the signs were everywhere
you kept your head down

face to the glare
hammering bevelling punching
all that noise and smoke

no wonder you didn't hear
you were wreathed in the heat
and darkness of your craft

never stood upright except
to hammer our silences
with ringing cries of grievance

peculiar to your class
eyes clearer than yours Hephaestus
were noting the lack of new orders

we don't deny you had skills
you armed the fighting gods
invented such curiosities

as the self-propelling tripod
the fire-breathing bronze bull
magnificent yet not

exactly what life's about
any more we have microchips
we have genuine automation

quiet machines that can reason
unlike your rough irons
clanking brainlessly filthily

think of your lungs black
as the grass round here your legs
bowed under you like pliers

you could have a job sitting down
somewhere warm and well-lit
where there's music plants fountains

imagine yourself with white cuffs
tapping a keyboard smiling
taking credit-cards only smiling

it's the future you can't fight the future
you can't argue with progress
Hephaestus look at it this way

My Two Muses

The younger would fetch you a slap round the face
And you felt it as the most whimsical caress.

But oh, the caresses of the older girl
Were stinging-nettles shoved into the soul.

One taught me the skin's delight, the other, its pain.
I was in love with both of them at first
But my eyes were opened by the older one
Who said: *don't believe a word my sister says.*

I won't, sweetheart, I swear. I swear I never have done.

Charm Against the Virtuous

There's a phoney cow you think's your friend, but her milk will give you rabies.
When you want to play at Mums and Dads, she wants to play Mummies and
     Babies.
And if you're feeling a little bit low, she'll tell you what you need
And she'll give you a couple of Nurofen, but I will give you speed.

She's old as your gran, she's got no man, she's never been out of this city.
She's nice as pie but it's all my eye, don't ever swallow her pity.
She wants you soft, she wants you sweet, but you'd better be hard and brave.
She'll carry you off to a ceilidh, but I'll give you an all-night rave.

Oh you're the wildest of any of us, I've seen it in your eyes.
You know I know what turns you on and I know you like a surprise.
You've been fucked up and so have I, let's get fucked up some more
And take no shit from that holy cow, but show her the old barn-door.

That Bloody Kid Again

My estranged body came back to me one night.
It said 'Aren't you going to kill the fatted calf?'
'No,' I said, 'But sit down, any way.
Not too close, please.' 'Well, have I changed much?'
'No, you were always ugly.' And I smiled
Because, to tell you the truth, in the dimmish light
It looked OK. 'What are you doing these days?'
My estranged body pointed to various marks
On its hands and shins, and grumbled 'Moving house.
I've moved so much I don't know who I am.
I'm always encountering chunks of furniture,
Walls, et cetera, that say I don't exist,
Ovens I haven't got to grips with, burn me.
One day my hair caught fire. It's a miracle
I'm still alive.' 'And yet,' I said, 'You are,'
Hating that note of self-pity in its voice.
There was a long silence. 'What are you thinking?'
'I think I'm bleeding.' 'How original.'
'You couldn't lend me...?' 'No. It's time you went,
Anyway, I'm expecting my lover.'
'How can you make love without a body?'
'I see you're still a megalomaniac.'
My body lurked at the door aggrievedly.
'It's raining.' 'So? You won't be washed away.
Come back when you've grown up. If you ever do.'
'I'd rather die than grow up into you.'

Midnight
(i.m. Jerry Orpwood, 1942-88)

The day was a difficult child.
Now it's fallen asleep,
You can hear yourself breathing
Evenly, without fear.

The emptied hour-glass shines,
Sealing the last room,
The last absence, like a mirror.

Why should you turn it over?

At this moment only
The silver pathway lies
Open at your feet.

It will mount the stairs with you
And unfurl into the stars,
Their distant dream-school.

Stretch your hand to the light-switch,
Press your face among feathers,
The soft pen-nibs scratching
A peaceful nonsense.

Think dizzily of the tilt
Of the world again, the weight:
How its dark sands are massing
To drop another day.

The Lost Language of Birth

To be here, to be nowhere, nervous as the wind
Or the landing-lights at ten thousand feet,
Systole, diastole, hanging by a thread

Over the reticent, brick-humble roads
Which turn their backs on me like men not guilty,
Not going anywhere, their eyes hilly:

To be dropped in my own pocket, my own excuses.
To ripple like a blue pain through the lough,
Mountainous hands arranging the hip-bones wide

For that great loneliness, birth. To walk across carpets
I must have stolen, out of rooms that drain
The heart of colour from my children's faces.

To know which side of the road death lives, yet love
The youngest tones of white, from blush to faintness:
To enter like a girl, pushing lips and elbows

Up into the breathy climate of lycra,
Emerging sleek and weightless, the wild glass
Gaping forbidden words like 'swan', like 'girl'.

The Fuchsia Knight

(for Medbh McGuckian)

You gathered his yarn onto unfamiliar looms,
And the vowels you dropped, the soft-signs you appended,
Brindled the cloth and changed it, like the tears
Forged in the hedgerows, bending the thick stems
With weights not even a god deserves to weep.

You bore him flowers which seemed so abundantly
Indigenous, he forgot his planter's rank.
His head grew misty with heather: luminous roses
And the never-heard song of his native nightingale
Brimmed between him and his sword. He learned to drink

Your consonants with childish intensity
As you chased them towards him with a dry-lipped stammer
Less part of the need for love than the search for perfection.
He learned that to open the veins of speech is sometimes
To unzip the fuchsia linings of live skin.

Stealing the Genre

It was the shortest night of the year. I'd been drinking
But I was quite lucid and calm. So, having seen her
The other side of the bar, shedding her light
On no one who specially deserved it, I got to my feet
And simply went over and asked her, in a low voice,
If she'd come to my bed. She raised her eyebrows strangely
But didn't say 'no'. I went out. I felt her follow.

My mind was a storm as we silently crossed the courtyard
In the moist white chill of the dawn. Dear God, I loved her.
I'd loved her in books, I'd adored her at the first sighting.
But no, I'm a woman, English, not young. How could I?
She'd vanished for years. And now she was walking beside me.
Oh what am I going to do, what are *we* going to do?
Perhaps she'll know. She's probably an old hand –
But this sudden thought was the most disturbing of all.

As soon as we reached my room, though, it was plain
She hadn't a clue. We stood like window-displays
In our dawn-damp suits with the short, straight, hip-hugging skirts

(Our styles are strangely alike, I suppose it's because
Even she has to fight her corner in a man's world)
And discussed the rain, which was coming down, and the view,
Which was nothing much, a fuchsia hedge and some trees,
And we watched each other, as women do watch each other,
And tried not to yawn. Why don't you lie down for a bit?
I whispered, inspired. She gratefully kicked off her shoes.

She was onto the bed in no time, and lay as if dumped
On the furthest edge, her face – dear God – to the wall.
I watched for a while, and, thinking she might be in tears,
Caressed the foam-padded viscose that passed for her shoulder,
And begged her not to feel guilty. Then I discovered
That all she was doing was breathing, dead to the world.

It wasn't an insult, exactly, but it was a let-down –
And yet I admired her. Sleep. If only I could.
I rested my hand at an uncontroversial location
South of her breasts, maybe North, I don't remember,
And ached with desire and regret and rationalisation.
I'd asked her to bed. And she'd come to bed. End of story.
Only it wasn't the story I'd wanted to tell.
Roll on, tomorrow, I urged, but tomorrow retorted:
I'm here already, and nothing ever gets better.

But then, unexpectedly, I began to feel pleased.
To think she was here, at my side, so condensed, so weighty!
In my humble position (a woman, English, not young,
Et cetera) what more could I ask of an Irish dawn
Than this vision, alive, though dead to the world, on my duvet?
What have I done to deserve her? Oh, never mind,
Don't think about words like 'deserve'. So we lay in grace.
The light. Her hair. My hand. Her breath. And the fuchsias.
I thought of the poem I'd write, and fell asleep, smiling.

I woke in a daze of sublime self-congratulation
And saw she was gone. My meadow, my cloud, my aisling!
I could hardly believe my own memory. I wanted to scream
All over the courtyard, come back, come to bed, but how could I?
She might be anywhere, people were thick in the day
Already, and things were normal. Why are things normal?

I keened her name to the walls, I swam bitterest rivers,
I buried my face in the cloth where her blushes had slipped
And left a miraculous print that would baffle the laundry:
Oh let me die now. And the dark was all flame as I drank
The heart-breaking odour of Muguets des Bois and red wine –
Hers, though I have to admit, it could have been mine.

Chippa Rippa
(for Elena Seymenliyska)

Re-wakened memory-sound: the rustly chip and chock
As the poker rummages: the obedient mutter
And gush of the stirred coal, relinquishing
Its ardent childhood wish – to be immortal.

Variant Readings

I expected bleachworks and burnt-out cars, not fuchsias:
Not cedar and sky-trickling larch, their remote massed shade,
Nor to hear my footsteps, lonely in streets of wet hedges
That tell me: here peace, and love, and money, are made.

Home was like this long ago, but can't be again.
I'll have chosen guilt and illusion, if I choose this
Most English of Irelands, our difference seemingly less
Than that between neighbourly hedges, depths of green.

Visions of a Protestant

I saw a city paved with stretched-out people.
They were clothed but their feet, for safety's sake, were bare.
Toes nestled lightly in all colours of hair,
Fingers in fingers. It was a jigsaw puzzle
Solved in heart-pains, headaches, watering eyes:
Death shrank to a speck high on a cliff of sighs.

I heard a city drowned in crystal thunder.
After a moment's silence, passionate saws
Were arguing chipboard into doors and windows.
A chalk-stick stumbled, broke itself in two.
Prices slashed, it screamed, *business as usual:*
The speck was a huge, cruel face. The crowd walked tall.

Cold Dawns

1 *Nightmare*

Busy as paddles in liquid, ratchets in clocks,
   An army is making new clouds above the Falls,
   And the rain-thin quilt we wear for rest unravels
And some are lulled, some trapped behind rattled locks,

And none can wake. Adrift in the bickering flow,
   That fills my kitchen with questions, still asleep,
   I pick up my kettle, turn, and almost leap
From the drawn blade flashed across the dawn-dark window.

2 *Maryville Avenue*

The frayed orange rug of a single lamp
Covers most of the street. Awake already,
The cement-works pants like a thirsty taxi.
The sky is one shade lighter than the tarmac,
But ghostly, still, in night-colour. Night-cold
Blooms in my doorway, solid with amazement.
The shiny, tidy dark of all I can see
Like the child's address – house-number to universe –
Or the confident water-rings of a thrown pebble,
Ends nowhere, has no end. How little the world is.
How it touches at every point, since your footsteps died across it.

Schoolgirl's Story

The news stayed good until Monday morning
When a taxi-driver was shot in the South of the city,
And his un-named schoolgirl-passenger injured.
Outside the window, clouds made changeable bruises
And spillings. Bad weather, taxi weather.
I picked up my dish, poured everything down the sink,
Unclogged it with bare fingers, ran for my coat,
Played back a dream of how it used to be,
Hearing about these things every day of the week
And not feeling cold and sick and hot: the beauty
   Of being nobody's lover.

I could hardly breathe as I reached the school railings.
The clouds turned heavy again, opened fire
On my face and eyes with stinging rice-grains of hail.
Bad weather, taxi weather. *If it's not there*
I'll run, and my screams run with me, from here to Balmoral.
But the bike was on its stand in the shed as usual.
The square-root of the frame, graceful, ice-blue,
Cut me the old two ways: her nearness, her distance.
The sky paled. I began to look for her
Without seeming to. I stopped feeling sick for her.
    Another sickness took over.

Sunday Evening, Belfast 9

The family cars pour with a limousine swish
Down the sequestered avenue, their style
Not quite at ease, still conscious of arrival
And settlement in this almost solid parish.
Their careful drivers dipped as carefully to
The service, dropped the occasional autumn cough,
Then rose, shook hands, went fed and gilded through
A trace of mist, impatient to be off.
Under familiar trees at last, they bring
Magnified, watery shadows of good news
To driveways flooded with the shine of home,
And let the ritual die. A dog barks welcome.
The gravel settles down after applauding
their buoyant tyres, the highlights of their shoes.

Were their mild hopes alerted, for a mute
Second, as creed went naked on the street?
Walking the other side, I could have slipped
From any congregation save their own:
No stranger's guaranteed in a darkening town.
But I proved harmless, too. I read the pavement
And found the place where all the petals, blown
From yesterday's weddings, might have been translucent
Evidence of imaginary bushes,
Their everlasting roses specially bred
To shower a bride in delicate, soundless wishes.
I picked them out, like moonlight from stained glass,
Like glass from skin, waiting to cross the road,
Thinking: the gods will pass, the gods will pass.

The Lisburn Road List

(Variations on a Theme of Philip Larkin)

Glooms of old stone between shops,
And flat oases that blaze
All night, as ubiquitous
As copywriters' full-stops;
Churches and garages, both, in their different ways
Telling us this is a road going somewhere else:

And the buses to *Silverstream*
Via Shankhill, crowded as far
As the bone-hard, low-church seats
Punishing each rear,
And the dozens of other competitive notions of 'home',
And the eyes gazing carefully down on each 'somewhere else':

And the dusks, as mornful and slow
As the queue at the road-blocks,
A fire-engine screaming through,
Past the heavily-macintoshed barracks,
And the passers-by and the drivers thinking 'what's new?',
Thinking 'Jesus Christ, why don't I live somewhere else?'

And the gentler fantasies
For sale – a new colour-scheme,
Facials, cheap holidays,
And, if all else fails, an ice cream;
And the intricate, well-worked hills undeceived by the dream
That life could be utterly different, somewhere else.

And at last the ephemeral I,
Observant or bored, but never
Doubting that summer will soon
Arrive to unveil a vast sky
Of rooftops and trees and the hard bright light of that question:
Where is your love for the life you had somewhere else?

Snowfire

The chimney-stacks had been variously feathered
As the north wind pushed across Maryville Avenue,
Whitening a corner here, a full side there,
And sometimes leaving the odd stack disregarded.
The roofs were white, the clouds a little less so.
They moved on fast, as if from the scene of a crime
They'd merely witnessed, but would be accused of.
At first, I thought it was only chimney-smoke
From a late-night hearth, trying to join the cloud-rush.
Then came a flashing, lit from beyond the apex.
Something on fire? It was bright enough, but silent:
A fire can't work without muttering, carelessly
Giving itself away. And now the wind
Was gushing up and up, and the roofs were dissolving,
And all the street was fainting and dazzling itself
In the fumey blast. I watched till my face went under,
The fire wanted in, and I had to shut the door.

Head Cold

River-mouth world, is it really a surprise
That a new tenant has judged your sinuses
An ideal home? Your breath aches through his coal-smoke –
Smell of the ancient tenderness of cities –
His fumey speeds sicken you like catarrh.

So many clouds, heroes of stone and shell –
The loveliest headache, if you could bear to look;
Every street laid with a different carpet,
Each garden its own mist of imagined spring,
Though a gloved thumb could wipe out any petal.

Strange city, doped and bright in your frosty vest,
Keep to your bed today, and fall in love
Again and again with the childhood illnesses
When your hands, unusually clean, turned the pages
Of adventures you could not possibly have.

Et Incarnatus Est

Windows are often loneliest when lighted,
Their silvery plenitude a kind of treason.
They smile, they seem to offer invitation
Between the last-leafed branches, but their eyes
Are kind only if you possess the keys.
Journeys towards such stars are best diverted.

Desire, though, being the senseless thing it is,
I know a certain window from all angles
And frequencies. The city's whole galère
Contains no poorer version of stained glass,
But it's among the daily miracles
When I check anxiously, find it still there,
Glass being so promiscuous with its spangles,
And light so frail, in cities such as this.

I'm happiest when it's invisible,
Sunk in the fireless black of the night sky,
A lovely emblem folded, put away,
And nothing left more innocent and hopeful
Than life itself. *There's no epiphany,*
No magic room: this is an empty house.
I can unthrone it, if I trust that blackness.

But when, through the burnt-out December trees,
The window shivers dreamily, plays at being
An earth-bound moon, then shows me, bright and full,
That soft shoulder-like curve, that frame of grace,
I breathe like a runner though I'm standing still.
I know what it is to have been a king
Once, and now to be frightened of a stable.

Some windows pierce the flesh but this, when lighted,
Is flesh itself, those fluids, sighs, word-world.
Other lights vanish or become blurred.
This burns the mind – not light, but living eyes,
Faultless, candid, where my last hope dies,
A child of hell, its death never completed.

Genius Loci

And through the blind glass that swings over every threshold
    I meet her eyes, touch her sleeve in an unfelt greeting,
And all the sad elms at their winter soliloquies, strive
    To copy her gestures, the grace of her clarification.
Each passage of footsteps insists on my terrified waiting
    Because she is all these opacities and rehearsals.

And in all the bright precincts we claimed, the ingenuous windows
    That gazed at the sky and saw nothing, are shocked into candour
Again as my hand cups a waterfall, studies a burning,
    Refining the one possibility, blatant, addicted,
And my lips brush a snow so unsettled and warm, with such lack
    Of demand, there is scarcely a trick of the air or the climate.

And if as I hurry home, rain-dazzled, down the long road
    With its blown-about pearls and its tapestry rucksack of hills,
She's there at the bus-stop, shivering, cloud-breathing, earthed,
    Waving an uncertain hand to attract my attention,
It's not in a wish to avoid her that I almost pass her;
    Simply, reality's never itself but a vision.

I have held her and lost her and lost her so questionably
    There isn't a stone unbereft nor unconsecrated.
All the hurrying cabs catch her up to some frangible safety:
    All the hedges weave gardens for her. She is every wind blowing,
Each darkness that's dressed in an impulse of light or water –
    An identity left, for a dying moment, wide open.

In Memory of a Friendship

Winter has reached the Spanish Steps, advancing
On tides of dirty suds like the landlady
Who mopped her way past literature, enticing
Tubercle bacilli from every mouse-hole.
The red street-carpets, swaggering muddily
Persuade the tourists to the Latin Quarter.
Hawkers, pipers, backpackers, gypsies, thieves,
Unabashed by the civic or the tonal,
Go on arguing as they've always done.
If someone's down to his last adjective,
Why should they care, among all these words and rain?

Joseph takes the day off for gardening.
He'd mentioned violets, and his friend forgot
The taste of coughed-up rust, fed on their sweetness.
The gifts seem lame, now, curiously weightless,
Loveletters to a sickbed, crushed unopened.
His own hand clenches, but he crowds the plot.
The buds twist on their necks to look at him,
Measure his skewed perspective, his unquickened
Muse. These were his painting-days. The rest
Is a double-grave, much visited, but modest,
The young men in it sharing, like two students,
Who think they've all their fame ahead of them.

Now sunlight soothes the convalescent steps
Where the tourists never leave, but simply swap
Countries, friends and occasionally, their jeans.
Epiphany's over, and the filthy carpets
Rolled and trucked away to be drycleaned.
The landlady mops the hall again, re-lets
The rooms to the one tenant who'll never leave.
The rooms learn to be quiet. But youth can't learn.
It takes offence at barely lived-in bones,
Watches, distraught, its ownerless name become
Less than the rain, less than the grave that drowns
Each spring, in earth-rich violets, acts of love.

How Can the Living Mourn Enough?

A car fled by with a shriek
And a wail. The trees fell down
And the dead were their thick green leaves

But the river that ran between us
Was the bright, dangerous one.

Heads hung between shoulder-blades
Like February flowers, intent
On the darkness at their feet

But the river that ran between us
was the bright, dangerous one.

Fingers pushed against eyes
Because tears let loose would become
Another universe
At the exit of our own

But the river that ran between us
Was the bright, dangerous one.

My fingers bunched cold cloth,
My lips were bruised by bone:
I wished to God I was dead.
The only loved are the dead.

But the river that ran between us
Was the bright, dangerous one.

Clouding the Borders
(View from a train window, Belfast-Dublin, March 1992)

The small hills glow their rain-deep green
In March as, in November, those
That hugged the sky round Iniskeen,
And fixed clay padlocks on our shoes.

Newry – where clouds already trust
Frail bodies to the most distant peaks.
North's westering gaze relaxes. Mist
And heather do their vanishing tricks.

No shadow of this landscape's mine:
No stick of it estranges me.
Kavanagh sowed his hills with coin.
We share the transient legacy.

I watch a ewe fold round her lamb,
Her brownish, and its snowy, fleece
Making in soft, unbroken form
The oldest word for *native place*.

The Release

When the plane lifts for the last time in the damp, grey, tender air
Over the small fields neatly swirled with mowing-furrows,
The Friesian cattle jumbled like dominoes
By their rusty out-house, I shall take one harsh breath
And fall instantly to dust, a thousand years old
Like the sybil freed from the curse that had kept her from dying.

Imperial Carbon
(for Frankie Sewell)

>   i love my sounds my sounds
>   i love my sounds my sounds
>   i love my
>   i love my
>   sounds sounds sounds sounds
>   my my my my

West London nights, can I never stop coming back to you,
to your antediluvian plane trees, hanging on at the edge of the Green
where the still-companionable winos paddle the ring-pulls,
to your pavement-stash of papayas, red peppers, green peppers, plaintains
and your *English Pot's* peeping through curtains of coriander,
to your underpass charity-beds, your shop-doorway care-schemes,
where the one-to-one lesson is *spare us a bit of change of please*?
to the stains I don't want to explain, that will never wash out of the granite,
to your cop-cars stalled in the bottleneck, top-knots pulsating
but cool as a hand tapping time to the Kiss FM cauldron

>   i love my sounds my sounds
>   i love my sounds my sounds
>   i love my
>   i love my
>   sounds sounds sounds sounds
>   my my my my

West London nights, I've been stuck in your skies for a century,
waiting for clearance, for mercy, rolling from sunset to sunset,
thinking I'd missed you in Marrakesh, burnt you in Belfast
but gravity turned out a winner. I'm yours, so don't watch me,

style-eyes appraising as if I'm a stranger. Don't bet on it, baby.
I'll just redistribute my weight a bit, look, now I'm moving
a treat to your beat, I'm native, I've family connections
among the neurotics of Acton, my Great-Auntie Mabel's
out pruning the roses or painting the railings, though really
the roses aren't hers, nor the railings – *Baby, the fifties are forty years old now*

      i love my sounds my sounds
      i love my sounds my sounds
      i love my
      i love my
            sounds sounds sounds sounds
          my my my my

West London nights, if you want some identification,
the turbanned Muslim who keeps the off-licence knows me.
By the way, here's my key-of-the-door to my door of the day.
It leads to a well where the suicide speakers and systems
plunge in but keep swimming and scrabbling their way up the walls –
The Sultans of Ping, The Pogues, Petula, Deep Purple,
Vivaldi, Vysotsky – it leads to a holiday sadness
where I unpack those troubles, those overdue books and tall stories,
& my lungs ache after one night & no letters arrive & my typewriter always
needs the old kind of ribbon, a carbon, the buggers don't buy any more

      i love my sounds my sounds
      i love my sounds my sounds
      i love my
      i love my
            sounds sounds sounds sounds
          my my my my

FROM

BEST CHINA SKY

(1995)

Railway Lullaby

Little train-lover, there's pink sky in your speckled window.
There'll be a bridge, a bay, a child's sea, rippling:
All the details exactly as you'd have crayoned them.
I promise, I promise, to take you nowhere but home.
Lean your brow to the glass, I'll shake very gently.
The dragon's in his box, his breath pure puffs of snow.
Five decades later, my gas-dim stations
Will glow for you again behind your drifting eyes,
Go out, one by one, and be gone for ever.

Distances

When she falls backwards and meets the fire and the rain,
Last of her generation in this absurdly continent family,
Who will remember her, make a note of her overwhelming virtues,
And colourful evasions: who will truthfully describe
The face that always remained a stubborn child's,
Outstaring us with hardiness, impudence, fear:
Who will follow that stare to the father:
Who will stand at the grave and tell him she was hurt:
Who will show the mother and sister what they stole:
Who will ask the young man, disappointed and disappointing,
For one of those Valentine poems she smiled at and soon mislaid
(The ever-blue handwriting knotted with shyest self-declaration):
Who'll untangle the whiteness and free all the numerous shapes of her lips?

They will say, those greatest of aunts, those most-removed cousins
Whose names she almost remembered, that it's not up to them
Since she leaves a child: this is the child's business.

Don't look at me. I'm innocent. I'm not the one
To speak of the dead. I can't even speak to the living.

A Short Life with Gratispool

Another Soldier (1945)

The Baby's only ever snapped
In Daddy's arms, maybe to bring it home
How like as two peas their heads –
Though Daddy usually hides
Most of his in one of them forage-caps
Which, thankfully, this nipper won't have to wear –
Though Old Jeremiah, snooping in the pram,
Puts Mummy's back up, whining, 'What you got there?
    Another soldier?'

Workers' Playtime (1948)

There's no room for any more,
Mrs Moore. No more twinkles
In Daddy's eye. We try. We're on the Housing List.
The LCC Man wrinkles
His nose and says our drainage is A1,
And tons of space for another tot. But what
If it's a boy? And even if it's not,
Four in a room's a bit much.
So, hard luck, my old Dutch.
Soon as we can we'll follow the van.
Meanwhile, on with the show.
Turn the pages, stay as sweet as you are.
Mummy's gathering moonbeams home in a jar,
Daddy's singing Oh, Mein Papa,
And occasionally getting pissed,
And the Victory Baby's growing quick, quick, slow
Into an Only One. Ain't we got fun?

Scarlet Ribbons (1957)

'By twelve years old, everything is accomplished':
And now you can see
That, despite puff-sleeves and plaits like paint-brushes,
She's almost made up her mind to run away.

Though the snaps are posed and dead,
She's always almost in motion, half up a tree

Or straddling a bike. (You can't see,
Of course, but bike and ribbons are red.)

Soon as Dad's boxed the Brownie in, she's gone,
Pedalling up a speed
That makes a mockery of holding on.

No hands, no hands, watch me
Never never never going home for tea –
The loose ribbon flying its trickle of blood.

What Can I Say About My Grandfather?

You were born in March, good month for a blusterer.
Sixty years on, you lead me up the garden-path.
I am accused of beheading chrysanthemums.
Your rage convinces me, I'll sign the confession.

You turn dull cloth into suits in a cedar-wood shed.
I thump my ball at the side when the treadle's silent.
You've lost your famous account with the local convent.
You call the nuns *sharks* or *schneiders*. You call me *Saletch*, and *Missie*.

And you're in a rage because your baby son died.
And you're in a rage that you fathered 'an old woman's child'.
You say: 'Leave them on the window-sill, it's kinder.
You don't know when you're well-off, Missie. You're *all right*.'

You give me a fiver for passing the Scholarship.
But my craze for classical music's 'all put on'.
Your fingers swell. It's rheumatism. It's cancer.
The room where I played the piano becomes a sick-room.

Fierce light leaks under the door on the day of your funeral.
I stare in the hall-mirror, between the permed heads
Of the shop chrysanths, to study my Christmas sweater.
The sweater's hairy. Tight. I'm too old for Christmas.

I still hate remembering how you'd looked in bed.
You seemed so meek and thin, so bloody grateful.
Mum said: 'Pop was a first-class tailor and cutter.'
She'd never learned to sew. I've never believed in 'all right'.

Curriculum Poetica

Fountains are mostly light:
   A lough or tarn
Is the bland, incomparable
   Centrefold
Where breathless mountains yearn:
   Waterfalls dramatise
Earth's slightest *Oh*.
   But a stream, star-crossed,
Learns from the grass in its eyes
   Its profile's low.
Good enough to undazzle
   To the valley's level,
Still it's begrudged:
   Poor tinkling harper,
Pebble-prospector, tapster
   To witch and woad-man;
Hanger-out in the sticks,
   Grateful to be lodged
In cul-de-sacs blessed by
   Local voluminous slops.
How can it shine without sky?
   Without fire, foam over,
Lusty as loving-cups
   At the gods' table?
Mud is its pulse if mud
   Its course and kiddle,
Its art, a lament
   In curious hieroglyphs
Some clever-clogs will propose
   Is just the usual
Nattering on about
   Old roots, lost nymphs,
   And, any way, in prose.

England

It became so old,
It turned into a baby.
Teach it language, world.

From the Anglo-Saxon

Visit me again, one of these evenings.
Bring the gift of your small self, wisely hooded in wool,
The cold-blush winging your face, your eyes all flight.
Let my shadow befriend your slowly settling shyness.
Come without being called, without first calling.
I'll have the coal bright, the bottle cold, in no time.
Tap at my door, my window, I'll welcome you always –
I, who rise helplessly when the hollowest fingers
Flutter and flap at the letterbox-flap, let it go.

The Con

There's a knack but it's a bit of a con, like.
Don't ask me how I first twigged.
I prob'ly just want to kid meself
I always knew in me bones, like you did.

It wouldn't work now, that's for sure.
You'd say: you're kidding, mum, you're a fucking
Lezzie, you are,
If I told you how, when me tit, like,
Poked you in the mush, you'd do a double-take

And, quick as a flash, start sucking.
Even when I'd just got you fed,
You was still the same little clinger.
You come on like a limpet,
Even when I was just messing,
Just tickling your mush wiv me finger.

The Purr

When the boy knew he would never be listened to,
He fell asleep. This photograph confirms it:
Sleep in the boy's hand, reaching absent-hearted
To smooth the equable forehead of *Morsilka:*
Sleep in the purr we hear from her tabby frown,
Her barrelled rump, the powder-puffs of her haunches:
Sleep in the stern, near-masculine little profile
That denies itself a study, though the father
Shouts *Keep still,* and the glass eye glares: that denies
It could ever meet desire in a woman's look.
Morsilka, the boy's slyly parted lips
Are saying in cat-talk: *Morr, Morr, Morsilka.*

Dormancy's always attractive in a man –
Ask the rise-and-shine brigade of his admirers.
When he was 25, they'd have cut their names
In his skin to see the colour of his eyes –
Too late, by a hundred years!
He slept and slept, heavy as the Ukraine
In Europe's gut, as vodka on the liver,
Woke to father a child or two, fell away
To deeper sleep, his electrician's hands
Curling into their knowledgeable darkness.
Now when I pause, the last straggler, coldly
Equable in the beam of his sleeping vision,
I deem it a privilege not to be roughly parted,
And thrown on like a favourite dressing-gown,
But wear my own hand, guiltlessly and lightly,
And murmur self-talk: *Morr, Morr, Morsilka.*

Because my foam will never trouble him,
I leave it on his lips, free of charge.
Because it speaks my favourite language, silence,
I make sleep-love to his carved and studious back.
His rest and my retreat are perfect partners
Like boy and cat. Or, like a woman, found
By the only woman, when the long notes drawn
At length from one another's sleeping fur
Call back the dawn before we fell asleep
To bear the breaking day, that utterly clear
Wakefulness. *Morsilka,* our smiles say
Might be the first word of a flesh-language
We always knew but only now have tasted
In the strong original: *Morr, Morr, Morsilka.*

War and Soup

(i.m. Georgi Valentinovich Drobyshev, 1907-1995)

Rear-Admiral (retired)
Of the Soviet Fleet,
Your father, wearing
His soiled cook's
Babushkin halad,
Manhandles down
From its several hooks,
The ticklish weight
Of the Samurai sword.
Losing no face
To the chopping-board,
It flashes before you
What it did in the old days,
And still might do
If it weren't a ploughshare.

In a distant kitchen
Forty years later,
You recall the scare.
Sand-speckled mortars
Rear up for food
As we watch the slow fade
From suits to bellicose
Huddles of khaki.
There was a peace plan:
'Our hopes are high'...
Now I want to cry
Oh, let me see
That old sleight-of-hand –
Catastrophe twirled
To the windfall or wedding
Where good stories end!
But the telly glows
And roars. War wins.

The Samurai Chef
Keeps humming a tune
In your home-grown *skazka*.
He shifts a serene
And fabulous grip
As the sword makes deft
Green lacework of each
Noble napper.

Then he gathers the threads,
Lets them whirl and skip
In his own fairy-tale.
When the rumour is rich
Enough, he'll announce
The feast, and share,
Golden, unbloodied,
His bequest of soup-moons.

Even now, our spoons
Could kiss the breathing bowl.

Antrim Road Dream-House

The house hangs in the balance of our pockets,
As near, as far, as a remedy for cancer
Or love-in-absence, when we climb its core
To open rooms like gifts you rarely find
In January. A wing of summery light
Sheers up the highest wall, sinks to the raw
Wood of the staircase like a contract signed
In sky, a god's impulsive, longed-for answer.
Room, it says: room to repair homes broken
In haste, to be together and yet spacious,
Hospitable... The frame jolts forwards, then.
A wailing car warns us not to forget
What quality of mercy holds the keys
Of all this luxury, suspense, regret.

A Small Incendiary Device on Eglantine Avenue

After the bang, seven globes flowered softly
On their seven stems, curving
Tall above the roofs and the long street.
Hot grain ran down the night in fading tracks
And a stick with which some child
Had touched the sky, fluttered,
Star-burned, to our feet.

University Square Glue Groove

You are not fooled, as the young are often fooled,
By local sound effects, light–shows in the sky.
You'd never trust a tomorrow you couldn't buy
And clutch, close as a lover's face, as food,
Today. It looks like honey, it looks warm.
You chase it with an earful of some beat
Safe as bad news, the eternal bytes that swarm
Round blunt machines for making human meat,
And wave to say that everything's dead-on
From up there in your personal pleasure-dome.
Elsewhere, God's air is smoking round a ton
Of slithering bricks, but this is Sweet Life Street,
The customs tightly zipped as 'formal' dresses.
Our chestnut empires, steeply, aptly, fallen
Though they appear, aren't metaphors – just guesses.

Transfusion

How can you learn to treasure what you have?
Not by watching the wing of day's no–colour
Smearily born from dawn's attempt at blue
Like a ghost's ghost-child. Not by trying to count
All those closed eyes that might have cupped with love
The coldest light. Not by telling your story
In a different voice, because it might have been
A different story, had you not guessed too late.
This breath you gather daily to regret
All your cast bread, which rots, contemptuous
As a road-block on the one road you must take,
Will be treasure only if so deeply given,
That, on some border, miles, or a mile, away,
Feathers of air begin quivering, in pulse-time,
The shirt-front of a child, who may lie stiffly,
But seems, all the same, to point to the future
In an eager, jerky line, from soles to scalp.

The Stowaway

Shiver of air
In a mean angle of my sliding door,

My hand, a cup
That dances with you, tries to catch you up,

How many hits
And misses till you're crushed, your wings in bits?

Last night, the friend
Driving me home talked politics without end.

I got so dull,
Spooled in the thick of the theoretical;

I wanted grief
Even for the smeared fur, glazed disbelief

That cried in front of us:
Gods of the hedgerows, hell is also this!

This morning, you
Are the only nightmare I can make untrue:

Two lace-snippets, brown,
With one pink thread in each, to tease a bald pink clown,

A monster, blind
And heavy, not unkind, but not your kind,

Stunned by her own
Haphazard wits, admonished when you turn

Your shy skull-face
And trust a finger for your perching-place.

You pause, intent
On measuring with some secret instrument

Where on earth you are,
Relative to the moon or some moth-star.

What's in the mind
You wear outside your delicate head? The wind

May know, not I.
Has autumn touched your pulse, said *time to die?*

You won't find rest
In this back yard. A beech-wood suits you best,

Not human sighing:
Have roads and rooms destroyed your mood for flying

Or is what slows
Your take-off just the cross-wind of bad news,

The stench and sirening where-
Ever a human breath enters the atmosphere?

The Border Builder

No sooner had one come down
    Than he began building again.
My bricks, O my genuine bricks
    Made of my genuine blood!
What would we be without borders?
    So which one are you? he said
And stuck out his hand to me.
    Birth certificate? Passport?
Which side are you on, which side?
    Merrily he unrolled
Starry dendrons of wire
    To give his wall ears and eyes.
Qualifications? he said.
    Residence permit? Tattoo?
Which colour are you, which colour?
    No colour, he said, no good.
He took my only passport,
    He slammed it down on the wire.
My hand, O my genuine hand!
    This is a border, he said.
A border likes blood. Which side's
    Your bloody hand on, which side?

Variations on a Theme of July

I said *Where am I?*, thinking love said *Home.*
Instead, the light remarked on absent eyes.
Quicker, then, than midsummer could revise
Its plans, clouds take apart their moonstone houses,
A ship of iridescences went down
In slights and tears and lies.
The light is matt and noisy, now, marched flat.
Ridiculous flags stick out of windows. Lies.
(My native land could tell you just what size.)
They close in shock, the rock-scarred irises
Of never-golden hills, the blanching skies.
Where do they meet, these blues, this greenishness,
And mix the colour, *home*? Is *home* more lies?
This valley is a confluence of lies,
A conference of doubling, turning faces.
They tried to be true colours, but kept shifting
Climate, slewed by something that could kill,
Pretending kindness, suddenly unpretending.
I know these Sunday paramilitaries
Who build in stone inside a child, make grey
Warships that can't be lifted
By love nor sea. But what is lost, can't find
A name and cannot tell its colour, cries
In me, touching the nerve of a like mind.
Poisoner, realist, filterer, fantasist,
I bed and breathe, dress and re-dress the lies,
Homely as rain, all-coloured as young eyes.

Two Windowscapes

(for Jean Bleakney)

I

I watched a pulse of rainbow as it faded,
A sky-traced heart-beat, strong at first, but failing
And lost before my light-enchanted cones
Could mix the waves, my mind still lost for labels.
A rainbow's something else than seven plain tones.
It's less like paint than pastel, hazy, shy
With inbetween shades, namelessly embraided.
That's why it seems so human and so tender.
A rainbow surely views us through the eye
Through which it's viewed – the cataracts, the floaters,
The dazzle and the weather-scattered panes.

II

The sky was milk, plum-frozen to the bottle.
Suddenly, it had drained. The light went dead.
Something was slowly puzzling out the world,
Groping along strange airways, lost, and then
Boldly it took possession. Like a playground
My window teemed, all moving, all enchanted.

Original human sin – to be enchanted!
To see a freckled girl emerging where
The laurel glowered – north her safe house, Apollo
Slack in Ash Wednesday shrouds – to say it's hope
Or faith, at least, in the wingbeat of that sparrow
Who skims the yard wall, shivers so strongly up
Through the caves and pantries of cotoneaster,
It seems she's got a site marked out, already
Becoming fact among the water-nests
The snow keeps fixing and dissolving there.

The First Storytellers

They said there was a house, and something in it
Formed by the satin-finish light would give
An indoor-courtyard, by the dusky sift
Of irons welcoming fire, and duckdown, sleep.
There was a rind as well, where pigeons shuffled
And shook their iris ruffs, and lived aslant,
Happy as slates, as clouds in a cloudy heap.
Some say that Time had found a place to live,
But Earth would not move in, so no one did,
Though there was flesh, and blood, and voice, and feeling,
As the first frightened witnesses declared,
A hand in water, a shadow on the ceiling,
Senses that knew light died each day, and grieved
And invented a demon to be tender with.

True North

Here, every man claims to have a brother.
The women say nothing.
Men kiss each other's faces with their fists
Till womanish blood flows.
The ladies know that's foolish.
They put a cheek to a cheek to keep it cold.
Here, scholars agree
'Cunt' is a generic noun,
So how can a poet possess one?
Here, women use themselves
As scissors, files, dividers, compasses.
They make out they're not murdering each other.

The Close Reader

Calmly and very carefully, like a thief
Of the old school, silk-fingered in the drawer
He'll leave not quite just-so in the master bedroom,
I check each word until a troubling, low
Vibration earths it, and the author's voice
Sing-songs, harsh and playful, from the drive.
I go on searching, even as I hear
The lighter footsteps, innocent on the stairs.
Face meets astounded face. But nothing shatters...
I move back to the drawer. Carefully, calmly,
I turn the jewels to light them with reflections:
The husband-soiled, husband-enchanted lips,
The sometimes eager, sometimes clouded, eyes.

The Safest Grazing

The faults in your secret, most unwashable linen:
A dot of iron-mould, a thread of hair,
The crumpled proof love packed you without care;
A wax seal, shiny with old needle-pain:

Is there no dusk so kind you'd release its hills
To these small scapegoats, roam with them to where
A thirst might lose itself in thirsty ripples,
And blushes close both eyes, or sly and lively,
Notice the look that declares their causes lovely?

Peat Fire

I broke into archaeology, uncorked
Death-champagne, gold fizz for the black throat,
But all that's left in my small-hours hearth is flaked
Skin from her rough heels, and her tattered sandals.

Song of the Non-Existent

This is the hour between dog and wolf, when the first
Anxiety walks across to the polished counter,
And the sky becomes lighter and darker at the same time,
And the moon, if it shows, is a pale, inessential detail

Because this is the hour of glass, the age of souls;
Gold is in every leaf, and to walk in the glow
Between traceries is to be among the angels:
This is the page on which you write the word 'angels'

And the muse, though stern, doesn't flinch: when impotent wings
Of learning stretch to the cloudiest stony hill:
This is the net of desire, where something adrift and homeless
Is caught and pronounces itself a nightingale.

This is the wolf's hour, after all; he turns it between his teeth:
The watery city thickens, blackens: all that the angels leave
Is this: your sudden reluctance to remember
How hard it was, and how beautiful, to live.

To the Spirit of My House

By the fire for the last time in Maryville Avenue,
Will I sit watching your hair unscroll in the flame?
Your hair's not red, not a mass of flowing curl,
Though perhaps it was, when you were a little girl:
Nevertheless, you brought to my hearth one night
Your paler colours, flowing to fill your name,
And, as you left, the coals seemed sunk in regret.
The fire has known ever since how to conjure you.

And when I eat my last meal at the book-strewn table,
Carelessly heaping rice from the foil tray,
Will I glance up and find you opposite me,
A guest, reduced to fast food by an unplanned visit?
Will one of us remark – 'Not too bad, is it,
Considering it's the local take-away?' –
And, smiling, suggest we make the informal a habit –
Two women who rarely cook, and never feel noble.

And when I go to my last sleep under this roof-space,
Will I think how a miracle just might have occurred,
Though miracles don't exist in any world
I've ever lived in, and find you casually pressed
To me, no edge, no softness, uncaressed?
Dazed with belief and disbelief, shall I stroke
Your crisp, un-flame-like hair, shall I lie awake
To study the miracle of a sleeping face?

And when I've shrunk it to boxes, this life I had,
Will I slam the door for the last time, locking you in
Firmly, leaving you ample time for despair,
While the orchard screams, and the dryads rend their clothing?
Will you tremble slowly to dust, and then to air?
Will I at last be alone, moving freely, breathing –
Or, as I turn the new key, sense something familiar
And wounding there, and be idiotically glad?

Math, Remembering

From long-stemmed words with their tender, watery perfumes,
I, no god, somehow created a woman.
For the first time, magic was simple.
I wondered: had I not known this all along?

But my flowers were only roots, sticky with soil,
Screaming in ugly voices – *we are not yours.*
Stems became bony, petals sharpened and fledged
And drew on my skin with long, scarlet claws.

To Blodeuwedd, Flying

Though hidden from me now, you're changing as if
The weathers of my heart still poured across your face,
And my hand-made sighs kept rearranging you.
What use are the winds of absence, strong and scentless,
When you constantly swing round like the month of April,
Flaunting different petals, letting me touch you
More artfully and hopelessly than ever
For having let you loose from earthly keeping.

Flauer-Mush

Cradle-snatched, done up like a dog's dinner,
    Leaves, buds, stalks an all
        Shoved in the kisser
Of some Lord Muck I never clapped eyes on before,
That can't tell a buncha dandelions from a gorse-bush,

I'm soon browned off being 'is precious Flauer-Mush,
    Trimming me follicles, touching up me roots,
Balancing bloody great jew-drops on me eyeballs,
    Poncing around in clothes
And sniffing meself and forever squirting me doodahs.

'E never fancied me. So when yours truly
    Feels Muvver Erf comming on strong,
        And, *Duckie*, she says wivver eyes, *Come back to nature!*
        I says to is Lorship, *So long!*
        And dig me roots in. Lovely.

I'm *the flower of the oak and the broom and the meadow-sweet*
    Till it seems I got 'old of the wrong end of the stick
        And I'm sweet Fanny Adams. Chucked.
    Blow me! The glamour puss the lads lapped up
        Given the bird. Tweet tweet.

Ole Wiz pulls out me ribs, snaps 'em in two, makes wings.
    Go on, get lost! 'e says. I don't need asking twice.
        I'm staggering up into space,
        Screaming blue murder, shitting
White, dropping bits an bobs from me brain an fings.

Now the cockeyed buggers've got me where they always wanted.
        I'm mangey an gory an queer,
    Old Flauer-Mush, off me rocker, outa me tree
And a bird into the bargain – well – I ask you –
    A bleedin owl – a bloomin old softie like me!

Tír Fá Tonn

I was plunged in your dampest mood, my face had pearled over
Like the skin of an aeroplane suddenly scarfed by cloud.
    A second higher, I found your shining mirror.
Rose-petals stained us, as if we had swallowed too quickly
    Too much new wine, and we were a compact, opened
Shyly as Venus's shell. Well, that day's skin is all dust now.
    We've rendered to Cloacina, who weaves the world,
The gifts that are hers, and the troubled streams of those fingers
    I stilled without touch, have become the geologist's nightmare –
    A rock-formation unique to vanished islands.

Best China Sky

A primrose crane, a slope of ochre stacks,
Stencilled on tissue-thin
Blue, and, flung between
These worlds, a sword-flash rainbow,
The cloud it lies against,
Metallic as its topmost skin,
And, round the eyes of hills,
The tender bluish-green
That quickly yellows.

The prism comes and goes:
Wonderful stain, transparency of art!
A smoke-wraith sails right through it.
But now it strengthens, glows and braves its span,
You'd think it was the rim
Of some resplendent turquoise plate,
Offering hills and cranes and streets and us
Fancies designed to melt
As our fingers touched them.

Prayer for Belfast

Night, be starry-sensed for her,
Your bitter frost be fleece to her.
Comb the vale, slow mist, for her.
Lough, be a muscle, tensed for her.

And coals, the only fire in her,
And rain, the only news of her.
Small hills, keep sisters' eyes on her.
Be reticent, desire for her.

Go, stories, leave the breath in her,
The last word to be said by her,
And leave no heart for dead in her.
Steer this ship of dread from her.

No husband lift a hand to her,
No daughter shut the blind on her.
May sails be sewn, seeds grown, for her.
May every kiss be kind to her.

Riddle

Moving and still
I try to fill
The space I had –
An inch of hair,
Erect with fear,
The rest, melted.

Portent

Over patches of bloom that might be frost, or where frost lately died,
The little bird runs like a rumour, dark as the road, with a snow-streaked side.

Lament

You'll die, and never again will my lips have touched you,
Your living mouth, nor my sleep have known such stillness.
Like a slow wave, phosphorescent, your voice will have risen,
Will have fallen, too far off to have left my thoughts shining.
Never again, from your vivid, familiar cursive,
Will my name have leapt, like a loved child, into my arms,
So that I silently tell you: though *love* means anything, nothing,
In your hand it's my life. Nor will I wake as your birthday
Dawns on my powers of blessing, desires all the colours
Most true to your faithless iris. And still that day
Will come back and tear wound after wound in the calendar,
But you will have died. Or I'll have. What's the difference
    In the eternal absence of all cherishings?

Sickbed

I would have washed flowers for you.
I would have washed water for you.
I would have fed you sunlight from the bowl.
Too neat. Too simple. You were already ill
From the words I couldn't wash, their being true.

Literacy

Only once, not asleep, I met you.
  A book gazed into your face.
  Your woolly chrysalis hung
  At your side, untrembling as
    Your 'heaviest of flowers'.

When you sensed I was near, and looked up,
  Your eyes were between-coloured
  From the world of names. Your smile.
  Sightlessly kind, and your blush
    Belonged there, not to me.

Only once, not dreaming, I found you,
    So still, I could have touched you.
    If I were that book, I thought,
    That fingered, lingering page,
      Not this human nothing...

Circle

Suppose God only imagined Lucifer's slight
But, locked in a mask of injury, so revised him,
He, God-adoring, fell from the perfect dawn
That fleshed and winged him, into perfect night.
Suppose you are Lucifer, who were thus rewarded,
And suddenly the night is a dawn of flame.
They'll say you hurled the torches out of vengeance,
But you, confused, half-shining, will repeat
That everything you burned you burned for light.

Months

1 *Months as Mirrors*

September's light falls so like May's,
    You could forget the year had moved
At its grave, water-burdened pace,
    From, not towards, the place it loved,

And, moving, stretches hope too thin
    To bear a moment's fantasy
Where dead leaves fill their hearts with green
    And flock home to a sun-caged tree.

My last children tip forwards, as if for bunny-hops,
Big forehead moons to little shapeless knees.
They had just begun to tumble into nowhere,
Still wrapped in their nesting-silk, when something froze them,
And they die into this photograph I'm making
From a sealed box and a last thread of mucus.

Death of an Afternoon Woman

Something is pushing them
To the sides of their own lives
        PHILIP LARKIN, 'Afternoons'

A hand, was it? Or something heavier,
Swooping with the down-swing,
Its shoes packed with meat
And little bones chipped from my own?
At first I didn't resist:
I'd be kicked anywhere,
Sit smiling on the farthest seat.
Was life mine to be lived?
Almost against my will,
As the chain-swings swooped, I heard
The seas divide.
I was walking a paper stillness,
A perfect centre parting
Through the roar of weather.
My life? Thanks. I'll rhyme it.
I'll keep it.
Keepers losers, they whispered
And I woke up.
If this is my house, it's mist,
If this is my land, water,
Constantly traversed
By miniature heels, child-hands,
Wide open, chainless.
The force I feared is so small,
I could catch it in a caress
And run with it to wherever
It tells me our home is.

The Amateur Electrician

Engineers make good lovers, they know how the body works
And with tender skill arrange small tributes and pleasures.
I'm no engineer, but I understand low forms of practical magic.
I'd give you a city Christmas, fountains of colour, lacings of wind-shivered
        brilliance,
If you would trust me to be your electrician.
But if you just wanted to sleep undisturbed in your deep country nightfall
Of fading rush-light and stars, that would be fine with me, too.

The Hag of Beare in Limerick

Suddenly, most of me's useless,
My cunt, unattended and juiceless,
   My tits, never sucked,
   My thermostat, fucked,
And my brain, like old Newsletters, newsless.

From a Conversation During Divorce

It's cold, you say, the house.
Yes, of course I'll go back one day,
Visit, that is. But the house

Will be cold, just as you say.
Two people have left home,
One of them me, and one

Our youngest child. So of course
It's cold, just as you say,
And big, too, bigger at least

Than it was with everyone there.
Don't think I don't think about you
Being cold in a house that size,

A house that gets bigger, too,
And colder each time I dare
Think about you and the house.

It used to be warm in the days
Before I decided to go,
And it didn't seem big at all,

In fact, it was rather small,
Which is partly the reason I...
Don't keep on asking me why

And telling me how it is
In the house. I don't want to know.
How can I go back, how can I

Even visit a house that size,
And getting bigger each minute
With all the cold rooms in it?

The Resignation

The mother we were free to hate is dead.
The last we saw of her, her face was breaking:
Only the palace of her hair still stood.
Her sons threw off their sullenness and cheered.
Her daughters, too, denied their hearts were aching.
We knew she'd leave us nothing. She loved men,
Next to herself, and we were none of hers.
But, yes, we thought her of some consequence –
Stronger than us, because she'd had to be;
Stronger than men. This proves the fallacy.
Her triumph, like her wealth, was all men's making,
And now she's in their funny cupboard world,
Upside down, her voice a box of holes,
Blue sparklers jammed in the hollow of her head,
While they charge round the room with guns and shrieking,
And swear they'd rather die than play with dolls.

Summer Time Begins

(for Joan Newmann)

In a surprise of light
My chimney props its shadow
On the house-front opposite,
And the shadow-stack lets flow
An upward skitter
Of dirty curls, unstable
As local crosswinds.
If smoke and shadow-smoke
Changed place, how could we tell?
And which sign to trust:
The hills' milky sheaves
Of blizzard, swept low
By the gale's cutter,
Or the slow-widening
Harebell dusk that says
Kind days will soon come
Newly relaxing through
Each loaf-small home,
No smoke, no shadow-fire
Riddling, deriding,
But all we dared hope for
Made tangible: a second
Chance, an extra hour?

About the Jews

(from the Russian of Boris Slutsky)

Jews don't plant wheat.
Jews trade in corner-shops.
Jews go bald earlier.
More Jews are thieves than cops.

Jews are adventurers,
No good at war.
Ivan fights in the trenches.
Abram minds the store.

I've heard it since my childhood
And soon I'll be decrepit.
Still I can't escape it:
The chant of 'Jews, Jews'.

I've never been in trade.
I've never stolen, once.
I carry this damned race
Inside like a disease.

The bullets didn't get me
Which only goes to prove
None of the Jews was shot.
They all came back alive.

1950

(from the Russian of Evgeny Rein)

The cable-car rises, a red-hot blaze, to the Sanatorium Frunze
(Named after Ordjonokidze), sends a mirror of light to the coast-road.
There's plenty of choice in the shops here – from eighths of litres to halves.
On your left, the Diplomat's Rest House. Journalists go straight ahead.
We're not far from Sochi. I'm seeing all this for the very first time.
Wearing my jersey-knit trunks with the sky-blue *Dynamo* band,
I lounge in the shade of a beach-umbrella, or hurl myself through the frontline
Of the quarrelsome breakers pitched steadily over the sand
By some Lord of the median term, some Black Sea spirit,

Looking out of the depths at the twentieth-century's backside.
There's womanly flesh in abundance – milk, terracotta, chocolate,
But the tastiest colour by far is that of a dumpling, deep-fried.
Everything's fine and appalling, and something is almost made clear.
Around sunset, a sense of foreboding creeps out of the Caucasus.
Closing your eyes, you're alarmed when dull, reddish pimples appear
In the lids like an eczema-rash, or some kind of horrible pox.
Koba's sun is still high; over Moscow and Ritsa, its zenith.
This same mountain eagle sees all, his attention is double-bright.
Whatever you know, protect. Keep your head down. Cherish
Yourself like your sight.

Here I Am

(from the Russian of Bella Akhmadulina)

Here I am at two in the afternoon,
Held up by the midwife like a trophy.
Lutes play over my head, fairy-wands
Tickle me. All my soul understands
Is a flood of golden colour; here I am
On a burning day the summer before the War,
Gazing around at the beautiful creation.
With lullabyes and Pushkin ('The Snowstorm'),
I get into the habit of being alive.
But here I am, ruined by war, alas,
Subject to Ufa's gloomy supervision.
Winter and hospital, how white they are!
I notice that I haven't died. Those called
Instead, are blurry faces in the clouds.
Here I am, brimming with eagerness,
Ugly, bluish, body just set free,
Alert to something tinier than a sound.
Not until later will I value this
Habit of hearing an eternal roll-call
Of nameless things in my name-giving soul.
Here I am, decked in purple, haughty,
Young and fat. But I have trained my mouth
To shape the smile of a poet before death.
There is a game between word and word
That's like the trembling between heart and heart.
The single obligation is to trace it
Flowingly, with a casual, careful art.

These words are bride and bridegroom. Here am I
Declaiming, chuckling like a village priest
Who prays the secret union will be blest.
That's why the good fairies scatter whispers
And laughter. I'm extraordinary, marked out
By my forehead, my singer's curving throat!
I love these marks of singularity.
My hand dashes off like a young hound
After her prey, bringing it to the ground.
Here I am. But my soul stops. I can't move.
I curse and cry. Let the page stay white!
Even though it was given me from above,
My task could not be honourably completed.
I bend my neck to the torment of a harness.
How others weave their words, I couldn't say.
I haven't got the nerve, the craftiness.
Leave me alone. A little person, twin
Of everyone alive, here I am
Dozing on the train, my nodding face
Homely against my bag. I've little fame,
Thank God, and no more fortune than my neighbour.
I'm with my weary fellow-citizens,
Flesh of their flesh. It's good. Last in the queue
That stretches endlessly from the cashier's
In shops, cinemas, stations, I'm the one
After the cheeky youth and the warm-shawled
Old woman, merging with them like a word
From my language and a word from theirs.

The Stone Butterfly

(for Kelsey & Rebecca)

Slow days, as a life prepares
To leave, discarding all
But its lightest necessaries.
Once we followed it
Through vivid stories, woven with our own.
We called it *Mum* or *Gran*, intimately.
Now, tired of our familiarity,
The life shifts, moves on
To a part we can barely read,

A hard, mysterious page, on which we glimpse
A figure so unselfconscious,
It could well be the long-ago child,
Scolded early to bed in her flowered nightdress.
The V-neck straggles across
The bare, innocent breast-bone,
The face, a kind of violence
To the face we expected, almost
As the child's must have been –
Flung open in grief or fury.
Fixed, now, beyond soothing.

But these are appearances, partial
Views from where we sit,
Tangled in life, still bound
By its tentative aesthetics.
The rich, layered protein bundle
Was meant to unfold, has always been unfolding.
When the molecules first talked and had ideas
That would be this particular person,
They allowed the heart a pause,
A moment's doubt for every great iamb,
And cells, already orphaned,
Were drifting from the untouched skin of the new.
The losses, heavier now,
May seem more soul-like:
A little blood that darkens
In the crook of the catheter,
Hunger, proprieties, the speakable words.
But this is her soul, too, this make-do-and-mend,
This Londoner's painful wit
That almost cheats each shortage
By a shrug, a *good riddance*,
And the sudden panic when
The black-out curtain slips.
Her hands fly into the night, then, signalling,
Lost and raw as fledglings tossed on a wind
To practise, until space
Becomes feathered, homelier.

That's when the slow day slows
Again, curves inwards.
We arrive again, and find
The curtains have closed ranks,
Broody as women in smocks
Waiting delayed appointments, the bare

Night-bulb burning as blue
As the dry blue dawn, and on other, less smooth pillows,
Eyes making out the grown-up shapes of day,
The dice swept back into the misty dream-cup.
She travels with quiet hands now,
And has taken only the smallest morning with her
For the sharp descent that cannot
Get easier.

But it does get easier:
The bundle almost peeled, only a little
Breath still saved in the lining,
To be spent in precise measures
Like childbed breath, but less,
Much less of it. And we must concentrate
On a new, exacter climb,
Feeling for toe-hold, stooping
Sometimes to pick up a keepsake,
Greedy now we know how small and cool
A hand becomes, a shell
Though we bind it, warm it, in our drowning fingers.

There will be harder things:
Keys that open wounds, rings to be counted,
Skins to be cast or worn.
Ghosts will leave dust or mist on the least expected
Surfaces: an envelope, which states
In familiar wobbly ovals
And swoops of cursive: *everything in order.*
And at once the bent white head and aching fingers
Will be an image I
Wipe off like tears, freeing
Something clear and achieved, its pride, its kindness:
The mind-thread glistening black
And alive as the veins on wings,
As if an envelope could be
That brilliant, weightless life she always wanted –
A butterfly. A manila butterfly.

For a time, we'll throw the dream-dice
And thoughts will flutter and play
Over a different horizon.
The world, we'll say, is sufficiently beyond us.
Rich postcards will arrive
From Eternity, a resort
Not yet built, but scripting its foundations

In super-matter, somewhere.
So we'll fly as far as we know
And come back sad, because gravity
Seems to own every airline,
And sit like children again
Being shown how to read
One more time, till slowly
Words become things, things become words, souls
And proteins pool their resources
And matter's highest kite –
Poetry, love, whatever –
Is tenderly reeled in through the dusk. Never mind.

Large-grained, each moment now
Widens, becomes a breath,
A sip of breath, brought
In a cup, by a machine,
But work for the whole feather-weight musculature,
The hand pulling from mine, a tiny pull,
As the lungs are forced to accept it
Again, again,
That punch of oxygen
Which starts the crying, rhymes the story on
And on, through chapters of plot
And counter-plot, into flashback
And metaphor, until wordless,
Hard-won, thread-like whispers are all that remains.

The day retreats a step.
The eyes close, choosing,
With sweet honesty,
To make it night. And still
An after-thought, an ellipsis,
The tongue in breath-space, trembling
As if it could offer us
A small 'and then'. And then
The forehead, huge and distant,
Suddenly whiter and, though quickly pressed
By lips, much farther away.

How can we say what happened? What we saw
Is all that can be said.
We can wish, of course, so fiercely
We nearly pray: that the body forgot to feel
How hard breath was, that the grace of all it had loved
Was received in every cell.

But for you and me, the end
Of the story is still guesswork,
And it's only my search for a not-unhappy full-stop
If I say how it seemed:
That something slipped very quietly
And unhesitatingly over

The edge of the day. It didn't
Flutter, fan itself up
To the lapis gates, the open halls of nectar
But fell like a stone, a fruit-stone, newly folded
To re-unfold, its contract with the earth
Binding as that of the sky-winged butterfly,
And death, no less than flight,
A natural miracle.

FROM

HOLDING PATTERN

(1998)

Kilkenny Castle

Over the bridge it appeared –
a castle grown from the same mild stone,
    rounding a net of fine rain –
a castle that gazed, shivering, back from the river.
    I crept between those walls
of stone and stone-brown water
    where small swans paused and circled,
and climbed to the cup-shaped window
    of a high, lit room.
Ancestral portraits slanted looks at me,
    but I was not besieged.
I wore the castle as if it were mine,
    the breadth of its kingdom fallen
beneath my gold-dressed hands
    that were white like swans, and clean,
though the rain hung dark with twilight
    and the moss deepened on paths
between the listing black headstones
    down in St Canice's churchyard.

1976

My Dark Windows

1

The voice said: *Come on in.*
Here are your naturalisation
Papers. You're one of the chosen
Few. Wilkommen. Bienvenue.
Welcome to the land of the frozen-
Out. And I went on in.

2

Wiping her hands in the Arrivals Hall ladies,
She sighs to me in the mirror: 'Grand to be home!'
In another mood I'd smile: 'It certainly is.'
In another, I'd joke: 'It's grand *not* to be home.'
But today my tongue has found a troublesome root
Which it's bound to touch and touch till the point of pain.
I simply shrug and refuse to demonstrate
How different 'home' is on her lips, and on mine.

3

The slow dawn of familiarities:
Walking the length of a street too sparsely peopled
For the victory cut of its buildings:
Even at dusk, the complexions
Of stone and glass perilously heightened
As if the sea had washed them once and might
Come back: finding my pen
In the same place under the bed where it rolled
Three weeks ago: nothing at all to keep me
From language – neither the sound nor the silence, *home*.

A Hiccup in the History of Belfast

In my new city street-plan, the big names
Try to slip through the pages incognito,
Blending with the crowd. I corner them
Heartlessly: 'I've seen you on the news,
Sobbing, with rain and soldiers in your hair,
By the burning takeaways and the black taxis!'
They look askance and beg to be let go.
I stand and gasp the legendary air.

I make things stranger making them familiar,
Taking the plunge past windows in steel vests
Where a boxed blowlamp and a sponge seem settled
For life on a cardigan's well-buttoned breasts.
I'm served with rough aplomb, and think I'm poorer
Only because I took the reddish-tan
Ulster Bank five for a Bank of England ten.

When I get lost, it's on some new estate,
Fences hugged to the end of every path.
A danger to cartography, I'm met
By a man with food and anger in his mouth.
'Looking for somebody?' He gives no hint
Of registering my accent and odd manner,
But clears the air, shaping the road I want,
Then saunters back to his gate and watches me –
The afternoon's bad news that proved to be
Merely a hiccup in its Sunday dinner.

November 1991

St Peter's Welcomes the Peace Walkers

Mini-skirted sixth-formers smile in the doorway,
Rattling donated boxes of Tunnock's Caramel Wafers.
Across the hall, their mothers and grandmothers
(The kind of women churchmen of all colours
Call 'our ministering angels') work with teapots.
The young priest welcomes the Methodists from the Shankill:
'We even painted the walls, look – just for you!'

I sit with two crisp-denimed Catholic women.
And soon we're friends, chatting about 'Queen's':
Maybe I've come across their student-children?
An older woman hovers, wants to join in
But won't sit down. She says she's not a marcher,
So it's not right: displays her ruined slippers.

'I'm on three types of pills,' she says, 'It's dreadful,
So it is. Abyssinia Street. A hell-hole.
D'you really like Belfast? Are you going to be staying?
I'm frightened to go out.'
                              'Couldn't you move,'
One of the women says kindly, 'to the suburbs?'

Something collapses in the long silence.
Call it religion. Say what emerges, naked
And guileless as the orange walls, is Class.

A Singer Too Soon
(in memoriam J.S.)

March has no summer manners.
The fragrance of grass at first cut
Is the gale's first hostage.

Unwillingly solo beside
The lough, the little bird
Has risked the gold of his life.

But the frost claws back the whole bet.
There will be no feast, no nest.
Or not today. And never for you, bright blackbird.

Boating in a Border County

Windless January dawn: the long rose-gold
Pulse across the lough so regular
It might have been an athlete's ECG.
The air glowed blue; even in the shed
Something filled the muddy pane like sky
Dreaming of itself.
                              You said: 'Too heavy!'
'Och, no,' the owner said. 'But she wants cleaned.
She's not been touched the year.' You both kept on,
But I kept on against the two of you,
Woman enough, for once, to get my way.

The oars slither fractiously as you struggle
To get a grip, and then they're under orders,
The boat tastes open water, and we're moving
Sweet as a late quartet's deep-carved legato.
Your gaze relaxes past me into pleasure.
This is your art, reflexive as the waves,
And like an art ingrained the shore goes with us,
Shuffling contours, altering a tree line,
Losing one white farm, adding another,
But never past redemption, as we steer
Horizonwards, our quest, of course, an island.

Those distant, sombre, unrequiting islands! –
Mythic as winter wheat till we get near
And watch them fall apart like old rush-mats,
Such sloppy nests as wouldn't house a duck egg.
But when at last one offers foothold, homesick
Almost at once, we roam in circles, back
Through the thin coppice to our sidling craft
And there we broach the picnic like two babies,
Dandled, replete with liquidness and light.

We barely noticed, but a trail of mesh,
A few splintery stakes, have placed us south
Of where we woke, doubled our emigration.
I want to smile, imagining contraband
So simply shipped, but when I glance across
To see your happiness, that other border,
As vague, as definite, shivers between us:
The soul stain of your cancer diagnosis.

A turn so sharply wrong ruined our maps,
Roughed up our boat at first and nearly sank us.
Today, it marries us. The shudder passes,
And it's as if you've rowed us out to where
The future meets us, settling round our breath.
Enough, it sighs, enough!
Our precious future...
It was a form of childhood; we could leave it
On such a day, in such circumference.

Fermanagh, 1995

Winter Travel

On the dirtiest winter nights they keep arriving;
Bringing the smell of snow, they squeeze themselves in
At the too-few miniature tables, flushed with achievement,
Or queue for carry-outs, collars ear-high and dripping,
Shuffling a slushy thaw right back to the painted curbstones.
The cars swap spaces, the counter girls swerve and signal
Faster, have to lean farther, have to dig deeper
To fill the gleaming flavourscoops, build up the pokes and cartons
With doubles and triples of carefully picked, fairly sick, combinations:
And in tucked-away terraces all over town, where the sleet
Is flowing in heavier folds and not even a robin
Would dare his faint rose ember, his watery winter flute,
Where Advent is fairy-lit advert, the slow van stops and peals
A humdinger peal of a glockenspiel reel that unwraps
The children from the TV sets, hurries the grownups, shivering,
Grumbling, searching their purses, beginning to die
All the same for the tooth-shocking, tongue-tricking, slippily swift,
Yet measured, dissolve. Yes, pleasure is snatched like a windfall
These nights when the city goes dancing in the ballroom of ice cream.

Absent Weatherwomen

I'd like to believe your hills controlled the weather.
I don't disbelieve. I know the clouds
That bloom and fade faster than weekend bruises
Are not marshalled by the weathermen
Nor the military, for all their satellites
And calculation. Those that squeeze their eyes
Tearful with prayer don't cause the mists to thicken.
I know the harebell dawn is not God smiling
Encouragement to his momentary chosen,
And that it isn't women that cause the rain
To daub and chill this city in its heartbreak
Maytime – nor the absence of those women.

The Island

Its contour rises softly as the death wish
When the Gartan mother sings her lullaby.
Belatedly you learn all seas confess

This landfall, though some blame it on the sky.
The harbour's rumoured safe as flax. But first
Some fate or fury, not to be confused

With Scylla and Charybdis, lesser Greeks,
Must check your passport and may hurl you starboard
To the gut-strewn kippering sheds of Nemesis.

That's why I pace the shore, procrastinating
With needles, mermen, dockside politics,
So Englishly. I do like being beside

The seaside but the sea's another thing.
One mouth could sing my uncertain own to it
Multas per gentes, kiss goodbye to bookish
Skills like divination and safe sex.

Characters

So often, as day ends,
It's not to lamp-warmed faces we return,
Not to our hungry friends,
But to the children of imagination.
They live in us like memories,
And yet belong to nowhere we could name
In our own stories.
They can't converse
Except by weaving patterns like their sun –
A strange, interior sun
Across their strange, dark-edged, interior days –
Yet we know their voices.
Lock both doors, now, curtain the river. Night
In real-time, with its tracer fire
Of meetings and desire,
They've learned, like us, to hate.
Permit them this, their only happiness
Of knowing they became our only light.

White-watching in Cork City
(for Sinn Féin)

Seagulls that sipped
The outflow, searched the tip,
Lift shining caps and sleeves
For the sun's approval.
Even on Ring Mahon strand,
You could fill sieves
With clean shell-petals.
Is nature a witch?
Abused and weary, still
Her whites excel,
Shine without bleach.
But what of these
Fine human feathers –
The satin alphas,
The snowy-braided
Manes, the lamp post doves
That daintily fly down

Onto sticks paraded
By our local dreamers,
Wearing their spring fleece:
How white is their peace?

March 1996

A Day in the Life of Farmer Dream

In the morning light I stand outside my limits,
With equanimity survey the fields,
The thorn-hemmed acres that I call my land.
Some are ploughed, some newly sown, some thick
Already with astonishing wheat: some wait
Under a tat of kelp, or bask in clover.
In the morning light I lightly weigh my tasks:
A strong-jawed tractor stands on the hilltop,
The day burns to be off, time is enormous.
What happens in between I couldn't say,
But the grass has grown, and I return on foot,
A tinker or a tourist, one who gambled
Perhaps, or dawdled over skip and scrapyard,
Or slept because the blue was cradle-curved,
And ownership a gleam under a shawl.
Back west, the lying day projects its harvest
Of goldshine; dew is deepening round each stone,
And mist and I will climb the hill, soon, seeking
A house that wears the plume of our dissolving.

Thirst For Green

> *The trees are coming into leaf*
> *Like something almost being said...*
>   PHILIP LARKIN,
>   'The Trees'

Now their dreams are letting them through to the top of their wet black sleep
Though nothing has heard them stir yet. Only the hyacinths beading
The bed-fringe of each gaunt Kali, patient to match

Five o'clock's lavender cloud, and, along the square,
The lights coming on in the seminar rooms a little later each week
Seem to remember the trees will soon be awake.

It's easy to measure, still, the uneasy length of that street,
From the windows arched like prayers round the heavily pencilled
Shamrock and tudor rose, to the wish that, whatever occurred
In my chest, it was less like the trapdoor drop when the noose
Drags up a life in its fullness for the last breaking,
And hemp says to bone: your incident is closed.

If it had just been a season, a hibernation,
This grief-time, why is it growing, why is it rhyming with leaf-time?
There should be haulage and transport, the great distribution of sap
Flowing like silk through the restless loom of veins:
The story was written in water, I'd say, but listen, it rebegins
With a sigh from the root to the crown's wind-shaken, smoky tip.

But something as tight as despair winds round the throats of these thoughts.
Pathogens crowd where a thirst is disturbed by rain.
Is something wrong with the rain? It pales, refusing to climb
Towards the clamped buds in their dream of making light.
And then I remember: elms are cursed, spoor-thick with an old disease.
And the spring crawls in like nothing on earth, with no leaf-heraldries.

An Answer

How perilous is it to choose
Not to love the life we're shown?
SEAMUS HEANEY
'Badgers'

Perilous as two planes on one flight path,
As the cry of a mother for her mother, lost,
As faith in a man who's sleeping with his past,
As the Bay of Biscay in an inflatable life raft.
When, like a soldier, you ran from one collapsed
Study-house to the next, you sinned against
The protocol of an ambitious host,
But not, I think, against the Holy Ghost.

Two Belfast Beasts

1 *Paranoia*

Yes, all roads lead to an Ulster Bank or a hill,
But the only way there's through Paranoiaville.

Now Paranoia's a wild colonial beast:
He rules in the West, he's got dens all over the East,

And he's so at home in the North, it's sometimes said
He grows another equally paranoid head.

In the South he's lying low, but he's seen at parties,
Boozing with poets and other mad arty-farties.

So visit that city of riches if you will,
But remember you're entering Free Paranoiaville.

2 *The Ice Dragon of Great Northern Street*

Some things simply can't be got right.
For all that I tried to research
The ways of my solid-fuel heater,
The fuel never wanted to catch.

My lighters, my high-grade coal
And my coal-coaxing implements
Might have been buckets of soil
And a draft of discouragements.

It's not that it never took pity:
Sometimes, the great northern pipes
Would murmur a small northern ditty
Hushing my huge southern gripes.

But I couldn't rely on it ever;
The same kind of treatment next day
Would leave us both cold. So I never
Learned when I should turn away

And when to keep stroking my dragon.
I suspected some faulty design
(Either the dragon's, or mine).
Though I'm just the usual woman,

And it seemed just the usual fire,
We couldn't reach mutual delight.
With the staunchest resolve and desire,
Some things simply can't be got right.

No Man's Land

Places are perfect for belonging to:
They can't get up, they can't walk out on you.
Whatever clever tricks the planners do,
The same old place, the pained old face, smiles through.

You can walk out on places, certain they
Won't mind or try to find you. Places stay
Put; however far you move away,
One of those streets will take you back one day.

And if it's been unmapped or wrapped in steel,
With tripwires lurking for the mortal heel,
Run down or stunned with an official seal –
Pick up your place and walk. Its weight is real.

A place is home, however dim or dead.
It's much less trouble than a double bed.
You think your place is someone's heart or head?
Forget it. Love geography instead.

The Photophobe

A house can be haunted by those who were never there
If there was where they were missed.
LOUIS MacNEICE,
'Selva Oscuras'

You have to leave a haunted house. Of course.
And so she did. She found one with no ghost,
No perfumes, chills, nobody to be missed,
And nothing to be kept but regular hours.

Plain views look in, confirm their lack of past:
A toytown bridge, one figure glancing over;
Electricity's tall exoskeleton;
A pine's display of brushes, the red downpour
Of dogwood, and four windows like her own –
A random hand she's no wish to uncover.

She wants a word-tight solitude, not response.
Her words have eyes, her views, blinds that displace
Each winter morning dazzle of pinpoint suns –

Her wasted breath, staring her in the face.

Street Snapshots in a New Peacetime

Late afternoon is best, when the sun has softly sidestepped
To the other tradition, the one that sips black water,
Its head against the hills, half waiting, half asleep.

By now, the sky's so tired of appearing patriotic,
It yawns a teatime colour where the evangelist falls
Into his own happy grave, and the junkman rises again,
His one loud yelp expecting nothing more
Addictive than a day no longer treasured.

My childhood ragman wove among Routemaster buses
Steamrollers, grown-up trikes, and other post-war traffic,
His pram wheels picking up shreds from the hay pancakes.
I never believed there was sense on my ragman's tongue.
When the words dawned I lost some god of language.

Junk, yelps the old man, Jesus, yelps the evangelist,
But across the street a different language is growing
In a blue-jerseyed, gate-swinging child who'll speak it tomorrow.
Puzzling herself, then, she'll remember the details:
The stiff little horse on his flapping flag, the three bright antique curb-colours...

Longshot

The city that tried to be hope's capital drowses
In a bluish scum, perhaps being bathed, or printed.
As three new skeins trickle white from the cloudmakers' chimneys
And the first buses edge towards filmy heartland,
You would need more words than spires to be persuaded
That the usual business had tested its connections,
And finds them this morning in perfect working order.

Tea on the Fifth of July

In the countdown days, she agreed with several women
The merits of oestrogen over testosterone,
Then that seemed too black-or-white, too us-against-them,
So regretfully she abandoned the oestrogen
In favour of long baths, spliffs and chocolate (hot) –
Such stuff as would fell the feistiest patriot.
Under the influence, no doubt, she began to fashion
A joint so huge it was still a long way from ashen
By the time it had travelled the tremulous, sweet lip-line
From a terrace in BT6 to another in Portadown
And back. Old men were leaning against the murals
And vaguely planning cross-community fleadhs and festivals,
While the young saw reason at once and unravelled the charms
Of the two traditions known as 'one another's arms';
And if something somewhere was marching, it was only a poem
That was late for its tea, and anxious to get home.

Words for Politicians

The Party of Frogs is the Party of Toads
The Party of Corners, the Party of Roads
The Party of Gloves is the Party of Glands
The Party of Whispers, the Party of Bands
The Party of God is the Party of Good
If you haven't learnt that yet, you bloody well should

'Cos the Baseball-Bat Party's the Party for Learning
The Book Party's party to Naughty-Book Burning
The Bring-Back-the-Past Party's fighting for Progress
The Yes-No Brigade utters nothing but No-Yes
The Green Party's Pink and the Can Party Couldn't
And if you believe me you bloody well shouldn't

'Cos Doubt is the Party of Bold Self-Assertion
The Party of Faith is the Party-Sized Version
The Idiots' Party's the Party for Smarties
The Party from Hell is the Party of Parties
The Party for Fish is the Party for Bait
And you'd swallow anything, wouldn't you, mate

'Cos the Anything Party's the Party of Sellers
The Bendy Spoon Party's that Party of Geller's
The Party of Saddam's the Party of Freedom
The Party of Women is out – we don't need 'em
The Party of Lagan's the Party of Boyne
And if you don't like it you still have to join

'Cos the Party of Like-It's the Party of Lump-It
The Party of Muffin's the Party of Crumpet
The Bakery Party's the Party of Ormeau
The Sunny Twelfth Party's the Party of Lawn-Mow
The Party of Nine is the Party of Six
If not then there's nothing a penknife can't fix

'Cos the Party of Cut is the Party of Run
The Popular Front is a Party of One
The Smoke-Alarm Party's the Party of Fags
The Party of Gays is the Party that Drags
The PUP is a Party no doggie wants in
If you start a New Party don't think it will win

'Cos the Fresh Approach Party's the Party of Same
The Alzheimer's Party's forgotten its name
The Residents' Party arrives by the coachload
The Pesticide Party is really a Roachload
The Party of Bread's on the Party of Shelves
If you want some more Parties, twist words for yourselves.

To His Coy Mistress, from Beyond the Grave

Cargoes, The Copper Kettle, Ruby Tuesday's,
Maud's, The Cello, The Manhattan Diner –
These were the places (not
Very private, but none finer)
Where, in the 2020s, we would meet
For morning coffee or a teatime snack.
By then, we both wore black:
I'd learned to be discreet,
You, to be kind. And if the gossips still
Said I stared rather strongly in your eyes,
What was a stare?
At least it proved we were there

It would have been eleven years, one week,
Past the millennium,
Before I'd touched your wrist –
Only to ask the time.
Another decade on, my withered cheek
Brushed yours to simulate
At the conclusion of each date
The Regulation Feminine Irish Kiss.
We had no scores to settle now, despite
The odd arthritic sulk, dyspeptic rage:
No debts, but those of age.

That famous winter struck in '29:
And took away our breath.
From *Bluebells* to the *Nonstick Frying Pan*
Our olde-worlde tips and mostly charming ways
Were mourned, but not for long. And when
In a plush-lined booth beneath
A mound where excavators had been poking,
Your walking stick and mine were glimpsed
Stiltedly necking,
So many centuries had elapsed
That who could blame us?
There was not one biographer to name us.

The Lightest Dancer

(to Michael Longley)

A bee, drawn earthwards
By the breath from a tuft of clover,
Went from choice to choice,
Fanciful, hovering.
There seemed no itinerary,
An improvisation, merely.
But, by the time it was over,
No flower had been left untouched,
And no flower, touched twice.

Song of the Gsohs

We're the gsohs of Little Ads.
We're slimmish lasses, solvent lads,
And wltm other kind gsohs,
With a view to taking off our clothes.
Ala's our promise, though we're Ps,
NSs, Christians, or RCs.
Our gods have words like *sin* and *blame*,
But we're the grins skimmed from their shame.
Come giggle with us, nose to nose,
And found the future race of gsohs.

Insight in Lavery's

A harmless drug, a harmless friend? –
Never, till Homo's sappy end:
But if you need some harm, you mug,
Choose a young friend or an old drug.

Céilí in Belfast 9

Your man plays cool, your man plays safe
But wouldn't you like an acrobat, a tightrope-walking waif?

Your man mustn't know, but don't you ever go
For the disreputable charmer or the milk-white dairy farmer?

Your man will never go, but couldn't you, even so,
Fall for a wheeler-dealer or a two-hand reeler?

You're fine, you're Belfast 9, but why shouldn't you
Go west, go south, go sip at the mouth of the wild child-stealer?

Where the Rainbow Ends

Halfway down Cranmore Park, it becomes clear
    That the road is heading straight for the roots of the hills:
The trees descend like a wavy slide at a fair:
    The city's abandoned, green will flourish for miles.

Up go the hills to heaven, as sinlessly
    As pets, with their velvet flanks, their stripes and tufts,
And down, down slips the road, black gravity
    Tarring my feet while my gaze, free-floating, lifts.

The trees soon tire of the game. They block the way
    Scots pines, chestnuts, larches – glorious things
But proud and a little cold, inclined to weigh
    And sift their shade above fussy gardenings.

And then there are so many chimneys saluting the sky
    Their fists have all but obliterated the blue
Not to speak of the green, which looked so near, so true,
    But now seems merely the memory of a trompe l'œil.

Mourn as I might, I haven't any choice
    But to turn my rise to my fall, and let the hills
Dissolve, as a face dissolves into a house,
    Leaving the stranger nothing but roads and rules.

Sans Souci Flats

I am my neighbours' lives, their woodwork parties,
The war dance of their lust, their shoe grenades,
The no-surrender dialogue of their doors.

My skull's the hollow kitchen where their Hotpoint
Scrambles the wash all night, and gender governs
Each quarrel in remorseless stereotype.

And what am I to them? An ancient deafness
Under the floor? A quaint old beam, or buttress,
Oak, of course, proof to all blasts and shaking?

I couldn't hope to speak their rip-tongued jabber,
Yet listening to them now's my one obsession.
In this, I'm an example to my country.

Chrisnin Gifts

Me Sarfa-the-River whine's got some Belfast vowels
By now, but it aint dead yet, not while we can cross
The wotjamacallit, *sheugh*, and Ole Muvver Lee still pulls
A pint of Watney's Brown in the Duke of York's.

That blank on the *A to Z*, down the Plumstead Road –
That's Woolwich Arsenal – stuck behind ten-foot walls
With a great big black steel gate, and two squat black steel shells
Sunk in concrete, one on guard each side.

They trooped through here for their "call-up", aunts and cousins,
Dressed to the nines and getting the giggles. See,
It's offices now, top-secret, MoD –
No chance for us to go snooping. Lousy work, munitions.

But at Charlton Pier where the Russky sub was packing
To head downstream for Folkstone, who should I meet
But an old great aunt of mine – well, the dead spit,
Skinny and permed and dyed and yakkety-yakking.

'Me son's a marine, we both worked on the sub,
Showing the tourists round, like…an now I'm out of a job.
Ee's going off to is ship.' It was like in '46,
Not a barrel of fun for the girls sent back to the sticks.

Them blown-up empty sweetie-bags of war
Musta been what the fag-puffin Fates set down
Beside the engraved serviette ring, the silver brushes and mirror,
When I basked in me hyphened name and me chrisnin gown

To be tickled pink by 'the tale of the old iron pot'.
There was singsongs in shelters, Messerschmitts in the park.
'The war was murder,' they said, so you knew that what
They really meant was, 'Lor, but it was a lark.'

Well, I've tidied my tongue, flown back to my second home
And I'm peeking into gigantic paper-bags
Full of stale hot air and bull's-eyes and prophets of doom
And lads on the march, and an empire's worth of old flags.

Round Trip

This must be home when a voice returns from floating
    And sinks into the dialect of a bay.
Its wonderment instantly becomes dismay.
    This must be home when a voice returns from floating
Out among islands, sheds protective coating,
    Achieves itself, then catches itself self-quoting:
'This must be home when a voice returns from floating
    And sinks into the dialect of a bay.'

Ineducable

Looking out on that drenched street my heart
half-listening as I say not this again
it echoes *this again* and I continue
to look half-seeing am I not alive
to all rain does to stone isn't my passion

for being free for being sensible
to all rain does to stone isn't my passion
to look half-seeing am I not alive
it echoes *this again* and I continue
half-listening as I say not this again
looking out on that drenched street my heart

Conversation with a Seagull

(in memoriam Joseph Brodsky)

Poem-maker, your guild disbanded, not one
    Man left at his station:
Love-adept, at last unbefriended, no-win
    Your situation,
So what if some cloud from your most Aquarian mood,
    Or a snowflake of brain,
Drift above Shandon, prospecting for Leningrad
    Through thickening rain,
Puzzling in vain for the wobbly Venetian Os
    Of arch-backed embraces,
The aristocratic self-disregard of *palazzos*?
    Such weathers aren't voices.
Say the feathery soul of your river-love just gave a cry
    As it dived from the railing –
A gull is a Soviet type, mass-produced, sly.
    Your wings would be flailing.
Whether nature plays God is still what I want to know.
    Can selves be re-formed
Like the river from rain? And now I can hear it – abseiling
    In spirals down from your vast oratorical
Rucksack – the question. *The question, Kerol, you're saying,*
    Is surely rhetorical?
The self is – well – imaginary, and it will go
    Nowhere – or wherever imaginings go.

Cork, 1996

From a Lexicon of Unlikely Couples

Looking up *dene*, I saw it stretch a slender
   Palm across the downscape, north, to *dun*:
Southron and Scotsman, borrower and lender,
   Lay cheek to cheek as two sides of a coin.
Next, stranger still, *desire* and *lack* made one
   Honeymoon pair, a Paolo and Francesca,
Whirled among fiery stars, yet never warm,
   Their special hell the absence of all friction,
   Their married name *desideratum*.

To Poetry

My darkest eye, the one I've never seen
In any glass, changes the day with you,
Colouring bridally, though out of season,
Like hills in sudden scarves of frost or bracken.
It knows your fiercest winter hex, but stays
Patient, snow-lidded, meeting dark with dark.
It loves the rose-bright pulse of you in health:
Its vein runs to your heart, picks up the song.
It sees you best when everyday eyes sleep,
But should these daily eyes lose sight of you
The meanest light will never meet my road.

The Burial

Once fairy-struck in pine-dim light I watched
A fern become alive, tremble and speak
A thousand contradictions, terrified
Of how I stared until I prayed it back
To some tired metaphor that it could bear –
The quaint *fiddlehead*, the ancient *pteron*.

Stanzas for a New Start

Home for a long time fought with me for air,
And I pronounced it uninhabitable.
Then, in an old tradition of reversal,
I understood I'd left my future there.

I chased across the badlands of recession:
I'd make a bid for any cuckoo's nest
That sang the joys of owner-occupation.
No loan shark lacked the details of my quest.

Now it's acquired refinement. It's a passion
Long-pursued, a serious late career.
I've shelved my dreams of contract and completion.
Haste doesn't suit the eternal first-time buyer.

Home, after all, is not a simple thing.
Even indoors there should be garden voices,
Earth-breaking rootage, brilliant mirroring,
A constant foliation of loved faces.

Doors are a must, but let them make a palace,
Let each room smile another, on and on –
The glittering, the plain, the small, the spacious,
The sacred and the haunted and the one

Hope rests her case in – windswept, cornerless.

Holding Pattern

(Belfast–London)

There were the rag-rug streets looking like silk
As light burst from a different angle, floating
The tiny mop-head trees on rafts of shade;
Old Thamsey, too, on form, busily twisting
Out of her rat-gnawn, matt-brown Gravesend stocking
To shake a rippling knee-bag for a brighter
Putney mood. That sudden rash of glitter –
Of sweat and spills and goosebumps – got me thinking
How, if you'd choose an island for its windows,
You'd go for this one, never mind the quick
Clearance of Aldergrove, the fields you reckoned
As space, the opened rainbow-mines you sank through.
And then I knew – this was my holding pattern:
To circle hopefully, never admitting
Before this moment (and not really now)
Which self, which well-embroidered plot, which mainland,
Which graveyard, I was travelling with my back to.

FROM

HEX

(2002)

December Tennis

Winter's first ice!
Green pavings of it, smashed
and sealed on the little lake. No swans,
mallards, kids – only an old ribbed dustbin
rolled on its side like the park drunk on his seat.

To make you growl
Carol, Carol,
I volunteer a toe
and up comes bold black jack-in-the-box, oh
wicked, delicious, soaking one new Nike.

We're for the courts.
Is it Lux or Dreft
they're powdered with? Such velvet
beneath our heels of sky!

Play is the rosebud gift
we gather yet.
Our old wood low-tech racquets
can flash, trampoline, taking
bows when we're in our stride – although
my first shot slugs the net – too low.

There's a circle in Hell
for love like ours. But the ball
survives the serve, the beautiful curve of our planet
reels from our palms, and the sun,
a toe-dipping god, is splashing the trees and the fence
across our dance in huge harmless meshed
Xs and Ys!

Kings of the Playground

All to get the Bully – who hid in a steel-clad cupboard –
the Bully Bashers stormed the trembling school.
They bullied the Bully's kit, his grubby blazer,
his sports-bag, his bully-beef flavour crisps.

They bullied the kids with the bruises
that showed the Bully's shoe-print.
They bullied the gerbils he'd teased, they bullied every computer
he'd slimed with his bully virus.

They bullied the prefects and teachers –
the nice ones first, then the bullies.
The kids who had conduct stars, the kids in detention, even
the football team, they bullied, yelling 'Ya bullying fairies!'

They bullied the books, though the Bully didn't like books:
they bullied the white-boards and black-boards,
they bullied the wall-charts, the registers, the sick-notes,
the pass-notes. They bullied the two-times table.

Then they thundered out and bullied the empty playground,
they bullied the big round sky that covered the playground,
they bullied the rain, the bushes, the used needles,
the trembling waiting parents, the tiny brothers and sisters.

Bully TV was launched. There was only one programme
'How We Bashed the Bully'. Anyone who switched off
was sentenced to 25 years community-bullying.
The Bully-Bashers relaxed. Gave themselves medals. Flew home.

The Bully listened a while, and grinned in the dark cupboard.
He combed his hair. He opened the door wide.
He sauntered through the wrecked assembly hall.
Scared faces turned. Eyes that remembered his bruises

clouded over, younger eyes grew shiny.
Suddenly someone shouted, 'Look, the Bully!
Them liars didn't get him! Three cheers for our Bully!'
And everyone yelled and stamped: 'Three cheers for old Bully!'

Old Bully mounted the stage. How tall he was,
what a lovely speech he made. The big boys lifted him high
and they all stormed into the trembling streets, yelling
'Make way for Old Bully, ya cunts!' And the people did.

Shade

might seem pure negative. But do you remember
when it was solid, delicious as a late breakfast?
We'd been in the fields since 6 a.m., training
the new kiwi-plants to weave thick cool tunnels
for next season's pickers, stringing the wayward tendrils
to the trellises that would lead them up and over.
There were few leaves on those apprentice vines,
nothing to beat back the power of the sky.
We watched our forearms shrivel like eggs in a pan.
What amateurs of the sun, what holy fools
we were, out there in the desert in our tee-shirts,
as if a god would pity human skin.

At noon the day was over, called off.
We crossed the fields to the avocado orchards
where we flung ourselves down, the team of us, speechless.
The cool-box broached, we dived into whole grapefruit.
Can you remember what the word *shade* meant there?
How we pulled it on, over our scalps and eyes,
and it was the end of all headaches,
how we rinsed our faces in it again and again,
how we buried ourselves in its arms and heard our names?
If death were to be like this, would we call it loss?
We'd know, long before we were cold, that a great wish had been granted.

Droplets

Tiniest somersaulter
through unroofed centuries,
puzzling your hooped knees
as you helter-skelter,
dreamy, careless,
without a safety net
into an almost-ness
as uneventfully lost,
your house re-let,
guiltless defaulter:

sex: un-noted: weight:
a minimal gravity:

whatever you'd have tried
in time amounting to,
unguessed, undone –
I'd have your cry
brought home – and yet
when you demand to live,
these hands that blessed
your hopeful forehead, answer
only in negative.

Nadir

Then the last luminaries went underground.
The sea expressed its characteristic view
With sighs, and raked harsh echoes from the strand.
Someone pressed at the window to remark
Spring's whitewash on the shit-house good as new.
There was smoke but no fire: there was almost no smoke,
But these would later come into their own,
The luminaries said. As sure as corn
In August, as the rising of the lark,
They'd wet the baby's head, declare it sound
And send it on, green-lit, to Tyrone.

The Perfect War Machine

They fall into line without question and thunder home,
    White as a childhood of happiness, pelting head-on,
Spit-stringy muzzles in wreathings of mane and steam.
    But *is* it happiness, whipping these gallopers home,
Reigning them in, colliding them, laying them down
    Suddenly meek on the shore (which also once leapt in the sun),
The strong white bodies dissolved to a few grey blisters of foam?

And now come the reinforcements, another disciplined team
    Over the top in a tumult of energies.
Happy? Of course. They run with the herd, and every herd is the same
    As far as they know. This lack of significance frees,
Surely, the blind white horses, who gallop and die with abandon,
    Having no myth of themselves, and no desire but the sea's?

Rigor Mortis

Someone should tell them they're dead.
Two rigid soldiers
are facing across a bridge,
facing at point-blank range:

two rigid soldiers,
both men ready to fire,
facing at point-blank range
the shot that stops the war,

both men ready to fire,
when the starter signals,
the shot that stops the war
of two land-eating lands.

When the starter signals,
watched by the empty children
of two land-eating lands,
they fire at each other's frowns.

Watched by the empty children
at either end of the bridge,
they fire at each other's frowns,
two soldiers, sights re-focused

at either end of the bridge.
It's like science fiction:
two soldiers, sights re-focused,
swallowing shot like bread.

It's like science fiction.
This can't be ordinary flesh
swallowing shot like bread,
and poised to fire again.

This can't be ordinary flesh,
its weaponry always loaded
and poised to fire again.
Two bundles of riddled land

in a carcass of battle-dress
are facing across a bridge
they think is worth dying for.
Someone should tell them they're dead.

Starlight: A Story

When we abolished nightfall from our cities
stars by thousands died. Died like the small change
in the pocket-linings of a lottery winner,
or like the secrets of a world language.

Never again would couples, naked-eyed,
point to the true fidelities, dividing
into the one who sees, the 'nil' or 'plus'
dioptric millionaire, and the one who skims a wish-spoon

through inner space and smiles, 'Oh yes, I see.'
And yet our easy neighbour went on rising;
the massive dishes murmured. Stars weren't apes or coral
(we blushed), but where we'd left the future niche-less,

north and far west, they peeped through the FOR SALE boards
and swam the flooded fields. Imagine it,
a land so old the only animals,
the only birds, were stars! 'Back,' we cried, 'Back to the starlight.'

We made them ours, quick as the half-farmed acres.
We didn't ask, they burst out of the foaming
tantalus of that clear, black, country sky
into our mouths, eyes, hair, mineral as raindrops:

copper, quartz, sapphire, marquesite,
brown diamonds, white. *Not in lone splendour*, no. We dipped
into the bubbling universe of memory
to name the striding lovesick giant, the bears, the twins, the huntress.

Some of us found our god-folk, some, our folk gods:
all the tutelary spirits of our sight
embraced us now we'd dumped the grid to mine
our little clinkable purse of sixpenny physics.

We'd seen the light. And then we saw the dark,
and how it wasn't to be brushed aside
as backdrop to the true show. It expanded,
it gathered speed, rolled in like loosened mountains –

impacted, dayless night. We watered down to shadows.
We were the planet's after-life, its memory
of dark-adapted eyes and hunting glamour,
alerted, impotent. We snapped our press-stud torches

to spots of frost and listened, saw new species
muscling between the trees, and sighed for the slip-roads,
while stars went on being stars, pure brilliance,
of course, but selfish, worse than genius.

Starlight. This, we've learned, was our illusion,
oxymoronic, untranslatable
into our puddled tracks and inked-out signposts. *Starlight*
that dies before it touches us, like love.

We swear – *de mortuis nil nisi bonum*
but each of us has stroked the reeds, confiding
to their long mouths that the dead have cheated us.
We pray, but I believe our prayers have changed

as prayers do change when a life-or-death desire
no longer knocks us out, jetting like water-cannon,
no longer knocks at all, and we drop into our place
at the key-holes of the earth. We are a solar people,

clichéd through with the flash of one near star.
These were our darlings all along: the rock-throwers,
particle breeders, sperm-merchants, suns.
To every brightness its reflective pattern,

and sight, perhaps, but not within our time-scale,
our curvature. To us, the low horizon,
the soiled cloud where we look round for our neighbour.
When the world tilts a little to the right

we say – or is it to the left – we'll see her,
luminous, unoffended, on our wave-length
still – the only one we touched and did not haunt.
'The moon,' we sigh, 'What happened to old moon-rise?'

The Thingless Phrase

(to Edward Thomas, after reading 'The Word')

Though I'm not sure if I could recognise
The voice from that of any song-rich bird,
Now you've marked for me something audible
As *pure thrush word*,
I wouldn't need to hear it twice,
I think, to trace the call
Out of that moment of parenthesis
(Not tuneful, *tart*; translatable to nothing
But un-romantic thrushness):
And if I never have the luck to hear
A thrush text-messaging,
It won't be lost, the mystery of your *thingless
Name* – I'll just keep coming back to where
The poem hears it, and wait there.

Just as in 1914

You can sell the young
A spell, a pill, a look, a grudge, a land,
Life insurance, God, a band,
A pup, a truth, their youth.

You can sell the young
Girl her own white unicorn.
You can sell the young
Man his own shite uniform.

Name it 'gallantry' or 'martyrdom',
You can sell it. You can sell the young.

Religious Education

The god of human love was king of kings,
Then, to our wooden classroom: where a child's
Finger moved, a small star cruised above it,
Nervously eyeing shapes beyond the wind.
I could dim any light and see it now,
The silver-on-black word, *epiphany*,
And find, brimming my hands, the charged rewards
For having, being, nothing. Is there mercy
In any universe for us, who knelt
Crownless among the hungry, kicking lambs,
And touched the star, we numerous underlings
Who now believe in all kinds of imaginary things?

Eichmann in Minsk

> *As I arrived I saw a Jewish woman with a small child in her arms
> in the pit. I wanted to pull the child out, but then the bullet hit
> the child's head. I got back into the car. 'Berlin,' I said to my driver.
> I drank Schnapps as if it was water. I had to dull my brain.'*
> THE DIARIES OF ADOLF EICHMANN

Drinking Schnapps like water, stare
Until the moment's hardly there,
Until the shapes in the forest's floor
Stiffen, fade and rise no more
As limbs and mouths with claims to air,

And trees fly back to the clearing where
The bony-shouldered spades prepare
To meet the load from the lorry door,
On schedule, as you'd planned before
Drinking Schnapps like water.

Nothing's there! So grown-ups swear.
So history lies. So bodies bear
The heavy measures ordered for
Disposal. It is only your
Child you pity, almost spare,
   Drinking Schnapps like water.

Falling Man

From another angle,
it's as if the lens
had caught him asleep,
dawn-lit, gripped
by one of those vivid
pre-waking bad
dreams, where the brain
e-mails itself:
this isn't happening.
Not the illusion
of stillness, but
the lack of distortion,
casualness, almost,
in his posture, his body's
so-far unflawed
completeness, muddles
our narrative grasp.
He can handle this.
It's only air,
air that was always
our element, made
to breathe and burn,
to be built into,
and risen above,
the trespass-inviting
pitch whose one
amazing floodlight
names us co-stars.

We had to look up:
we bathed our eyes
in light so they learned
colour, stretched arms
and lungs into Os
of desire: we found
trees to feed us,
mountains to teach us,
like sleepers waking,
kept ascending,
poised on the tip
of our soaring backbone
until there was less
and less air: maladapted,

enchanted, we still
saw ways to increase
height, flung up towers,
flew fortresses, looped
skyway to skyway:
we 'conquered space'
as we phrased it, trawling
our own supplies
of oxygen, rushed
up, floated down,
not quite admitting
what thrust had been required,
suspecting we'd grown
at least one small wing.

But the love of surface
stuck to our soles.
And our sun-gods, turning
to stone, sang out
from their beautiful hardness:
dive, plunge,
be scattered over
your disputed cities
and shine beyond memory!
Gods need our trust:
then they'll catch the shadow
of a man, falling,
or a man, flying
into his future,
who smiles as it stops
and spins him a tunnel
in which he hangs
as others are hanging
outside their windows
and walls like pupas
waiting to split
into moths, new man-moths,
and fly away, lighter
than poetry.

The steeper the fall,
the wilder the angle
of rebound: this
is emotional physics.
We sting as we die,
like ants, we roll

our alchemical dead
into thunderheads, gather
as balled-up stars
and pelt the world
with skull-bits, billions
of crumbled backbones
to feed the soil,
to grow the new tall.
From the air, nothing hurts.
The air itself
is nursery blue
and safe as steel-
threaded towers. And our hands
move over the face
of the deep, they are all-
powerful: look,
they can dump fire
on selected targets
while turning a page
horizontally,
to pause this diver,
laying him safely
on Slumberland foam,
him and his heart-plunging
nightmare, his billowing
shirt, his scream
fading to daybreak's
patter of shower-tiles,
running-shoes, pavement –
the usual welcome
of nearby earth,
G-forces impalpable
now to one quick,
finely-braced ankle,
one kicked-back heel.

An Unsentimental Education

Now it is settling down, the scream.
ELIZABETH BISHOP

When the room toppled slowly round that cry
Your narrowed gaze went sightseeing. Perhaps
Sleep would fall on the effervescent air
If you were kind and studied all the gaps
And quirks in things, exchanged a cheerful sigh
With the white paint-crumb in a portrait's eye,
And tamed with tea those mild ambiguous cups
Whose peep-holes, grains of rice, 'weren't really there'.

In time, you found the sanest point of feeling –
The earthquake zone. A shock-absorbent ceiling,
Slide-away walls in natural-seeming blue,
Turned into planes, boats, buses, with their stock
Of very proper windows. Dared to look,
You'd see the poems, waving hard at you.

The 'Pastime' School of Poets

Poems I might have written for my father,
had he lived long enough, had I learned quicker
to find the vital signs inside the daft
corseted minuets and crumbly sword-play
of borrowed language: had I not ranged against him
my revolution, where a poem was measured
beside the shapes of things just made, lit blocks
I loved, wrought in Black Mountain foundries or
night-brilliant power stations in the depths
of Europe – poems my father couldn't see
at all, and wouldn't touch because they'd burn
harsh chemical shadows, blanching rays
into the poems he loved, the lines he whispered
to make them breathe and enter, turn, and echo
through courteous archways, genuflecting slightly
towards that dangerous place, the margin: poems,
once gifts, now telling him he had no gift,
a man who scribbled 'poems' as a pastime,

a man who *scribbled*: – poems he crushed in bins
or ashtrays, draw their smoke, flatten their crinkled
surfaces and flow across my keyboard
as poems I might have written for my father
for him to love, and to be loved by others;
I stand back as they pass, admiring how
simply they press towards their vanished moment,
freed from gentility, made truthful by
the silence darkening round them, as I once
darkened my poor father with my silence:
poems too late for giving, poems that whisper
if poems don't hurt us, are they truly poems?
but claim no power to burn, are almost weightless
among the graves of books and revolutions
and old beliefs that such things are immortal:
poems I'll write for no one, for a pastime.

Uxbridge Road: Sex & Charity-Shopping

Don't think, because we're poor, we don't touch dreams
When we tweak cuffs and spin the rainbow rail:
We know the stars are moved by colour-schemes.
Don't think we're merely taking cover. Style
Just named its price – or these are not my jeans –
Leather-look retro, darling, not has-beens.
Ask anyone, the winos, the old biddies,
Our one-pound coins buy love, like everybody's.

Kitchener Street: Flights of Fancy

I want you to be real again, bluebird.
If these villagers can grow palms
And pinwheels, father forty moss-cheeked gnomes
And paint girls' names on side-walls, can't you quietly
Take a moment, skim my red-brick rhymes,
Lately so back-to-back, and be the new word
Granted only when space is taken lightly?

The Quest, The Hex, The Alkahest

Hate – what a whirlwind ride
from love to there:

star into black hole, white-hot Mr Hyde
into flaky Jekyll –

believe me, this
wasn't like turning a coin.

It was radical re-design.
So I gathered glass blackberries

from the only rose too wise
to wear fancy suits –

the *alchemilla vulgaris*
and revised my solvents and solutes.

I'd been chucked out of O Level
Chemistry (Cookery, too)

but I knew how to blacken a name,
cure desire and divine the healing kiss

sent in a bubonic bubble
of spit: if love was shit, whatever else

would be no syllogistical trouble.
I turned up the flame, threw in

a flash of salt: as soon as my world of dew
rose to the boil,

I added the can of worms, the tin of stew:
the love-thing. Oh, it glowed

deeper the longer it rode,
slow-tanning to a hepatitis shade

in an ooze of gas on the hollow
crux of each second-hand ring

I rented as I travelled.
I knew I was chemical king of the rolling road

when water was just a ghost
on a distant cheekbone (whose

I didn't care – not mine
any more, ever, amen)

and I stroked its face as the matter cooled
and I called it *the most*

malleable and ductile
metal, miraculous *gulth*,

glitter of wealth in the froth
of my gullible self –

no, wait. I was better than that.
I called it hate.

I'd lost my sense of shame.
Soft parts are first to get fucked

as that Hazchem Eucharist
rinses your mind, but

it's the bargain you strike
for the twenty-two carat product.

I played with the target, zapped
some shy peripheral *putti*

(split–splat) then aimed point-blank
at the former seraph –

you. I wanted blood and tears, no pity,
so here was the set-up:

your favourites walked the plank
in front of you. I had you hexed,

hoaxed, on fire, hung from a spike,
gnawed out by cancers,

wild-eyed with Alzheimer's,
laid low by machete attack.

Blood? *It* was only ketchup,
the *kitsch* of the poor, the *kvetch* of the hated

bouncing back, twisting the tale
begun with your very own knife-

thrust through my hero's life: reversal,
darling, the oldest trick:

revenge, if you like. Now, though,
it had your sheen, your brow:

it would last forever, my septic
passion, tender and true

as erectile tissue,
secreting radiant ink

like the real thing. Not so.
Think, if you dare,

how the dead live. A new
corpse is a gas,

all go in its green-blue-pink
bio-bright kit, it dances

a day or two, yes,
then slithers off back to bed, lies down

abandoned, random, done.
When the last degradable bit

has gone, the glamour has.
And hate's like that.

Dead love is jazz. Dead hate is zilch,
zero, the emptiest flat

in the writer's block, the binned obit.
It's a legless bug, a glugless sink:

it's darkness visible –
but you need to be Milton to see it.

After a final belch
at the dizzy alchemist

to deliver a knock-out hit
of isopropyl methyl-

phosphorofluoridate,
it pisses off to wherever

Stork lies down with butter.
And maybe, somewhere, the difference doesn't matter:

Base and Precious wed in a silvery mist
on an aisle in some Tescos

for stars – that's Chemistry
for girls. But Alchemy? Sheer spin

and greed, like the other thing
which makes the world go round

the twist and reappear
decidedly pear-shaped.

Don't think I'm being moral:
given a local fount

of elixir, a pinch of salt,
a body that seemed to count,

I'd kill tomorrow.
But no one's there. Or here.

Hyde snuggled back inside
Jekyll (*Look, no hair*).

Dew's dew. My rose, you
aren't much of a rose

since the alkahest jumped cup.
Tin of course continues

to be tin: functional, cold,
often found empty. Gold? We made it up.

Last Minute Gifts

A cool Talk Pen (*record and play back your own message*),
one litre of ten-year-old Laphroaig, some Re-Vit Body Massage,
a sweater-bear, three hundred grams of Continental Truffles,
a box of Lancôme's *Couleurs*, plus a few other cosmetic trifles,
were found untouched in a Duty Free bag in the dead woman's home,
like chromosomes that had never mated, planes that had almost flown.

The Arrival

There are days early in love when love knows nothing
but to exist between our thoughts, unremarkable, vaguely
grand – as the future did when we were children.
Nothing becomes love more than when he dozes
like this, a jet-lagged wanderer, curled over his wallet,
his possibly false papers. *I'm the one:*
arrest me! is the last thing he would say.

A Rarer Blue

Bluebells were once as common a surprise
for a London child as the sea. I used to cherish
their tiny pinstripe, curly nostril-whiskers.
How they'd make a whole wood wade in blue
interested me less than the shameless juices
webbing my hands, the questions of collection:
how many bunches to a vase, why death
had sealed so tight the newest topmost bells.

Now, it's always the wrong wood or season,
their ghosts a spiky reticence
and, any way, forbidden.
Now I would like to see the matter dropped
in a sadly unenlightened childhood
and give my gaze to the heath-dwelling solitary

who lets the island shine through all her panes.
She likes a northern coast, but she isn't snobbish;
she gleams on Sussex, too, my wakeful lantern,
eye of the grass, mouth of the dawn, stone's sea-glimpse –
the little shaken harebell that won't be pulled.

The Submerged Cathedral
(in memory of Phyllis Robinson)

> *I have made mysterious nature my religion...to feel the*
> *supreme and moving beauty of the spectacle to which Nature*
> *invites her ephemeral guests, that is what I call prayer.*
> CLAUDE DEBUSSY

It's an hour before the dawn of rock 'n' roll:
Music has not so far been made flesh –
Or not for a working-class girl of thirteen.
And then I watch you play, star graduate
Of James Ching and the Matthay School,
Your technique so physical, so lavish,
I'd call it, now, *l'écriture féminine*
For pianists: but in 1958
All I know is that you are what you're playing –
You're playing *La Cathédrale Engloutie*.

A camera's drawn to the concert pianist's hands,
Caressing octaves, palely capering –
Sunday *Palladium* stuff, with Russ Conway
Or Winifred Atwell (coos from the mums and dads),
To be filed under my new word: *Philistine*.
This is art so deep it's industry:
Music as white-water, which your spine
Channels, springing arms transform. That's how
You lift and tumble these ton-weights of bell power:
I watch you, not your hands. I watch the sea,

Out of my depth, though, like *La Cathédrale*.
I mean all this to last – the eight hours' practice
Each day, hopeless devotion – and it does –
In other contexts. Oh, I bury it,
Music, and you, and all the pain of childhood,
But lumber back like a medieval builder
With washed-up stones (some good stone, too) and prayers,

403

To raise another heaven-touching marvel
On the same flood-site, watch another tide
Swagger in and demolish every bit.

After the last wreck, when I'd declared
The end of building-works on any coast,
Strange bells began to ring for me, the tone
Rubbed ordinary by forty years, but true:
Ghostly but not damned. What if the ghost
Wryly sang, 'Promises, promises?'
It was a gentle challenge, after all.
The sacred stones were myth. The tide that reared
So vengefully, hauled by the same moon,
Was myth. Not so, my common ground with you.

How we talk up 'the generation gap',
Break our necks in it, and never find
The friendly criss-cross trails of co-existence –
That gift which is to pause at one epoch,
The people of one earth. Yes, the years wear us...
But may all years be worn as you wore yours
That day we met, with teacherly compassion,
Because the body knows when the brighter mind
Rejects it, sulks like an untuned piano:
You lived in yours (it knew) like the luckiest girls.

It's hard, though, for the tired cells to sightread
Their last prélude, fingers twisting palm-ward,
In search of rarer ivory, their guiding
Beat a laggard stone-deaf walking-stick.
Like Schubert's songs, off in another key
Before we can say 'swan', you were elsewhere:
And elsewhere, in a room nearby, your music.
I'd wanted you to play. I let that go.
You counted off your new pursuits, confiding
'I love the sea. I love to watch *la mer*!'

On Portrush Strand I watch it too, engrossed
Like a child beside a piano, half aware
That this, whatever 'this' may be, won't keep,
The waves themselves won't keep. But someone plays
Debussy. Something rescues the white horses
You're not admiring now – not from these shores,
And makes them flesh, as music was, for me,
An hour before the dawn of rock 'n' roll
When you, star graduate of the Matthay school,
Lifted the great bells out of the sea.

The Sky and John Constable

Portray the artist
   As justice:
In his scale-pans,
   Foreground and background.
He places an ounce-weight
   On foreground, adds another:
Tall background rises
   Like grief into his eyes
   And can't be wiped.

A widower has no hunger
   Except to paint
Sky, sky as it should be –
   Enormous dynamo
Of *brilliancy and consequence.*
   No cornered afterthought
Will not return its power
   Via the wisp of a mill-sail,
   A gilding of wheat.

How can bodies, food
   Exist in the light of death?
But he is entrusted with light:
   He is the artist. So
Portray him as division
   Between his torn sky
And his worked meadows,
   The perfect ounce of justice
   Weighing on him:

   Weighing his lightness.

John Constable and People

1

How many strokes to a hireling
   Compared to rich pasture?
He is an item, eloquent
   Only in gesture.
He never stops and stares,
   Being a nobody,
A loose hair on the sleeve
   Of things, a streak of texture.

But this is his gallery.
   He directs the vast
Herdscape of hills,
   Sculpts in mud and grazing.
He himself is grass,
   His only resurrection
Through steam and fire towards
   The frame. The funerals.

2

A boy too heavily scolded
   Dips his face to the beck
And tells it everything.
   He is not of the elect,
This portrait-hater.
   Though he'll yearn to please,
He'll not be watering down
   His clouds, his candour.

One day, when he looks up
   He'll see miles past his thumb:
There stands the rarest cloud,
   Its human features forming
Ringlets, necklace, snow-
   Fall of her Empire-line,
And, at the vanishing point
   Of generous laughter, him.

John Constable and Faith

He says: 'These pictures are experiments'
and he finds out how the cloud-shadow touches
the mill-stream, records its altered volume.
He plots effect to cause, measures the lean
of a rotted post, the sinkage of a cart-wheel.
But when the earth can't wait for Easter Sunday,
when the little starry blizzards
are whirling out of every finger of blackthorn,
there's nothing to test, to doubt, in the stun of that cry:
'I am the Resurrection and the Life.'

This is not how we do science, not what nature tells us,
speaking out of the slowing heart of summer,
the sharpest claws alert for what they can seize
in the fields we never paint any more, as in the desert cities
whose burning we will photograph tomorrow.

Is it knowledge, or some quick brush-stroke of faith
binds us to him still? We can't unweave them.
But if he says his clouds explain the velocity
of heaven's breath, we stare, and lower our voices,
as if we hoped to hear some new announcement,
or the old one, making sense in a new way.

Evolution, 12th September 2001

Some mornings, light is hard as the grassless mountains
and mis-timed adolescence breaks out in my bones.
When I try to look up, eye-remnants, fragments of chitin,
swirl and crackle together, aspire to a brain.
I have evolved into something that shouldn't exist,
optimal, powerless, hatched in the wrong house.
They've furnished it horribly: the hardwood frames
are prison surplus. When I buffet the glass
it stuns me like the language-user's lies.
I shall never grow up into *them*, never get at all human –
which is being the wrong way up in a body once yours:
torment worse than the cranefly's, haggling over a corner
until he finds the sky, opens out like a strange
tasselled parachute and floats himself, dying,
into mountains grassy and sleepy as last week's childhood.

Pietàs

You were my sweetheart. Can I say so, now
I'm almost old, with no further claim to gender:
Now desire is a word and has no pulse
Beyond its own faint sigh, and love speaks simple prose?

You know how the crayoned collars we put on the spinning-tops
Made colour different? So, if I tell you my body
Remembers you, that's how: in delicate pastel strands
That will never be teased out while the top keeps spinning.

The girl closed like the man, the man soft as the child –
Such ironies of touch are bound to upset our curators.
Sweetheart, my first love poems should have been yours,
But to dare to break the glass has taken so many years.

I made myself a dress of stiff-collared lies
And the wind blew us both away. Only now can I return
Like a stream of tears over the stones of my wedding
To where you wait, a man my age, not yet

Dismissed, because I've handed you my camera,
And perch in front of you in my quaint ruched swimsuit.
One knee bent, school-grubby hands on hips,
I twitch my lips at the light, and think *beauty queen.*

Failed curls, limp breasts, no waist – and I'm trembling, because
I'm seventeen and everything's possible.
Then, in an after-flash, I see my flesh unchosen.
Your eyes tell me I'm lovely, so nobody else's can.

I found, of course, the usual steely wings;
Left you among flowerbeds, transplanting small fierce thirsts.
Sweetheart, the dead are rewarded: the children learn
It is only next door where the ruined parents go.

Against Posterity

Gather round me now, you older poets –
Poets in your late forties, early fifties,
Mid-fifties – you who understand
The significance of these small demarcations:
Poets of three-score years and pension book,
Superbly unretiring, with or without a *festschrift*
Made by the admirers you'll never become:
Poets triumphant in your racy seventies,
And you, especially you, in your eighties and nineties,
Maire, Dasenka, Kathleen – marvellous sisterhood –
Bring your short breath and your dancing stanzas.
And don't be shy, you grandfathers and great-grandfathers,
Though poems may be your only progeny –
Hey, you with the tinsel beard, no bardish pride!
This is a call for solidarity
Surpassing miserly gender (oh, forget about gender:
By now it's surely forgotten about us).
Spread the news of your brilliant forthcoming collection,
The Whitbread and the Forward in the bag,
But raise a not unkindly eyebrow at
The Gregory girls and boys still trembling at first base.
Tell us your publishers love you more and more,
But if you've travelled the hard road from nowhere
To sunny fame then down to the council tip
Of the out-of-date, declare with modest humour
The world has yet to match your three-legged stride
Along the crest of that hill it hasn't noticed yet.
Be tacit, but imply you won't go gentle
Like clowning Dylan, nor in Plath's hard rage,
To freeze with those who would have graced our gathering
With wit and beauty and magnificence
Had they cherished themselves as they cherished language.
Poetry's for grownups. So gather round, who know
Their music isn't the new rock 'n' roll
But a late quartet that sometimes bursts out laughing.
Bring your sustaining harmonies, let rip with your solos,
Unfurl surprises till the final chord,
When we'll forgive your silence – as ours will be forgiven –
And make way a little grudgingly
For the new recruits, who'll seem a shade too youthful.

Anything/Nothing

He becomes lame
    she stops
        climbing mountains

he loses some of his hearing
    she loses
        some of her tongue

he forgets to admire her body
    she ceases to admire
        any body

young marriage doubles the joy
    old marriage halves it

    and so she begins
paring lengths from his sight

    but remembers to shout
a joke in his best ear
    clink of glasses

    they share the mountain
at the kitchen window
    determined to savour

    seagull, sheep, stone
he names the snowdrifts for her
    the half-measure

    oh how they work to keep
this earth that's so much harder
    so much bigger, now,

        than anything
        than nothing

To the Shipbuilder, his Tabernacle

Leave the shed-door open:
It's all that lights the garden once we've crossed
Your solstice-shaded birthday.
Dusty martyrs' crowns on the young ivy
Are the best we can do for autumn flowers:
Our rooftop-transept banishes the sunbeds
To Evensong by four.
But this door has a forest's eyes; when cedar
Bristles back to its origins, the day
Sticks like honey, never wants to let go.

Did we know we were buying sunlight,
Driving out to one of those desolate
Life-style hangers on the edge of town,
Strolling the wooden shtetl?
It was your birthday. I was feeling rich.
As if I'd been stockpiling English dreams
For the first Ukrainian-Jewish-Russian-Finn
Who'd crossed the border into B and Q.
I wrote a cheque to make the best and dearest
More yours than Moscow.

You got inside at once, opening crystals
Of space with a submariner's
Eye for horizons, deep in stacking-systems.
Tools lined the decks like sailors,
Some bright, some sleepy. Rusty captains stowed
Their wooden legs upright. Tins on tins,
Labelled *almond cake, pitted olives, ikra*
Rattled with machine-food.
You pinched the nameplate from your office door
When they 'retired' you, fixed it to the shed.

And if the wood by now
Is being turned by micro-organisms,
Glued with a frost of cobwebs,
The gentle molecules of oil and creosote
Tired of stretching: if I submit and say
That autumn's pollen, halo-ing the ivy,
Was gold enough, more than we could have asked for,
Don't go before I've told you, with a wife's sad humour –
Leave the shed door open
So that I'll sometimes see you.

Wood Lovers

And a time will come when we drive on, ignoring
The grassy welcome-mat outside the pine trees' barracks
And our infallible instinct to surprise
Some tiny village, light-forgotten, stained
Cupolas lined with pleated pearl and coral.
And a time will come when our legs refuse to vanish
Far enough to uncloud the bluebell islands,
Or the windflower archipelago, white as Sweden:
And then a time when there's no wood, no forest,
No signposts for the words that keep on saying your voice:
Gribochki, kolokolchiki, choroshi less.

Refresher Course

Drifting at dawn out of staticky hurricane dreams
to the clearest blue ever sieved through a wet tent wall,
to the shock of grass in its first-day sky, and the roar
of the river-beast, the whole sheep orchestra
sending each other a wobbly, hopeful 'A'
and never needing to reach the symphony,
we knew we had altered time. Time was our child
like the child of old parents, a huge reach
encompassed: we would shed years every day.

In or out of the tent, time flew: we caught it
occasionally, we gave it different nicknames,
to do with light. The only tune it knew
was *Variations of a Theme of Rain*:
gas-rings and rain, dishes and soap and rain,
blankets beginning to steam and sparkle; rain,
wood-fires spitting at rain, wine with a spritz of rain:
rain in the bones, pricking, darning, tugging.
Once, playing *Hunt the Sun*, it let us win:
we stood at the wet kissing-gate and felt
the brush of dim warm animals called rainbow.

Imagine a life as just-made glass, so clean
it was invisible, self-polishing.
It never asked us to notice it until
the leaving day. Stroke after stroke appeared
and wrote: *we were happy here*. And happiness paid
its last pound-coin to the casual farmer.
Our feet crept home as shoes, our wrists as sodden
watch-strap; we could see the day was filthy,
and time, drumming enormous adult heels,
hated our straw house, our joke umbrellas.
We talked about going back, perhaps next week.
But only one of us did. And only like this.

Swedish Exchange

When we entered the room it was white. The lampshade was
blue, circular, patterned with circular holes. A white half-curtain
at the window was printed with ellipses of different colours.
There was a flat mirror in a wooden frame that was curved,
lending the glass a faint concavity. A whitewood table and two
chairs. A red mat.

We made the red mat dirty. On the table we put a glass of lilies-
of-the-valley: they had cost thirty kroner on a street corner
somewhere near the Klara church. The woman who sold them
said: you must give them cold water! There is a blue dictionary on
the table containing 30,000 *ord och fraser* and, on the window-sill, a
lime-green tennis-ball containing a finite but unknown number of
bounces. The mirror is full of badly hung clothes. Light sometimes
leaks from the lamp-shade holes, the chairs refuse to sit at the
table.

To make the room simple again we will have to leave it. We our-
selves will have to re-complicate. This is a pity. We'd like to leave
the room not as we found it but as we made it, impressed with
our favourite transfers. The room would be grateful. And we
would be white, clean, with natural wood features and a few
splashes of primary colour, an excellent design for the modern
human. We would close the door and not invite ourselves back in.

Portrait of God as a Creative Writing Student

Such a long Sunday
in March: north wind
mouthing my letter-box,
edging its way
into the bright room
where I calmly read,
having discovered this morning
that God exists
and has made the world
much as a first-year student
makes a poem – from himself
and any available language,
with many slides and hitches
and hopes and misconceptions
about what the hell it all is.

I see my duty clear:
to foster his self-esteem
and his humility
in equal proportions.
He must learn how to listen.
He must get used to revising.
So when I climb
the thin blue tree
of my dying brain, in a chill
brilliance much like this
March day, I will tell him
some of his ideas were good,
lots of his images
I liked – for instance, grass.
I'll show him what I'd cut out –
the mistakes more sinister
than adjectives and adverbs
that smell of rot, and the rhymes –
their loud self-mockery.
God will be grateful.
I know his next world
will be an improvement
if not quite Shakespeare.
I look forward to reading it.

Quotations

What I like about quotations
is their loneliness

what I like about loneliness
is seven and a half vodkas-and-blackcurrant

what I like about blackcurrants
are the sharp little stones inside their burst cushions

what I like about cushions
is their lack of backbone

what I like about the backbone
is its perfection

what I like about perfection
is academic

what I like about academics
is the way they curl two fingers when citing quotations

(Etc.)

A Word I Used to Know

Lincrustra? (Link Ruster? Lynn Cruster?)
'40s brand-name? Pronunciation disaster?
      That it meant anaglypta
I've lately deduced, but deduction wasn't an issue
Before I could spell, when words were to squeeze or to chew,
      Or smelt of some picture.

Lincrustra: it was a playground of dancing, identical
Roses, each in its ring, with a diamondy spandrel
      Delightful between:
A child-high façade, nose-tip-friendly, that graced a fair portion
Of rooms in our tall end-of-terrace – some gloss, some emulsion,
      'Light Oak' or 'Nile Green'.

415

I'd read the Braille thoughtfully now, as a period detail,
A saleable feature: but that's not the reason, lincrustra,
I stroke you – my grandmother's pride, cherished weekly with Dettol
And Min-Cream, and, daily, for peak lower-middle-class lustre,
      Her soft yellow duster!

The Omen Bird

She flew onto the fence of every yard
And garden of our youth and raised, thrush-throated,
Her rueful, mothering, mournful little cry:
True love, true love, it's not true love, admit it.
You'll never have true, true love like Dad and I.

Why think about it now? Leave her to fly
The winds or nest where memories are more sheltered,
More sheltering. If he and I wrong-footed
The sex-dance, still its tune was in our blood
And it was rock 'n' roll, not some old lie:
True love, true love, it's not true love, admit it.
You'll never have true, true love like Dad and I.

And if one dawn I walked out of his garden,
Through mud and broken, lifeless stalks, the dream
That lured me was an orchard of my own.
Larksong was not more distant than that scream:
True love, true love, it's not true love, admit it.
You'll never have true, true love like Dad and I.

It's years now since we loved and since we hated.
I'm dead to him. The orchard's down. So why,
Why does she perch on winter's crumbless ledge,
Her head alert, blinking a bright tin eye,
Almost as if she saw our old pine bed
Still held the slumped conundrum, loosely knotted,
And she was trying to lure us to the edge:
True love, true love, it's not true love, admit it.
I'd never be surprised if you two parted.

The Tour

It was the Irishwoman's Auschwitz.
Her shoes whispered over the frail unlucky spades
slapped to the paths by the self-cursing poplars,
printed an ooze on the breathless linos: *you are doing this
to me, Englishwoman.* From room to room, worst to
worse, we stirred the unprocessed grains of murder
till different crowns of ash lit up the rival
colours of our identically dyed red hair.
In a last new graveyard, elegy
tried to take our hands, show us the way through
by lettered light, the faintly carved
relief-work of Babel. Had there been one prayer-language
only – say, immaculate pagan Latin,
or masked, tender Yiddish, we could have closed our eyes,
but she saw the whole of Europe signatory
to the old Sassenach crime, the ghastly omission,
and I bit my fist like a pale East German schoolkid
chewing the dirt and skin in *Nazi*, swapping
stars with himself, as she keened the severed tongue.

The ghosts pressed back against the walls,
trying not to feed the present indignation,
straining not to be swallowed, not to become Israel.

The Polio Cup

You couldn't catch their germs. There was no risk.
Some couldn't move. *Poor things.* The luckiest maybe
Lurched on crutches, each strapped leg a cage.
They cried to go outside, so they were set
In iron chairs and beds, facing the sun.
You waved to them from the bus queue. Some waved back

And you, fazed by the etiquette, waved back
So they waved back and you were trapped, at risk
From seeming soft or cruel as iron. The sun
Pinched your eyes, your arm weakened. Maybe
Nurse would march out soon and issue sunset
And roll the children back and lock the cage.

417

The bus rolled up, opened its friendly cage.
Your wave was strong, final. You turned your back.
Now you could show that in your cagey twinset
There was a tough kid who took the risk –
A tough kid going somewhere brilliant, maybe
The pool with its splashes, shrieks, delirious sun.

In fact, you went to the park. You walked in the sun –
Mummy, Daddy, Carol-Ann – a cage
With three gold bars. You rattled them gently. Maybe
One fine day…? You kicked gravel, dropped back
Then raced ahead, to be at your own risk.
You watched the tennis, half a brown-limbed set;

A bowlsman barked 'Good wood, sir.' How you'd set
The world to rights if you could rule the sun
And air: children would breathe and never risk
Losing their dreams to the grown-ups' jealous cage.
You swung from trees till your rulers called you back.
You asked for an ice. They looked uneasy. *Maybe.*

Now you were ready to run away and maybe
Join that clamouring gang of 'riff-raff', set
On a go at the drinking fountain, splashing back
And forth the chained cup with the slice of sun
In its mouth. You'd grab it, swig from the leaky cage
Of germs, and live! Oh run, just run the risk,

The risk of life's sour tin, filled mouth, sweet *maybe.*
Your heart's an aching cage. You lost the sun.
Your muscles set. A childhood never grows back.

Mothers/Daughters

Like natives of a country
who know nothing of that country,
we planted houses which shuddered,
pumped oily outflow
into fresh water, stole each other's air –
and we told each other it was them,
the men, who'd ruined our land.

Learner

She tried to make a life out of dead things:
A woman's gravestone eyes, a man's drowned smile.
With all her breath, muscle, cherishings,
She tried to make a life. Out of dead things
False life alone can come, but since 'hope springs'
Et cetera, for a long laborious while
She tried to make a life out of dead things.

A woman's gravestone eyes a man's drowned smile.

Letter
(i.m. Yehuda Amichai)

Love is not, you told us, the last room
In the long corridor that has no end.
Young till that moment, I had not imagined
Rooms beyond love – not rooms with life in them,
But now I felt a season of decorum
Cooling my breeze. I thought I too could rise,
Brush off my suitors, seek those ghostly floors
Most distant from the heart and the heart's heat.
Reaching at last the *sanctum sanctorum*,
I'd notice further doors, hemmed with faint rays
(The corridor was long, you said, was endless),
Find rooms it seemed too soon to talk about
While time could laugh. Clutching your groundplan, still
Convinced, I came of age. And here I've learned
That the heart's room, as well, may have no end.
Windows may seal and fade, and doors unhandle,
Lit outlines melting into wall-thick mist.
Wherever you are now, in rooms beyond
My grasp, I write to say – it would appear
That the first room, love's, may also be the last
Though love is now an absence, cornered there.

The Fitting Room

I was a legend in my mother's lifetime
And marvelled as the name I never took
Did cute or comic things in simple rhyme
Or dazzled like an easy-reading book.
'But I grew up,' I said. 'What happened after?'
She didn't know. Perhaps her heart intoned,
'They are not long, the weeping and the laughter,'
But, terrified to entertain such thoughts,
She went on joining up the dot-to-dots,
And, at her side, the child of fifty groaned.

I had no life to share, few words to say,
Till she lay dying. Then, the legend spoke,
Spoke legends in the colours she'd have chosen,
I hoped, to warm a cave untouched by day.
Words failed her, but her mouth, crookedly open,
Seemed to be laughing at the little joke
Death makes of life. Since then, I've found a tongue
Too quick, I think, at argument and blame,
And yet I've half a hope she sits among
My readers – those who know my grown-up name.

She'll tell the tale that fits like me like a glove
And I won't feel diminished, saying Mother,
Mummy, Mum. Why is so much of love
The kind of gift you know was made by hand
And not made well, some weird, tenderly-knit
Garment that doesn't suit, won't ever fit?
I'll guess it was her love I called a legend.
I thought it shrank me, sought an ampler space.
But she's the legend now – the way I tell her,
My funny gift. My loss. My crooked face.

Autumn Colours

High over Petersburg, gold and red
Like a Khokhloma soup-spoon, a kitchen gleams
And mists with fragrance, just as it did
When you were the boy with the bowl of dreams.
But the grown-ups died and the tall young man
With the lacquered money and laughing wife,
Can't be the one who fills the word, *son*:
As he shakes your hand he unmakes your life,
    Saying 'Pack up your troubles, Pa, let's go
    To the Fountain of Youth or some place you know.
    The fountain's fucked and the weeds smell vile
    But the fags are cheap, so smile, boys, smile.'

And you picture the banners, red and gold,
And all they meant or should have meant:
They've gone with the gods and the country, sold
For a song whose words aren't any you learnt
As a Young Pioneer. You can move as you please
But the town on your papers isn't your town.
Each rolling Mercedes is full of old faces –
Same apparatchik, faster gun.
    Then pick up your kit, that place is scary.
    Better retire to Tipperary.
    It's a long long way, as the war-vets sing
    But nearer, my love, than your Leningrad spring.

Rogue Translations

1 *Once*

(*After 'Ya Vas Liubil' by* ALEXANDER PUSHKIN)

I loved you once. D'you hear a small *'I love you'*
    Each time we're forced to meet? Don't groan, don't hide!
A damaged tree can live without a bud:
    No one need break the branches and uncover
The green that should have danced, dying inside.
    I loved you, knowing I'd never be your lover.
And now? I wish you summers of leaf-shine
    And leaf-shade, and a face in dreams above you,
    As tender and as innocent as mine.

2 *Special Exhibition*

(*After 'Mirskaya Vlast' by* ALEXANDER PUSHKIN)

A craftsman made an image of a crucified god.
His prayer, in time, became a work of art
And stood in a museum under armed guard.
2000 years ago, the original prophet,
A mystery to us now, hung slowly dying,
Dying, as he'd lived, among the undeserving poor,
Flanked by thieves, his cherished women crying –
One said to be a virgin, one, a whore.
Now, where they leant, impassive policemen reign,
And no one else gets near the exhibit.
Wannabes watch and pray and sip champagne,
The star's not here. He couldn't afford the ticket.

3 *We'll Meet Again*

(*After 'V Peterburge mie soidyomsya snova' by* OSIP MANDELSTAM. *The speaker is a South Londoner of the early 1940s.*)

We'll meet again in 'Peter'.
We'll dig up that Victory sun
and say the word again –
our blessed, daft little word.
The Soviet night's a nag called Black Velvet.
The empty universe is a pint of Black Velvet.
We'll bet on the empty universe.
Long as our favourites are on-stage, our troupers
who never say die – long as you never say die, girls –
we'll all come up roses.

Like a cornered moggie, the town
whips up a humpback bridge complete with sentry.
A wicked car rips solo through the gloom –
cuckoo, cuckoo.
I don't need your old pass, ta very muchly.
You can tell the guard where to get off.
Give me crimson velvet, a couple of tickets,
that hush, that nervous rustling,
silky as silk stockings.
A girl cries 'whoops' and Venus takes a bow,
up to her cherries in roses.
I'm praying to you, little word. My daft little wonderful word.

Boredom stares at the gas-fire, roasting its knees.
Was that the sandman passing,
leaving a smear of ash
on the arms we knew and blessed?

Those crimson curtains, deep as orchestras,
Those treasure-boxes, stuffed
like gran's chiffonier
with clockwork captains and their china dolls –
bastards and hypocrites haven't got an inkling!
Put out the candles, son, if that's the boss's orders.
Put up the old black cretonne. The women'll just shrug
their luscious shoulders, won't you, girls, and keep
right on singing. Bless you.

Singing shoulders, blooming banks of roses,
the sun lit up all night – and you never saw sweet FA!

4 *The Grape-picker*
(After Fasti, III. Non. 5th, by OVID*)*

By the fifth morning, when the dew has dried
   On the saffron cheek of Tithonus' wife, Aurora,
Instead of the Great Bear and the sleepy Herdsman,
   You'll see the Grape-Picker, curly-haired Ampelus,
Stretch out his boyish hand. This is his story:
   Child of nymph and satyr, he was playing
Among the Ismanian hills one day when Bacchus,
   Idly watching, fell for him utterly.
And he sang up a drunken gift, an enormous vine, fruit-laden,
   And trailed it over the highest bough of an elm tree.
Scrambling along to reach the glowing clusters,
   Ampelus lost his balance, pitched over headfirst.
Bacchus lifted the small corpse from the hillside.
   He placed it in a canopy of swaying, grape-bright stars.

5 *The Things He Liked*
(After 'On liubil tri veshi na sveti' by ANNA AKHMATOVA*)*

He liked secret agents, submarines.
He had a soft spot for the Thames Barrier.
And he was tied to me.

He read big books from remainder shops,
All about *things*, the things
He liked: secret agents, submarines,

Our Mysterious Universe,
The Volvo 300 Series,
And he was tied to me

Who couldn't read a fuel-gauge.
He hated long talks about feelings.
He liked secret agents. Submarines

Were a primitive fascination.
They were his youth, his memory,
And he was tied. To me

He was Naval Intelligence. I kept bugging him.
I stroked his prow, promised to play at whatever
He liked: *secret agents*, *submarines*,
And he was tied to me.

To the Future Generations

Sweeties, you can't all be carried.
Though you're almost as light as sperm,
you're almost as numerous
and we've only got two pairs of hands
as mother used to say.

Darlings, you can't all have names:
we've got hearts, we've got favourites.
Some of you are top of our pops;
a few are on the tips of our tongues,
but some (that's life) are not.

Ladies and gents, please wait your turn.
It's no use waving and screaming.
You're not the only ones:
we're making more babies each minute
and the body-count's gonna be fantastic.
We've only got heads on our shoulders.

Letters Back

Dear Muse, my female first (apart from Sitwell
Who charmed me hugely at the age of eight),
Whose poems I re-hashed like Holy Writ, till
I learned to honour, not to imitate,
Forgive this impudence. I'm not pretending
Your spirit spoke, dictating me your choice
Of addressees. It's awfully English, sending
Tirades by post. You'd never use this voice
I've wished on you: compared to yours, it's tame.
You're 'Sylvia Plath', you're almost my invention,
A thing of words. And all words cloud your name.
Yet fiction sometimes has a pure intention:
And monologue, which seems a selfish ruse,
May ring more true than monograph. Sing, Muse.

2

Dear Carol, I'm inclined to think you're bats.
But then I hear you've lately moved to Wales
And teach Creative Writing and keep cats:
Sorry to take the wind out of your sails –
Or should I spell that 'sales'? I do suspect
You're playing up, here, to the 'poetry scene',
Auditioning for a bit-part in my act,
The movie, even? Still, I know you're keen
(Who's Sitwell, by the way?) and fairly pissed
At critics and biographers and *men*.
(What's wrong with men?) OK, if you insist,
Take up your quill. Don't bother me again:
I'm dead. Just try to get the scansion right.
And don't come on all tragic. Keep it light.

3 *To the Critics who Judged me a Fake*

You customs-men exclaim and seize my *Letters*
Home. 'She's schizo.' 'Where's her attitude?'
But, guys, that's how it used to be. Our betters
Demanded both success and gratitude.
A daughter knew her mother's sacrifice
In every twitchy nerve. The least she owed
Was sugar, spice and all things nice as nice.
Not the truth. Jesus! Not the poetry toad.
Twice immigrant, we'd shrink and shrink to fit
First the glass slipper, then the slippery ring –
Mum's own arena – where they hose the shit
And keep the clowns from smashing everything:
Where any talent not a social grace
Is contraband, or dirt: stuff out of place.

4 *To the Amateur Freudians*

Oh please! D'you really think my road was down
To Dadsville that sad morning. *Dad?* Who he?
My prey was live and kicking. Object one:
To drag the schlemiel back, back, back to me.
And, two: if nearly dying didn't spark
The spell, to die for real and fix his hash.
I wanted him to cry, the little jerk.
Jezebel, too. I wanted them to crash.
Not nice, I know. Of course, what bright wives *should*
Do is give their genius-hubbies rope
And turn a blind eye while the money's good.
No, it ain't me, babe. Love was still my hope
That morning when I knelt in stink and grease
To tug his heart undone, whisper Oh please…

5 *To the Queen of England*

Men slaughter harmless mammals, act the shaman,
Rap with ghosts, conjure with goddesses,
And who in your establishment would blame them?
Then, if they're ripping off babes' bodices
Instead of helping put their kids to bed,
Your knights will merely smirk – that's poet's licence.
And any way the wife was off her head.
You nod: those vulgar tears, that shocking violence.
It's so un-necessary, going ballistic...
A little infidelity's old hat
Among you royals, n'est-ce-pas? Re-do your lipstick
And heap the laurels on this diplomat-
Diplopic. But don't swallow all the charm.
His stuff about you's bollocks. (S'cuse me, Ma'am.)

6 *To a Rival*

Adrienne Cecile Rich, you weren't exciting!
Back then in sixty-two and sixty-three,
I was the one doing the red-hot writing.
And then you added DC to AC
And found a style I can't exactly praise.
Postmodern, is it? Well, your sense of form's
Kind of unbuttoned, on its holidays.
You reached the wreck, though, flippered up some storms,
Found the drowned face. The shore-bound shiverer died
Painfully, her lycra skin ripped off,
Trim craft in ribbons. No, not suicide
But huge divorce, long labour. *Mazel tov!*
The truth is yours. Women poets must dive –
Not flay themselves. Glad you came up alive.

7 *Another Entry for a Revised Mythology*

Meet Mr Arachne of the Guild
Minerva founded, weaving the long tale
In twice-dyed threads: our psychic battlefield.
A lurid web of horror and betrayal,
It fills the museum mind of hoi polloi,
His cloak-and-dagger version, starring Daddy,
The Daughter and the Prince who must destroy
The Dad – who's dead, but still a real baddie.
This scene shows the dénouement of the plot:
The father hides behind the boy whose skinny
English chest the girl zooms through like shot.
So Dad gets girl and Hero feels a ninny.
This story's not original, nor proven.
Spiderman's threads are mine, wildly re-woven.

8 *To a Young Narcissus*

What are the lyric poet's proper themes?
Not 'self-discovery, self-definition?'
Not the 'Personal Helicon' and its streams
Where the drowned face shivers recognition?
Poet-Professor, literal and prescriptive,
The poet in you mars what you profess,
Versing his fields until they're fruitful, fictive
And dubious as 'self-forgetfulness'.
We warm the bones, arrange the stones again,
And it's our breath makes them extraordinary.
You knew this once, and carved it with your pen,
A mythic ploughboy in a mythic Derry:
Young poets sing themselves, themselves to hear.
And some, of course, stay young their whole career.

9 *To Mother*

Therapists and shrinks, amateur writers
All, made it come true, the Freudian gist
Of women's grief – a myth bound to delight us
College girls turned newly classicist.
I'm not denying my loss, the dad-shaped trauma,
Just claiming that the surgery went wrong.
After I saw the poem in it, the drama,
I pitched the story up and found my song.
Was I forced back or freed? I think I'd found
The balance, till the myth was darkened by
Re-telling, and got rooted in the ground
Of all my being, burnt into my sky.
It was one fable but I had another
Where you were loved and sought and mourned for, Mother.

10 *To a Playwright Collector of Buttons*

The saddest part of being fatherless –
You never learn to do the things men do
To save their souls; the way, from trash and mess,
They build their nerdy heaven. David, you
Are into buttons, tarnished eyes that stare
From walls and mouldings round your writing-den.
The cheap bright grins say, 'Anywhere but here,
Writing this bloody play!' I might have chosen
Stamps, but stamps meant letters, desperation
Of various kinds. My 'play' was tongue-and-groove
With work, no tiny holes for respiration,
A seamless miracle I wove and wove
From every thread that blew across my life.
In fact, there were no threads that 'blew across' my life...

... And that's what made me great! If love's mere part
Of life to man but 'woman's whole existence',
The same, I dare suggest, is true of art.
I courted poems, countering all resistance,
Till they were mine, my nerves, skin, hormones, breath.
They were the love, they were the death I chose.
With every year my corpse looks less like death
Because it's made of poems. And love. Who knows
How hard it might have been sustaining that.
What power has art to breed at menopause?
What form has passion when you're old and fat
And all you do together is the chores?
Those the gods love die young. Don't imitate
Me – or yourself. 'Bye now. I've got a date.

NEW POEMS
(2004)

To Save the Wheel

(after Highways and Byways *by Paul Klee)*

But the byways also took us
    to our only feasible
        horizon.

We hadn't got lost, turned
    at too sharp an angle:
        it was our road, we pressed

on homelessly, vaguely,
    to the blue,
        to the fire-face,

peeling off minerals, mammals,
    stripping and grafting,
        the only way we knew

to save the wheel,
    and the road that re-invents it –
        the wheel and everything.

Pastoral Among the Leonids

The sky was mud and oil, the fish scattered,
Their tabby skins and fans of spine melting
Like the corpse of Lycidas into Milton's sorrow,
Or pastures into running glaciers, feeding
The sea-bed no one made, but everybody lies on.

Under a guess of moonlight, owls exclaimed so faintly
They can't have been out hunting: maybe they were hooked
On a mammal-show called Man: Insentient Species?

Meanwhile, the nature-shoppers decked their trolleys
With Big Bang glitz: Helium, on *Big Brother*,
Made out with Hydrogen, their spendings shook
The star-small hours like a choir of babies:
In fact, at point of sale, there was too much earth,
To see, and all my salvage was this dream:

432

A sky of pale green water, lit by strings of bubbles,
Delicate oxygen fountains twinkling upwards
To form all breath, and breath's enablers – milt
And Milton, broadband ducts and oaten pipes:
No new gods; a sufficiency of shepherds.

The Baltic Swan

Steadily striving inland,
Until so close it was in the realm of the personal,
And we called it 'he', after *lebed*,
(Masculine, Russian), the single Baltic swan
Had the dangerous shape of two contrary instincts,
Hunger and fear. And, though hunger drove him,
His wide and zigzag course, the wind-defying
Braced flare of his archangel, Aztec wings
Signalled the cross he carried.

How dearly he wanted not to give up the sea,
But he'd sighted (scented, heard, felt in the tides
Around him, in him?) something
Half-learnt far back – a featherless ideogram
That pictured *Eat! Survive!*
And we, who spelled so much, watched and were gripped
By his translation. He was like the island;
He was its language, *Nature*: big clean words
Knotted in our own wrack, if we could only find them.

On foot, he at once lost style.
He wobbled, lurched, his splayed
Froggy webs and fine shins overloaded
With gravity, the sheer dry weight of him.
But he wasn't turning back. He aimed straight at us,
Huge shields ablaze. The almost comical
Face-mask – Loyalist-orange, ebony-trim –
Fixed just beneath his eyes,
Shocked us like a drawn gun: pure swan,
As guns are pure man, his diamond essence.
We tried not to gasp, we couldn't speak
As he squashed himself onto our picnic rock,
A swan eclipse, spilling all over the inch
He'd put between his tottery world and ours.

He rolled a little, like a sea-filled barrel,
Snorted, preened his foam,
Then leaned from the fleece-packed muscle of his neck
And probed the safest, nether bits of us –
Bottles, wrappers, my discarded sandals.
He tried my toes for texture, delicately.
I breathed my pulse to normal.
Showing fear was out: we'd refuse that exchange.
(Weren't we the brains here?) Slower than slow motion
One of us picked the loaf up, tore
Some small, sweet pieces, and we flattened
Our palms to bony plates, to say we meant
All the good he wanted (Eat! Survive!) –
And laid it out for him, our only meaning.

The neck dipped, the horn spoon poked and scooped.
We tore fresh pieces, ate our own scant share
Until the loaf ran out,
And we folded up our hands to show goodbye,
He snapped once at my sandal, and agreed,
Dragged himself to his feet, swayed back to the water.
He faded slowly, lingering at the margin,
Cruising the flotsam like a pro, at ease,
But vulnerable, now. We wished him wary.

He was out word for 'nature', we didn't ask
To keep him, we didn't expect uniqueness,
There were no thanks in his luggage.
And perhaps he was no more wonderful than a seagull.
But I translated his visit as unique,
And it entered our language for the ferry back
And the holiday talk, and has never been forgotten.
Longer than usual I kept his souvenir,
An amazingly soft, un-icy, ice-white feather.
I'd stroke its length, brood about swansdown fillings,
And quill-pens trailing poems – all those uses –
And when it hurt I'd pause the reel, and stare
The feather to its flight-shape, white and far,
Like staring out a word until you see
The perfect strangeness. The spectacular silence.

Exile: An Update

A journey always meant hope.
When they rammed the truck black, and you couldn't retreat
from so much breath, none of it wanting yours:
when you paid a Mercedes for the back of a lorry,
when you dropped yourself from the top of the fence and bounced it
at the Eurostar, and stuck there like a skingraft
or suture, knees hands fingers soles an agony of stitching
through steel, and earth's long wound flying beneath,
that journey still meant hope – if you could hang on, if
your mind could: hope, the lick of water,
hope, with the face of your child
at the end of the tunnel.

Graduates of transport, you mastered arrival:
the gun-butted tumble straight to bell, or the scenic
route; the lie on the gate, the shrug in the street –
a street where you built a pram of the things that would be your life
when there were walls again, and form, and shadow,
or a street where you looked for a coin:
someone had always dropped a coin, if you looked
hard for the little shine.
This time, it's different again.
The light seems right, you already know some of the language.
The village greets you at last. It's beautiful:
the hates are bricked and plumbed, the slight seepage
drip-feeds the perfect green.
You learn to wait, though nobody else is waiting.
You stand still, walk around the block, or stretch
carefully out on the pavement,
still hoping. But it's not
yours, that coin. It's ours. We lost it years ago,
you stole it. Look how strangely
it shimmers as you stare a thousand years down
in the island's mud. One kindly finger shows you
your place, the illegality, the proper
attitude, and the first flight home.
Another five say, Oi, Saddam, here's what
hope hoped, what journey journeyed to.

Baby Baby Baby

Something's using them – stronger than their strong bodies,
their pierced, unforgettable bodies. When the boys complain
Oh, baby, baby, their searing laughter's the sign
it's begun to own them, Holy Ghost or goddess
they got for free – full power, no sacrifice.

Cameras enjoy them, evolution adores them,
their peach-bloom shoulders, eyes' immaculate punk
moons in each matched sunset of shadow and highlight.
Their blood roars round at such a lick that the junk
and the junk food and booze haven't scrawled one mark on them yet.

Time has stood back for them, promised them a breather,
perhaps in a moment's weakness, perhaps because of a deal
with the power in them. Their minds are the lightest weather,
the landmass nobody worked or built on, primaeval.
You fear for them as they sashay across its fissures,

the terrible kneeling forms of the daddies and uncles
grabbing their ankles, howling, *Baby, we were joking*,
the thin white mother-claws wavering out of the funk-holes.
But they kick them to pulp, they're laughing, they chant love's karaoke,
louder than anyone screams in a land still reckoned lucky.

They glow, and the power boots up to deliver more
life, lots more. Oh, baby, baby, baby, they wanted
to love you, although they dropped you in hard cots where
it frayed to wet rage. The power can't stop, they can't
stop it. The pills are forgotten, the condoms tear,

the power grins, *Yes!* And it coils in the girl-power thing.
It boils in the swaggering boys and the shag-each-other-to-bits-
then-bash-each-other couples. The kids are swaying
their tiny peach-bloom shoulders, already certain it's
the only tune. *Oh, baby, baby*, it isn't – but it always is.

The Child Lover

It was a grim small ghost, a shamed child,
Tangling with me every time we met.
The come-on, the recoil, with which it smiled
Was mirrored by the twisting of a foot,
And shielded by the empty cup it held
Lip-high, as if smile-murderers were about.
It said, 'I want a drink.' Or, perhaps, 'I'm cold.'

Into its field I ran, a dream-paced fuse,
A hair-raised scorch-mark through imagination,
All dream-aware my name had been cried out,
And only love could be the breaking news.

An armed shape shuddered, drew its damage taut,
And so we both re-learned that conversation
Where every 'sorry' sparks some fresh abuse.

The Weather of Scarves

We were playing at adultery when we swapped them
And smuggled them into our marriages.
They were the candid opposite of our bodies,
Our other clothes. They had no wrong-side-out.
Any bit of the fabric could have entered
That almond-sized hollow behind our ear-lobes,
Or buttercup-kissed a chin, or crept beneath
The hair to snuggle with a feathered nape,
They were perfect hands for sex, never tired or heavy,
Never ashamed. Their only wash was rain.

We left them in public places to betray us
But no one noticed, heard a single whisper.
Everything in the wedded world we gave them –
Our pheromones, our microbes, particles
Of street and work and skin, our spit and matter,
All the souls of our lives, each soul an odour –
Yet nothing. They were nothing,
A mood, a smoker's sigh. Their dream was breath:

They wished we free them from our weight and tangle,
Un-noose them, let them fly. And so with denser
Threads and knots of air they were re-woven

Until the time when we could cease pretending.
The smell of your life faded, there was only
An image, then, of chequered ash and sky,
Too long kept to be returnable.

Danse Macabre

The clothes I've worn to advertise for sex
And since thrown out come back to me in dreams,
Writhing, wallowing. I wring their necks:
I make them beg. I rip. I razor seams
And hems. I shoo them hellwards in a hail
Of studs, a lightning crack of busted zip.
Their smatterings wriggle, frantic to regroup
And mend, but now there's less material
The awful pathos shows, although they bop
Like mad, so hot, so see-thru, so Top Shop.
The wedding clothes I've worn for one-night stands
Are billowing somewhere, sacrificial, spotted.
They say it's love, these man-made Havishams
And wear my flesh as though it had not rotted.

The Blue Jeans Monologue

Cloudy as the summer of '68,
we have that same light ache, filtering through us
as through the weave of council estate skies,
California-dreaming.
We walked beyond our logos and our labels,
talked with the smoky all-nite rasp
of thigh on thigh, found ourselves among
brothers and sisters anywhere we travelled,
and loafed and got above ourselves, the only
uniform, we smiled, apart from skin.

We are the medium and the message still,
though limper than a sigh,
intractable as our old-fashioned waistband.
You will never own anything again
as you owned us, the two legs of your blue
noon, the wings, the crux, time of your time.

We knelt to no one, yet,
as you observe, our knees are almost gone:
we must have had a god, then, probably
some youth in flares.
Our buttocks have been stone-ground, sitting out
the sit-in of the decades, sagging weirdly
when forced to stand. War isn't over. Our

particular war is over,
marched flat in the long strides you used to think
guaranteed the world. And now you recognise
our plague-spots, last year's one-coat aubergine,
the same as your front door and window-sills,
and ask what you've betrayed. But if
you could investigate, dig deeper
in the life-style of each fibre,
you'd find no proof beyond
some shreds of silver paper in our pockets,
a spot of bike-oil, cleaning fluid or tannin,
a menstrual stain just dawning
in the hard seam of the crotch.

Baba, Mama, Babushka

Here are three nesting dolls. The bud-like one
Seems to be pure prototype, a gene
For shiny, head-scarfed, match-wood woman-ware,
Virgo intacta, lucky charm for lovers:
The cherry with no stone, the shirt without a seam.

Round her a body forms, not quite religion,
But shaped for her alone. This one's a cloak
That spills red doves, a looking-glass that sees
And smiles those wide, slack mother-smiles, and barely
Winces when you screw her belly to her back.

The matriarch shell she's hardening seems timid,
All washed-out apron, chirps of 'Don't get old,
Darlings,' but take care: her sucked-egg shadow
Makes midnight of our fleshly self-esteem –
Even her own, that tiny rosy skittle
Of unforgiven life, ripe but already brittle.

The Dotage

Old age will surely be much like an only child's
Childhood, its preoccupations the body's,
Each act of bodily care a sacrament,
Though you yourself are the heavy ministrant:
And beyond the body, the *tabula rasa*, snores
In toy-cupboards, magic of a small outdoors;
The ball that's smug with disobedience;
The book smelling greedily of its contents
Where you are pictured, mobile, enviable
Among the animals, the younger people.

The Grandmother's Tale

What I once loved were lies. They had such nice eyes!
In the ice of his smiles, I missed the truth by miles
But cornered my unicorn, marred and unmythically horned,
   And his word was my sword.

This is a route that's routinely unsuitable: bull-
At-a-gate while the *latte* is hot, and the candle-light flatters
The cad in your abracadabra, the hole in the whole simulacrum
   Of plenty in Lent,

You offer your coffers of treasure, and he goes 'Sure...'
So you buy him the Kohinoor. And it's wild for a while,
Until he ships out to his isle, and its single file
   From hypnotic to *not.*

But your heart says it's owed. This is so. From the day I was widowed,
Wed to his ghost, I soon hosted my own Casanova.
He leans from the empty chair, and his breath lifts my hair:
   'There, love, it's not over.'

Where are the old and their dead but enfolded in *ars amatoria*?
Faces and arms we embrace in the car parks of crematoria
Aren't mere remembrance: embraces evolve in us till
   The final nil-nil.

Watercolour

(Late 20th Cent.)

The lake's a sampling of October:
Colour-prints of rust and rose
And peach, no brighter, no more sober
Than the banked originals,
Call the lucky seaguils over:
Sky-branch, lake-branch, all are yours.

Clouds load in, dissolve, re-double,
Till they've stained the whole veneer,
Burst the frail mimetic bubble;
So our sun-struck heads-in-air
Find, these days, that mirrors trouble
Bright ideas of smiles and hair.

Does art age, as artists tend to?
Mimics' skills commence with eyes,
Eyes get misty. Minds extend few
Hooks to recent memories:
How can brushwork, then, pretend to
Visions and agilities?

We are rooted where time found us
Through a thousand strokes of luck,
Like the fruits cascading round us,
Most to perish where they struck:
Though the splitting seed feels boundless
Greenest days obey the clock.

Blind reporters, filming neither
Solid nor reflected things,
We might easier claim another
Life, complete with harps and wings,
Than convince the changing weather
We are where the new bird sings.

A Postcard from the City of Learning

In a postcard *mise-en-scène*, the present pastoral
Continues mountain-making: slip and ring-
Roads, car-parks, *access*, retail hangars: more
Fat than was ever scraped from snack-bar Snowdon.

Like mountain-streams to sea, the bullshit gestures
Of footpaths fizzle long before the forecourts –
From whose vantage-point the brutal green
Leers at the back door, flakey Father Nature

Now as absconding Dad, his fist gone limp,
Returned not to abuse but praise his pram-trash.
We glide and shift in an educated trance
Across the playgrounds, or lie prone for hours,

Licking our crumpled kill. Look, Dada, flat-pack,
cold-pressed, sun-dried! Rural-plural, us,
Who stalk the curious urban moose called Lifestyle:
Who try to be the video and the popcorn.

It's not a case of Matalan versus mountain:
Nor can you blame the mountain altogether
For Matalan. Move-and-get-and-gorge is human:
All nature, ours or older, wrings the clay it's given.

Try slithering up that peak, even in Nubucks;
You'll see less sky than frames our sapling-dotted
Anti-skateboard feature. And if the peaks were trackless?
The metal park wet pasture...? Handbrake off,

I roll into my dream: carved shade and pavement-
Conversation in some pastiche High
Renaissance city, Wroclaw, say, its language
Risen, light and proud, its Tescos also rising.

Lullaby and Warning

(to the Field at Buarth Gwarchau)

Pause, field, each time the sky
Fails to dawn through its dulled
Barley haze, mysteriously like yours.
Earth has begun to separate from light
And though your grass-mind whispers, 'It's all right,
The usual separation, not divorce,'
Few businesses, you know, in your vast city,
Won't rationalise or fold.

The playground's destitute.
Your prettiest strippers, stripped from crown to root,
Can find no shoppers:
The tiny dealers, with their deely-boppers,
Tail-coats and shades,
Who cruised the gorgeous spectra, scored, sold on
The surplus bullion,
Freeze, now, in scentless beds.

But trust this scythe,
Its steel exactness, simplifying, clearing,
As necessary as breath.
And if it fails, because bad tenants spoiled
The sky, blunted the blade,
And goad you with their winter-free design,
Pause, field. A stalled September isn't spring.
No root of you should stretch. No stem should shine.

Welsh Stream

We heard no watery rustle, saw no movement
at first. And then we spotted it, the tic,
the one-nerve flicker, every thirty seconds,
and knew, with an absurd sense of reprieve,
that the dead muscle, brown as parcel-seal,
where clay sagged at the weight of fern and horsetail,
was in fact living water, weak but striving
with tiny shudders for a different place.

Fatherless in a Blue Language

In my absurdist pastoral
The mountains blend their tusks and flanks, defeat
Taxonomy. I blush:
I used to be literate,
And still the signposts flatter me with double
Ls and Ws, as if
I might, finally, utter
All the salivary cursive that joins up
Slate fence and pebble-dash,
Ring-road and rope-stain where the last
Drover lassooed the outcrops.
But it's all in my head.
No tongue, I think, no tenure.
Even the tongue I have could lapse.
Saesneg, I whisper, scaring
Myself with my own hiss and thud,
The trespass and the silence: here I steep,
Unfamilied, echoless.

'English' sounds kindlier
As if it might describe, not colonise,
The cadence of the bluebells,
Exiled, and waiting in
The raised beds, to rustle, *'Croeso, croeso'*
To my father next spring:
'English' in the way he was, half Welsh,
But scarcely knowing it,
Naming no place, sad for a green somewhere
I thought was downland Sussex –
The dense dark night-hikes, dawns
Risen from dewponds, meadows, frayed
By oxbow meres like exclamation-marks,
And every wood along the way in bluebells.
He found those woods for me.
In Fenchurch Street his shipper's smoky hand
Signs for the hated "maisonette" I sold
To buy this view, this flood of field and stone
And sky that leaves me dazzled, makes me cry
Because I'm in his dream, and he was never here.

The bluebells seem at home,
Despite the clay and wet and wind: they stand
Straight-stemmed, almost outstrip the faltering wall,
Robust, full of themselves,

Like children in sea-shallows
Lost in the joy of turning
Shivery flesh to ocean.
I find a word for blue,
And *glas* becomes glass fountains,
Whose conduits syphon and re-shower
The rain clouds' indigo. At dusk
Though, it's the quarry colour,
The purplish pewter grey of slate in shadow,
Of broken, re-peaked mountains
That put the sun out early, even in midsummer.

It's not the bluebells' story –
The story which begins when a young man,
All in the merry month of May,
Steps out one morning through
Hawthorn star-bursts, down a chalk defile,
White as white crosses, gradual as the drift
To war, but neither is it mine,
It's pure translation.
So let them write it in a Book of Kells
Or Mabinogion,
All curlicued with gracenotes, their
Welcoming *cynghanedd*
For you, dear father,
Since language will appear round any landscape
We choose to love, made up
By rhymeless winds and mountains,
Made true by speaking:
I'll wake you, Wilfred Arthur, as I wake
New chimes of English from the cuckoo bells,
The *clych'air gog*, the slate songs of Cymraeg.

Native, and Living in Wales

Thistly and poor as the fields, the thirsty anthologies
Spirit them in, the lost lambs, the odd fish, the not-even-slightly-Welsh
Made-in-England English who couldn't quite make it in England.
Whoops! Only joking! They came here to be self-sufficient,
Or something, maybe they wanted to be druids,
And they wrote the poems and the poems wrote them a nation,
A new DNA, switching the definitions
Miraculously. Now they're getting Academi grants

To bond with the Basques. And though the Eistedfodd boys (sorry)
Won't ever invite them, there will be plenty more platforms
To win in their own wonder category: English Welsh Writer in English.

Direct Train

The North Wales coast looked desirable in passing:
it always does. 'What a lovely seaside,' two
shy elderly travellers remarked. And I wanted to say,
'It's not, when you're beside it!'
and point out the proximity of track to beach,
not to mention the A55 and the typical prom,
with its burger café and shelters, and the miserable concrete walkway
but I merely glanced at the lovely illusion (to feel
nostalgic already would be ridiculous),
and noted the sullen herds of flat-topped caravans flowing
the sea-less side of the tracks at Abergele.

There was the usual hubbub of 'Change at Chester'.
After that, settling into the painless curve,
the steady, southerly glide, I could soften a little,
and say to myself, 'England, utterly England,'
suddenly wishing it summer, so London, four hours later,
would still lie canopied in a safety-net of daylight:
(there's something sad in arriving alone, at night,
and for a stay so short, a long weekend's-worth
I'll hardly notice, sitting at the computer
or pushing myself out to embarrassing literary soirées).

And as usual I felt that the place I truly desired
lay only within that inconsequential series
of miniature, minimal places which are the sum of travel,
and yet it was no solution to keep on leaving
one country for another, since this gave too much importance
to place, worked up a lot of un-needed sensations
hard to resist or outgrow, despite the years of practice
dividing my time, as they say. I don't want my time divided:
I want it always to be three o'clock, that most
indivisible time, in a field whose bushy, brown horizon
moves so much slower than the impatient embankment,
with terraced houses nearby, and a horse, and a grubby canal –
a time that not even December can spirit into nightfall.

And I want to be saying 'England, utterly England'
in a voice that doesn't imply I have locks and keys there;
rather, I'm gliding like blood, in complex circles, sensing
London down on my left like a gritty boot,
and the North Wales coast at my right shoulder-blade
with its little fleece of waves, stuck out like a curious wing
I sprouted once by mistake, imagining I could fly.

Do the Serial Monogamists Need a New Vocabulary?

Love's the word we use when the urge takes us
Above the clouds in piercing claws, and fakes us
A crown of stars. 'I love him/her to bits'
We say, showing how well the L-word sits
With GBH. Love has no qualms. It bakes us

A pie of children's hearts. Oh, but it wakes us
So gently, whispering, stroking. It re-makes us
Into the small fair-headed one, who fits
All kisses. When we write our greatest hits,
Love's the word we use.

Love justifies our sperm, our spawn, our acres,
And when, one day, betrayal or boredom rakes us,
And old names are spat out like bitter pits,
We mouth the sweet new flavour, swearing it's...
(Love's the word we use).

Finishing a Poem Can Be Like This, Too

Though the Nuns said they had no souls
We kids gave fancy burials
To birds and voles,

Laid them in lint and prayed that broad-
Church angels might put in a word
For them with God.

Today less piety informs
My shovelling into roots' and worms'
Tight catacombs

Until I've made a sort of nest,
Deep, damp and cold, for the fluffed breast
And school-cap crest,

Grieved that such colours, cornsilk bright,
The passerine finesse of flight,
Have lost their light

Yet not unconscious of the thrill
Of something near impalpable
Brought down, stopped still.

Whole Words
(for Rebecca)

Another mute bites down, a new mutation
Roots out its own tongue. We blank such losses
As 'friendly fire'. The language we shared round
With such imperial fairness, keeping only
What was ours, can't not be ours. But now it can't be ours.

We asked to be a voice, even a footnote
To February, a true note. That we drowned
In our own throats indicts us. But remember
We spoke that difference, felt the gathered fibres
Sweeping across our tongues till we vibrated wholeness.

Some tongues are quickly slit, some, broken over
Years, crushed into trade-route underlay
Till smooth and white enough to hang as local colour.
The exception goes on springing from the spring-less
'landscape where both people and books lived'.

Two tongues, two brother tongues, carefully write 'I hate you'
Carving the sand with accurate licks, eyes veiled
Against the reading: similar salt confuses.
Each tongue curls back in the hood of its own breath
And guesses: neither speaks the other's journey.

Whereof we cannot speak, keep talking, softly:
One howl awaits the mouths that make the holes
Made by their masters' mouths, at first with laughter,
Later, slack consent. Try 'no' again, and savour
The difference from their 'yes'. Words last a generation,

And only while our children still confirm the flavour.

De-Creation 2004

Think of a face
That bites its lip and twists its brow to bind
Closed eyes in place.

Over the brow, a hand
Searches the seam where bone and tissue, spurred
Viciously, fused into mind,

A hand like an absently-fathered
Cradle-word, half curse.
Repeated again and again, or the sullen tread

Of troops, unwinding the wars.
So the waters between them turned.
Again into blood or shivering truce: not yours.

You prayed for rain, you were burned
To ash. In the only dream
Again and again you are orphaned.

You play being her, being him,
Being loved by a god. But the child is always dead
Between them – between the leather-stain of her palm
And his tethered head.

Culture

Does a bird ever sing solo?
I think not: there is always a duet
Though one voice may be secret,
Whispered from a distant bush or hollow,
Or even silent.

A Gravel Cairn

1

How long does it take them to understand
that this dear thing which refuses to move, which turns dirty,
stinks and dries out and gets smaller, does not hear its name,
nor feels its broken places healed with wax or bells?

I think they will never completely understand it:
I think this might be the rather pointless point of them –
to stare at the horror that happens, that they know happens,
singing over and over it won't, it can't, it didn't...

2

Being carried to the highest point and dropped
did not teach them how to fall, but how to lie very still.

3

Don't drink the eyes in light, the lips in rocks.
Resist the deist slant of mountain-tops.
Time is not someone, dreary though it is
to glaciate those eyes, sandblast that special face.

4

Language unspeakable:
a clitter of musselshell slates in the abandoned quarry,
a chime of Spanish Bluebells. (Or English ones, for that matter.)

5

Stealings of ivy
through my stone wall –
fingers waiting to be snapped

off, or snapped – the test, the old stones say,
of whether law and order have gone west,
and what I mean by beautiful,
and what I fear about decay.

6

The little yellow lizard
is dead, belly up,
hands lifted in supplication –
or that's how it looks.
Though I don't really suppose
she cried out to Apollo
or Huitzilopochtli,
I protect the gesture
as it shrinks and becomes
hard essential pearl,
with a tiny gravel cairn:
back to square one.

Ordinary Soles

(Durham Cathedral, January 2003)

(for Anne Stevenson)

1

At first it was a view, sombre theatre
Staged for the tourists it had half foreseen,
Soon cancelled by the hills, their tinselly scatter
Of New Year's city. When it showed again,
Above the Bailey, looming on the crests
Of snow-lined slates, it seemed domestic, plain,
Despite its mass, some Palaeolithic hearth
For tiger-scaring fires and warriors' feasts.
But human pleasure wasn't in its myth;
Only some madness which had forced those vast
Spiralling trunks to the canopy, stained them with
Faintly Islamic chequerings, combed the light
To seven shades of glowing dusk, and crossed
Blood-sacrifice with something called salvation,
Wanted me there, made almost moral right
Out of the comfort-zone of awed sensation.

452

2

It was no shell. Hoards of the unadoring
Had trudged the aisles, acquisitive and blind,
And not destroyed the marrow: you could sniff
Its life-force, superstition, sure that if
Today, some loaded plane made light of it –
Light, and immense and simple dust, slow-pouring
Into the bedrock, next week's hands would find
The prototype, or young architects compete
With wilder plans for fusing sky and steel
And low-lit shadow-nests in which to kneel.

3

I wish some hand could stop this iron ball rolling,
Check the tumultuous spin, and wrap the year
And all its rage into some child-proof sphere,
With cotton snow the only debris falling.
Out of such simple-minded depths might not
An Angel of Self-Doubt unveil her face
At last, smoke-shadowy in the conjured heat
Of oil-fires where she floats, and bodies, rippling,
Half-melted, claw and pull at her in seizures
Of frantic hope? But when it comes, her shout
Is tiny, falters in the competition
Of manpower's engine-roar. Go back, she pleads;
Forget your tyrant-making, tyrant-toppling
Enterprise. Look close. Your war is terror
Itself: how can it cancel terror out?
This angel, talking to herself in error,
Is human, not an emissary from the skies,
But from the future. She is Evolution
And fades as I invoke her with these lies.

4

I laughed at history, once. A gimcrack vein
Of martyrdom pulsated, neon-red,
When plugged into my secular disdain,
The comic strips of family anecdotes
Reluctant to evolve into an adult's
Tentative research and imaging:
But how can it be kitsch to lose your head?
Later I found the words, The Pilgrimage
Of Grace, and I could hear those rude heads singing.
What chutzpah, when you marched against the king,
Were cautioned, and set off again! Oh, great
Great grand-dads, tearing at your feathery souls

To part them from the spiked mess on the Bridge,
You're bullying me again to demonstrate
That I'm a genuine relative of yours.

5

Perhaps you'd be appalled that there's no Cross
To head our march, shocked by the futile ease
With which we'll breast the democratic breeze,
Attracting cameras like a motorcade;
Perhaps you'd choose the Coalition's crusade.
But you would go with us as far as this:
That kings be questioned, unjust kings opposed.
And so halfway we touch, venerable ghosts
And common heretic who calls on God
Only when tube trains stall, or gangs are loud
In midnight streets. The window's prayer-wheel rises,
Nevertheless, lights webbed in fragile lead,
Like a mandala, beautiful but not
So beautiful it daunts and blinds, but rouses
In dust or memory gene some still-embodied
Arrythmia: the pilgrims' voices, flat
And hoarse with cold, their slow encumbered tread
Drumming the heartless miles and extra miles,
Until they sing no more.

And here's today,
The light like dirty ice, the still-white lawn
And melting roads suddenly footprint-strewn,
As if the first marchers were on their way,
And tired, contemporary, unmiraculous soles,
Metabolising grace from power restrained,
Were grinding out a different passage through
The fossil-heavy self and all its walls,
Sparking off synchronicities of new
Aerial pathways, choirs and towers of cells –
Not monkish ones, but growing-points of mind
Whose miracle would be this: a seventh sense
That leaps between history and consequence.

NOTES

NOTES TO THE POEMS

AZTEC SACRIFICES *(pages 65-76)*

Anahuac: Literally, 'The Land between the Waters'. It encompassed the US south-west (the ancient Aztec kingdom of Aztlan), Mexico and Central America down to Costa Rica.

Chapultepec: Grasshopper.

Huizilopochtli: The sun-god, and god of war.

Moctezuma: Moctezuma II (*c.* 1480-1520), the last Aztec emperor.

Nauhatl: The language of the Aztecs

Quetzalcoatl: Literally, Plumed Serpent. He was a 10th century priest-king, later believed to be a god who would one day return to lead the Aztec people. His reforms included the abolition of human sacrifice. It's said that the Aztecs mistook Cortes' fair-haired second-in-command, Pedro de Alvarado, for their lost god. In Chapultepec Park, Mexico City, Quetzalcoatl is represented as a double-headed stone serpent.

Tenochtitlan: The Aztec capital, and the site of present-day Mexico City.

Texcatlipoca: A god of light and dark, who tricked Quetzalcoatl and defeated him by sorcery.

A NECKLACE OF MIRRORS *(pages 77-84)*

Sappho. *Alcaeus* was a contemporary of Sappho, a great lyric poet. The 'later hand' belongs to Ovid who used the legend of Sappho and Phaon in the Heroides. *Phaon* was presumed to be Sappho's lover, a boatman. *Leucadia* is the rock from which she was presumed to jump when rejected by Phaon.

Li Ju-Chen's Dream. *Li Ju-Chen* was a novelist of 19th-century China. One of her novels conjures a feminist Utopia, in which male and female roles are reversed.

UNPLAYED MUSIC *(pages 85-108)*

Akhmatova in Leningrad. *The Kresty* was the Leningrad jail where women queued daily, hoping for news or a glimpse of imprisoned relatives.

THE GREENING OF THE SNOW BEACH *(pages 225-50)*

The Duchess and the Assassin. The Grand Duchess Yelizaveta was the sister-in-law of Tsar Nicholas II, and the wife of the Governor General of Moscow, Sergei Alexandrovich, who was as universally disliked as she was admired. The Governor General was assassinated at the Kremlin Gates by the Socialist Revolutionary, Ivan Kalyayev, on 4 February 1917.

Death of an Elder Brother. *Sasha* (Alexander Ulvanov) was Lenin's elder brother. He was hanged at the Oreshok Fortress, Lake Ladoga, on 5 May 1887, for his part in the attempt to assassinate Tsar Alexander III.

A Moscow Wife, Waiting. Larissa Borodin's husband was finally released at the end of May 1988.

Finding the Sun. Quotations from Mandelstam, *Tristia*, and Dostoyevsky, *Crime and Punishment*.

THINKING OF SKINS *(pages 295-324)*

A Prophet Unhonoured. After promising the dying Jan Palach to continue to fight for democratic socialism, Jan Kavan, exiled in London, founded and ran Palach Press. This was a news agency dedicated to informing the media about the activities of the Czech dissident movement, Charta 77, and publishing its own regular Bulletin. Kavan returned to Prague after the political changes, but according to reports in the British press, has since been severely criticised for previous collaboration with the State. The poem simply affirms my sense of the honest idealism with which Kavan worked in the days when I was a part-time assistant at Palach Press. *Living in the Truth* is the title of a book by Vaclav Havel.

BEST CHINA SKY *(pages 325-58)*

A Short Life with Gratispool. *Gratispool* was the trade-name of a photographic processing company that operated a postal service during the 1950s.

The Purr. Russian cats say *morr*, not *purr*.

War and Soup. *Babushkin halad* could be translated as Granny's gown, in this case, an ancient dressing-gown. *Skazka:* folk-tale.

Math, Remembering; To Blodeuwedd, Flying; Flauer-Mush. These poems draw on events and characters from the Mabinogion, but do not adhere closely to the original narratives. Various texts suggested strategies for some of these poems, especially Alan Garner's *The Owl Service*, which so brilliantly and faithfully casts the 'Blodeuwedd' story in modern dress. An uncollected paper by Nuala Ní Dhomhnaill suggested how Blodeuwedd may be interpreted as an earthy, rooted figure rather than merely flowery and ethereal.

Tír Fá Tonn: in Irish myth, the Land under the Waves, the happy Otherworld.

The Hag of Beare in Limerick. Probably a mythological character, the Hag is the speaker in the medieval Irish poem, *Aithbe Dan Cen Bes Moro*. There have been a number of English translations: the one I know is *Ebbing* by James Carny (*Medieval Irish Lyrics*, Dolmen, 1985).

About the Jews. Boris Slutsky (1919-1986) was a major poet of the Soviet generation. Many Russians know this poem without being aware that Slutsky wrote it. First published in Boris Filippov's *The Secret Soviet Muse* (Munich, 1961), it wasn't published in Russia until after the poet's death, in 1987. The poem is taken from Yurii Boldyrev's 1991 edition of Slutsky's *Collected Works in Three Volumes (Sobranie sochinenii v trekh tomakh)*, I, p.165.

1950. The original poem by Evgeny Rein was one of a sequence printed in *Znamya* (July 1991) under the title 'Anti-Clockwise'. M.F. Frunze was one of the founders of the Red Army. G.K. Ordjonikidze was a high-ranking member of Stalin's Politbureau. Koba was Stalin's nickname, and Lake Ritsa, in the Caucasus, was the site of his dacha.

Here I Am. Bella Akhmadulina (*b.* 1937) wrote this poem in 1968, presumably in response to government criticism and suppression of her work. Her collections of poetry include *String* (1962), *Music Lessons* (1969), *Snowstorm* (1977), *The Garden* (1987) and *Selected Poems* (1987). She has translated extensively from the Georgian. 'Here I Am' is dedicated it to E.Y. and V.M. Rossels. Ufa is an industrial town in the Urals.

HEX *(pages 383-430)*

Wood Lovers. *gribochki, kolokolchiki, choroshi less*: transliterations from the Russian for *mushrooms, bluebells* (diminutive forms), *a good forest.*

NEW POEMS *(pages 431-54)*

Fatherless in a Blue Language. *Saesneg:* English. *Croeso:* welcome. *Glas:* blue. *Clych'air gog:* bluebells.

Whole Words. Line 15 quotes from 'Speech on the Occasion of receiving the Literature Prize of the Free Hanseatic City of Bremen', by Paul Celan (*Collected Prose*, Carcanet Press, 1986).

Ordinary Soles. The Pilgrimage of Grace, a Northern movement opposing Henry VIII's Reformation, was brutally suppressed by the King in 1537. George and Richard Lumley, who were among those executed, are the figures referred to in section 4.

INDEX

Index of titles and first lines

Poem titles are shown in italics, collections in bold italics, first lines (some abbreviated) in roman type.

464